ASTON VILLA REVIEW 2002

Produced by Aston Villa Football Club

ACKNOWLEDGEMENTS

Aston Villa Review 2002
First published July 2002 by Aston Villa Football Club

© 2002 Aston Villa FC
Villa Park, Birmingham B6 6HE
email: publishing@astonvilla-fc.co.uk
website: www.avfc.co.uk

ISBN 0 9543120 0 7

Printed by Polar Print Group Ltd.

All rights reserved.
No part of this publication may be reproduced, stored in any retrieval system or transmitted, in any form or by any means, without the written consent of the publisher.

Produced by Aston Villa Publishing.
Editor: Rob Bishop.
Photographs: Bernard Gallagher, Neville Williams, Centrepix, Empics, Allsport/Getty Images and Raymonds Press Agency.
Design, layout and graphics: Bernard Gallagher, Phil Lees and Nadine Goldingay.
Special thanks to: Jeffrey Prest, Frank Holt, Ray Spiller, Rod Evans, Pam and Dave Bridgewater.

KEY
- ❑ Player booked
- ■ Player sent off
- g32 Figure in goals column indicates time of goal
- (77) For players in the starting 11, bracketed number indicates time of substitution
- (9) For substitutes, bracketed number indicates the player replaced

Notes
- ● Players are listed in squad number order, except for the goalkeeper, who is always at the top of the list.
- ● Substitute goalkeepers are in squad number order, with (Gk) after their name.

Also available in this series

Aston Villa Review 1993
ISBN 0 946866 09 0   £7.95

Aston Villa Review 1994
ISBN 0 946866 19 8   £8.95

Aston Villa Review 1995
ISBN 0 946866 23 6   £8.95

Aston Villa Review 1996
ISBN 0 946866 32 5   £8.95

Aston Villa Review 1997
ISBN 0 946866 39 2   £8.95

Aston Villa Review 1998
ISBN 0 946866 46 5   £9.95

Aston Villa Review 1999
ISBN 0 946866 50 3   £9.95

Aston Villa Review 2000
ISBN 0 946866 54 6   £9.95

Aston Villa Review 2001
ISBN 0 946866 57 0   £7.95

Pieces of silver at both ends...

If 2001-02 was a generally cloudy season for Aston Villa, there was, at least, a double silver lining.

The first layer was put in place with the Premiership campaign just a few days old, Villa completing a 4-2 aggregate victory over Swiss club Basel to win the InterToto Cup at only the second time of asking.

And although that achievement was more a means to an end, offering a route into European football rather than a celebration of winning a trophy, the club's other piece of silverware was meaningful in its own right.

In the week after the first team completed their programme with an impressive 3-1 victory at Chelsea, Villa's youngsters took centre stage to lift the prestigious AXA FA Youth Cup.

The home leg of the final against Everton was something of an anti-climax, resulting in a 1-0 reversal, but both in a superb first leg at Goodison Park and throughout the competition, Villa's young prospects produced some outstanding football to suggest the club's long-term future is in good hands.

Those supporters who hailed the final victory, of course, are anxious to see similar success in the short-term from Villa's senior side, and that will be Graham Taylor's priority over the next two years.

It came as something as a surprise to many that Taylor took over the managerial reins in February after John Gregory had brought to an end his four-year residence in the hot seat, the former England coach having indicated earlier in the season that he had no desire to be back at football's sharp end.

But if results were not always as favourable as would have been desired, the Villa faithful were certainly appreciative of the more adventurous attacking style employed by the new boss – and those positive tactics finally paid dividends with victories over Southampton and Chelsea in the last two matches.

Ultimately, too, there was the reward of qualification for the InterToto Cup for a third consecutive year, although the eventual goal is obviously to achieve success on the Premiership, FA Cup, Worthington Cup and UEFA Cup fronts.

The cups were a particular source of disappointment last season, made all the worse by the fact that Villa Park proved to be the graveyard on each occasion.

After the euphoria of an InterToto final triumph over Basel, when two-goal Juan Pablo Angel signalled his intentions for the new campaign, a first round UEFA Cup exit at the hands of NK Varteks was a bitter blow. Villa actually won the second leg 1-0 in Croatia, but that wasn't enough to repair the damage inflicted by a 3-2 home defeat seven days earlier.

The Worthington Cup trail was short-lived, too. Reading were duly despatched as Villa entered the competition at the third round stage, but Sheffield Wednesday shrugged aside their First Division struggles to deliver a knockout blow in round four.

A third round home clash against Manchester United hardly seemed conducive to a lengthy cup run, and so it proved, but not before Ian Taylor and a Phil Neville own goal had sent Villa's hopes into orbit. Sadly, they were brought down to earth as a 2-0 lead evaporated into a 3-2 defeat.

As for the regular business of Premiership football, Villa scaled the heights on numerous occasions. A 3-1 success over Liverpool at Anfield was undoubtedly the performance of the season, while it was the third week of October before the team suffered their first league defeat, going down 3-2 at Everton.

Seven days later, after consecutive home wins over Charlton Athletic and Bolton Wanderers, Gregory's boys sat proudly at the top of the table, and talk of Champions League qualification was in the air.

By the end of the year, however, Villa had managed only one more success, and although they arrested the slump with January victories over Derby County and Charlton, the game at The Valley proved to be Gregory's last in charge.

In stepped Taylor for his second spell at the helm, and the man who had guided Villa to runners-up spot 12 years earlier began the task of revamping the current squad. His positive brand of football raised hopes that things were once again heading in the right direction.

It was accompanied, too, by the emergence of Thomas Hitzlsperger, the rebirth of Gareth Barry as a midfielder, the signing of outstanding striking prospect Peter Crouch and the explosive arrival on the England scene of Darius Vassell.

With Peter Enckelman making his breakthrough as first choice goalkeeper and Jlloyd Samuel establishing himself as a fully-fledged member of the squad, Villa undoubtedly have an abundance of young talent on which the manager will hopefully build a team capable of winning major honours.

This 10th edition of the *Aston Villa Review* looks back at the events of last season, and features a match report for every competitive senior game, pen pictures of all the senior squad and coaching staff, statistical details of the club's principal teams, plus a round-up of the main stories which unfolded at Villa Park during the season.

Anyone who has purchased previous editions now has a collection covering a decade of Premiership action; those who are new to this publication will hopefully enjoy it enough to make it an annual addition to their bookshelves.

Rob Bishop

ASTON VILLA REVIEW 2002

CONTENTS

Foreword — Page 3

FIRST TEAM MATCHES

Date	H/A	Opponent	Score	Scorers	Notes	Page
July 14	A	Slaven Belupo (ITC3/1)	1-2	Ginola		6
July 21	H	**Slaven Belupo** (ITC3/2)	2-0	Hendrie 2	*(Villa win 3-2 on aggregate)*	7
July 25	A	Stade Rennais (ITC SF1)	1-2	Vassell		8
Aug 1	H	**Stade Rennais** (ITC SF2)	1-0	Dublin	*(Villa win on away goals)*	9
Aug 7	A	Basel (ITC F1)	1-1	Merson		10
Aug 18	A	Tottenham Hotspur	0-0			11
Aug 21	H	**Basel** (ITC F1)	4-1	Angel 2, Vassell, Ginola	*(Villa win 5-2 on aggregate)*	12
Aug 26	H	Manchester United	1-1	Vassell		13
Sept 8	A	Liverpool	3-1	Dublin, Hendrie, Vassell		14
Sept 16	H	**Sunderland**	0-0			15
Sept 20	H	NK Varteks (UEFA1/1)	2-3	Angel 2		16
Sept 24	A	Southampton	3-1	Boateng, Angel, Hadji		17
Sept 27	A	NK Varteks	1-0	Hadji	*(Villa lose on away goals)*	18
Sept 30	H	**Blackburn Rovers**	2-0	Angel, Vassell		19
Oct 10	H	**Reading** (WC3)	1-0	Dublin		20
Oct 14	H	**Fulham**	2-0	Vassell, Taylor		21
Oct 20	A	Everton	2-3	Hadji, Schmeichel		22
Oct 24	H	**Charlton Athletic**	1-0	Kachloul		23
Oct 27	H	**Bolton Wanderers**	3-2	Angel 2 (1 pen), Vassell		24
Nov 3	A	Newcastle United	0-3			25
Nov 17	H	**Middlesbrough**	0-0			26
Nov 25	A	Leeds United	1-1	Kachloul		27
Nov 28	H	**Sheffield Wednesday** (WC4)	0-1			28
Dec 1	H	**Leicester City**	0-2			29
Dec 5	A	West Ham United	1-1	Dublin		30
Dec 9	A	Arsenal	2-3	Merson, Stone		31
Dec 17	H	**Ipswich Town**	2-1	Angel 2		32
Dec 22	A	Derby County	1-3	Angel		33
Dec 26	H	**Liverpool**	1-2	Hendrie		34
Dec 29	H	**Tottenham Hotspur**	1-1	Angel (pen)		35
Jan 1	A	Sunderland	1-1	Taylor		36
Jan 6	H	**Manchester United** (FAC3)	2-3	Taylor, P Neville (og)		37
Jan 12	H	**Derby County**	2-1	Vassell, Angel		38
Jan 21	A	Charlton Athletic	2-1	Vassell, Angel		39
Jan 30	H	**Everton**	0-0			40
Feb 2	A	Fulham	0-0			41
Feb 9	H	**Chelsea**	1-1	Merson		42
Feb 23	A	Manchester United	0-1			43
Mar 2	H	**West Ham United**	2-1	Angel, Vassell		44

Mar 5	A	Blackburn Rovers	0-3			45
Mar 17	H	**Arsenal**	1-2	Dublin (pen)		46
Mar 23	A	Ipswich Town	0-0			47
Mar 30	A	Bolton Wanderers	2-3	Warhurst (og), Taylor		48
Apr 2	H	**Newcastle United**	1-1	Crouch		49
Apr 6	A	Middlesbrough	1-2	Angel		50
Apr 13	H	**Leeds United**	0-1			51
Apr 20	A	Leicester City	2-2	Vassell, Hitzlsperger		52
Apr 27	H	**Southampton**	2-1	Vassell 2		53
May 11	A	Chelsea	3-1	Crouch, Vassell, Dublin		54

FRIENDLY MATCHES

July 16	A	Swindon Supermarine	4-0	Cooke, Melaugh, Berks, Walker	55
July 19	A	Telford United	3-3	S Moore, Standing, Palmer (og)	55
July 23	A	Tamworth	3-2	S Moore 2, Walker	55
July 28	A	Gateshead	4-0	Angel 2, Vassell, Hadji	56
Aug 11	A	Juventus	5-1	Cooke 2, Hynes 2, Haynes	56
Aug 12	A	Racing Santander	2-0	Angel 2	56
Aug 15	A	Bowers United	10-0	Walker 3, S Moore 2, Hitzlsperger, Smith, Marfell, Berks, Cooke	57
Sept 10	H	**Nottingham Forest**	4-1	S Moore 2, Balaban, Walker	57
May 2	A	Shrewsbury Town	2-5	Hendrie, S Moore	57

APPENDIX

BOOKSHELF	Where to look for a good Villa read	58
TEAM GROUP	First team squad	59
MANAGEMENT	Men behind the teams	60
PEN PICTURES	Player profiles and playing records	62
OBITUARIES	Absent friends	73
PREMIERSHIP STATS	Final table, scorers, attendances and statistics	74
VILLA STATS	Club facts and figures from 2001-02	76
RESERVES & YOUTH	Results, appearances and goalscorers	78
ALL-TIME RECORD	Complete Premiership table (1992-2002)	85
OTHER NEWS	Happenings at the club	86
EURO RECORD	Match-by-match European results and scorers	88
CLUB STATISTICS	All-time club-by-club record	90
SEASON STATISTICS	All-time season-by-season record	92
SUBSCRIBERS	Supporters' roll call	95

INTERTOTO CUP THIRD ROUND FIRST LEG MATCH 01

Slaven away at a cooker

Date: Saturday 14 July 2001
Venue: Gradski Stadium, 4pm

SLAVEN BELUPO (0) 2
ASTON VILLA (0) 1

Attendance 3,000
Referee Massimo De Santis
Assistants A. Consolo and A. Stangerli
Officials from Italy

▶ On high heat throughout, Villa's European hopes were close to being fried to a crisp beneath an unforgiving Croatian sun, only for the brilliance of substitute David Ginola to hand them a lifeline.

The Frenchman's 90th-minute equaliser, curled home in the blink of an eye after a trademark recce along the Slaven 18-yard line, gave Villa a precious away goal in preparation for the return leg, yet it could have easily been a near-irrelevance, had the hosts not spurned several gilt-edged chances to build upon the lead handed them by Pavo Crnac in the 61st minute.

As it is, the men from northern Croatia gave themselves fresh hope in the dying seconds, when substitute Goran Gersak hit the winner after being set free by Miljenko Kovacic. Few begrudged his team their sliver of hope.

Inspired by their defeat of Bastia in the previous round, the hosts made a mockery of their reputation as a smash-and-grab side. Far from sitting on a 1-0 lead, they sought every chance to sweep forward against ring-rusty Villa, whose defence, with the exception of Alpay, was unsettled throughout the game.

Danger-man Marijo Dodik and Damir Muzek failed to capitalise on good openings in the first half, and it needed a finger-tip save from Peter Enckelman to prod a Renato Jurcec header over the bar.

As the hour mark approached, Dodik and substitute Miljenko Kovacic fed the ball out to right-back Petar Bosnjak, whose angled drive was blocked by Enckelman, and the Finn had to be quick off his line again when he headed away a through ball from the rapidly-approaching Dodik.

An upset loomed when Frano Amizic pushed a ball through into the path of Kovacic, who shot over with the goal at his mercy. But it merely suspended judgement for Villa, who failed to clear their lines a minute later, allowing Pavo Crnac to burst through and blast the ball home.

Villa had the chance for a swift response in the 62nd minute, but Alpay headed Merson's free-kick just wide of the far post.

As if temperatures in the high-80s on a breathless afternoon were not enough, Enckelman had his hands warmed further by a 30-yard piledriver from Petar Bosnjak in the 69th minute.

With Villa now pressing for an away goal, their defence continued to be stretched by Slaven, allowing Dodik space on the left, only for his shot to curl against the bar. The woodwork saved his own team just seconds later, however, when Delaney's low cross from the right was poked against the post by Petar Bosnjak in a desperate attempt to clear.

Hero of his team's InterToto campaign to date, with six goals, Dodik was in danger of becoming the villain when he headed Kovacic's cross too high when perfectly placed at the far post with seven minutes remaining.

He and his team-mates were left to rue their wantonness in the final minute, when another Ginola cameo resulted in a shot out of nothing which reduced keeper Ivica Solomun to a spectator as the ball flew into the net.

Celebrations were short-lived, however, as Gersak evaded Villa's weary defence to remove any element of foregone conclusion from the return leg.

▶ Villa's defenders build an effective wall. From the left: Lee Hendrie, Alpay, George Boateng, Steve Staunton, Steve Stone and Gareth Barry.

▶ **SLAVEN BELUPO**
blue shirts, blue shorts

1	Ivica SOLOMUN (Gk)	
2	Petar BOSNJAK	
3	Frano AMIZIC	
4	Pavo CRNAC (82)	61
5	Stipr BOSNJAK	
6	Hassan KACIC	
7	Roy FERENCINA	
8	Mario KOVACEVIC	
9	Renaton JURCEC (c) (50)	
14	Damir MUZEK (60)	
15	Marijo DODIK	
	Substitutes	
12	Robert LISJAK (Gk)	
13	Goran GERSAK (14)	90
15	Zdravko MEDIMOREC (4)	
18	Miljenko KOVACIC (9)	
19	Dario BRGLES	
22	Srebrenko POSAVEC	
24	Igor GAL	

▶ **ASTON VILLA**
claret shirts with blue trim, white shorts

1	Peter ENCKELMAN (Gk)	
2	Mark DELANEY	
3	Alan WRIGHT	
4	Gareth BARRY (73)	
5	ALPAY Ozalan	
6	George BOATENG	
7	Steve STONE (78)	
8	Lee HENDRIE	
9	Dion DUBLIN (54)	
10	Paul MERSON (c)	
11	Steve STAUNTON	
	Substitutes	
12	Darius VASSELL (9)	
14	David GINOLA (4)	90
15	Juan Pablo ANGEL	
16	Jlloyd SAMUEL (7)	
18	Thomas HITZLSPERGER	
19	Jonathan BEWERS	
20	Boaz MYHILL (Gk)	

▶ Villa's first match against Croatian opposition ▶ David Ginola claims the club's first goal of the season

INTERTOTO CUP THIRD ROUND SECOND LEG — MATCH 02

Predictable Lee-way

▶ They had partied long into the night in Koprivnica a week earlier, but the most telling noise of this tie came from Lee Hendrie.

After his football had done the talking in the first leg with one of the better performances in Villa's 2-1 defeat, Hendrie had insisted that seven days' work on the training pitch would be enough for his team to turn the contest around.

The young midfielder proved his own point with two goals which reasserted the natural order in front of a bumper crowd that was more the exception than the norm for this competition.

The previous Saturday had been Slaven Belupo's biggest night since clinching promotion to the Croatian first division four years ago, but this was reality check time for a capable side who were nevertheless always second-best against a Villa team in full fettle.

Having slammed home a cross from Villa new boy, Hassan Kachloul after 19 minutes, Hendrie enjoyed the luck of the bounce when a 39th-minute through ball rattled around between him and several Slaven defenders before he prodded home a shot through the crowded goalmouth.

He was close to a hat-trick, too, only to have the ball taken off his toe by a defender in the 62nd minute when lining up an open shot.

Soon afterwards, it needed another timely tackle, by sub Miljenko Kovacic, to deny Juan Pablo Angel, the Colombian substitute having been given a tremendous ovation when replacing Dion Dublin.

If it was comfortable for John Gregory's side, though, it was never a stroll, although Slaven's danger men Mario Dodik, Renato Jurcec and Goran Gersak were up against an altogether more composed Villa defence than they had faced seven days earlier.

▶ *The strain of playing on a hot afternoon in July is evident as Gareth Barry clears this Slaven attack.*

Even so, the visitors rued a break by Dodik in the 68th minute, when he first beat the defence only to trip over his own feet, and then sent a centre across the face of Villa's goal which found no takers.

Revelling in more forgiving temperatures than had accompanied the first leg, Villa were a yard faster, with Petar Bosnjak regularly bamboozled by Kachloul.

Villa's first clear-cut chance arrived after seven minutes, when a well-timed Merson pass left Dublin in the clear, only for the striker to pull his shot wide of the far post. The goal then loomed large for debutant Kachloul, but his header to a Delaney cross flashed across the face of Solomun's goal.

With Villa allowing their opponents too much space on the edge of the penalty area, Danijel Radicek squandered a golden chance to steady his side when he scuffed a shot while wide-open in the 11th minute.

With fewer unforced opposition errors upon which to capitalise, the Croatians were now clinging on to the tie by their fingertips. Yet Villa seemed to relax subconsciously after their opening goal, allowing their opponents to creep into the game, and Schmeichel had his first major task when saving a Mario Dodik header.

Villa look poised to nail the tie down in the 39th minute, when Delaney was released behind the defence, only for Solomun to block Stone's touch as the cross comes over. But Merson was to the fore again a minute later, providing the pass from which Hendrie clinched Villa's passage to the semi-finals.

Date Saturday 21 July 2001
Venue Villa Park, 3.15pm

ASTON VILLA (2) 2
SLAVEN BELUPO (0) 0

Attendance 27,850
Referee Georgios Borovilos
Assistants A. Kolokas and C. Psaros
Officials from Greece

▶ **ASTON VILLA**
claret shirts with blue trim, white shorts

1 Peter SCHMEICHEL (Gk) (13)	
2 Mark DELANEY	
3 Alan WRIGHT	
4 Gareth BARRY	
5 ALPAY Ozalan	
6 George BOATENG	
7 Steve StONE (47) ❏	
8 Hassan KACHLOUL (17)	
9 Dion DUBLIN (54) ❏ (15)	
10 Paul MERSON	
11 LEE HENDRIE	g19, 39
Substitutes	
12 Darius VASSELL	
13 Peter ENCKLEMAN (Gk) (45)	
14 David GINOLA	
15 Juan Pablo ANGEL (55)	
16 Jlloyd SAMUEL	
17 Moustapha HADJI (73)	
18 Steve STAUNTON	

▶ **SLAVEN BELUPO**
blue shirts, blue shorts

1 Ivica SOLOMUN (Gk)
2 Petar BOSNJAK (18)
3 Frano AMIZIC
4 Pavo CRNAC (13)
5 Stipe BOSNJAK
6 Hasan KACIC (60) ❏
7 Roy FERENCINA
9 Renato JURCEC (8)
14 Damir MUZEK
15 Marijo DODIK (73)
20 Danijel RADICEK (34) ❏
Substitutes
8 Mario KOVACEVIC
12 Robert LISJAK (Gk)
13 Goran GERSAK (45)
16 Zdravko MEDIMOREC
18 Miljenko KOVACIC (62)
19 Dario BRGLES
27 Igor GAL

▶ *Villa Park's first European action since the UEFA Cup-tie against Celta Vigo in 1998*

Don't walk away Rennais

MATCH 03

Date: Wednesday 25 July 2001
Venue: Route de Lorient, 8pm

▶ Just when Stade Rennais were on the verge of disappearing over the horizon in this InterToto Cup semi-final, another key contribution by David Ginola transformed the tie with a precious away goal.

Ginola, the scorer in Croatia 11 days earlier, this time turned provider, sending over the free-kick from which Darius Vassell headed Villa back in business in the third minute of stoppage time. But if there had been understandable optimism among Villa fans that this season's path to the UEFA Cup had no Celta Vigo blocking the route, they now knew that the French side were just as likely as the Spaniards to provide a stumbling block.

Stade Rennais established a lead more slender than they deserved on the back of a darting offensive and solid defence that illustrated only too well the trickle-down effect from France's World Cup and Euro 2000 triumphs.

If French cuisine can be light and fluffy, its football is now made of much sterner stuff, and Villa were aware at the final whistle that there was still much to do in the return leg.

2-0 ahead, the home side merely emphasised their superiority when they replaced their impressive forward axis of Olivier Monterrubio and Severino Lucas mid-way through the second half, with barely a break in their stride.

The duo had tormented Villa, Lucas running onto a loose ball after 20 minutes to open the scoring, and if Cyril Chapuis had a hard act to follow when replacing Monterrubio, he did it in style, arriving unmarked at the near post to head home Echouafni's cross in the 67th minute.

Some of the self-inflicted fraying around the Stade Rennais edges, which had seen them almost squander a 5-0 advantage against FC Synot in the previous round, began to reappear at that point, yet Villa rarely threatened to exploit the resultant spaces, until Vassell rose in a crowded box to set up a second-leg thriller.

If the consolation was fortuitous, Ginola's hand in it most certainly was not. His 53rd-minute arrival in place of Steve Stone had already created a succession of chances, only for Chapuis to provide an emphatic response by extending the home side's lead.

▶ *Dion Dublin and Alpay put the Rennes defence under pressure, but the French side get the ball clear.*

Villa might have been putting their passports away for another year, had Enckelman not come out sharply to beat Monterrubio to a weak Boateng backpass in the second half. Earlier, Enckelman had narrowed the angle when Le Roux burst out of midfield to let Lucas in from the left, the latter's shot slipping past the Finn but wide of the post.

Villa countered sharply, goalkeeper Eric Durand just beating Dion Dublin to Hassan Kachloul's low cross, although it needed an excellent tackle by Mark Delaney to cut out a promising excursion into the Villa area by Monterrubio.

The hosts' promising attacks finally bore fruit in the 20th minute. Monterrubio looked to have sacrificed a promising attack to play for obstruction by Gareth Barry, but the ball rolled through to an unchallenged Lucas, who calmly slotted it past Enckelman.

Chapuis' goal provided an even bleaker outlook, but Vassell's last gasp leveller put a totally different complexion on the proceedings.

STADE RENNAIS (1) 2
ASTON VILLA (0) 1

Attendance 15,753
Referee Lucílio Batista
Assistants J. Esteves and C. Matos
Officials from Portugal

▶ **STADE RENNAIS**
black shirts with red sash, black shorts

16	Eric DURAND (Gk)	
4	Michelon CESAR (84)	
5	Olivier ECHOUAFNI	
6	Dominique ARRIBAGÉ (c)	
8	Christophe LE ROUX	
14	Philippe DELAYE	
17	Julien ESCUDÉ	
18	Olivier MONTERRUBIO (62)	
19	Severino LUCAS (76)	g20
21	Anthony RÉVEILLÈRE	
26	Gaël DANIC ❑	
	Substitutes	
1	Fabien DEBEC (Gk)	
3	Gregory PAISLEY (4)	
9	Frederic PIQUIONNE (19)	
10	Jocelyn GOURVENNEC	
15	Stéphane GREGOIRE	
28	Cyril CHAPUIS (18)	g67
29	Marques VANDERSON	

▶ **ASTON VILLA**
claret shirts with blue trim, white shorts

1	Peter ENCKELMAN (Gk)	
2	Mark DELANEY	
3	Alan WRIGHT ❑	
4	Gareth BARRY ❑	
5	ALPAY Ozalan	
6	George BOATENG	
7	Steve STONE (53)	
8	Hassan KACHLOUL (62)	
9	Dion DUBLIN (78)	
10	Paul MERSON (c)	
11	Lee HENDRIE ❑	
	Substitutes	
12	Darius VASSELL (9)	g90
13	Boaz MYHILL (Gk)	
14	David GINOLA (7) ❑	
15	Juan Pablo ANGEL	
16	Jlloyd SAMUEL	
17	Moustapha HADJI (8)	
18	Steve STAUNTON	

▶ *Villa's first clash with French opposition since the 1997 UEFA Cup-tie against Bordeaux*

INTERTOTO CUP SEMI FINAL SECOND LEG — MATCH 04

Away goals rule as Basel beckons

Date: Wednesday 1 August 2001
Venue: Villa Park, 7.45pm

ASTON VILLA (1) 1
STADE RENNAIS (0) 0

Attendance 30,782
Referee Wolfgang Stark
Assistants J.H. Salver and C. Schräer
Officials from Germany

▶ For a team supposedly concentrating on the league, Stade Rennais have a funny way of going about it.

Bankrolled to the tune of £60m over the last three seasons by their wealthy owner, the French club are under strict orders to be a part of next season's Champions' League, yet they had made a pig's ear of the first hurdle when losing 5-0 at home to Auxerre at the weekend. If that suggested easy pickings to Aston Villa, come the renewal of their InterToto Cup semi-final encounter with the men from Brittany, they were in for a surprise.

Ultimately, Dion Dublin's goal after just five minutes secured Villa's place in the final, courtesy of the away goals rule, but 85 more minutes would elapse before he and his team could savour the fact, in the face of Rennais' continued appetite for this supposed sideshow to their main itinerary.

The visitors' starting line-up contained seven changes from the first leg, yet any deficiency was purely theoretical. Unflustered by Villa's perfect start, they quickly regained their poise and had their hosts on the back foot for much of the game, their speed and directness repeatedly prising openings in the Villa ranks.

The hosts might have been spared a nervy closing period, when a combination of Dublin and his marker Julian Escude forced substitute Moustapha Hadji's cross over the line shortly after the hour mark, only for the referee to blow for an infringement.

By then, however, the Frenchmen had fashioned what would prove to be their own make-or-break moment. In an echo of Marijo Dodik's crucial miss for Slaven Belupo in the second leg of Villa's third-round tie, Stade Rennais' striker Cyril Chapuis broke free of the defence to have two bites of the cherry, only to be denied first by Peter Enckelman and then by his errant stab at the rebound.

The game was just five minutes old when David Ginola took over where he had left off in Rennes, delivering a centre from which a stretching Dion Dublin was delighted to open his account for the season with a close-range side-footer past keeper Eric Durand.

The French side almost silenced the home crowd within minutes, however, when Yohann Bigne's pass left Chapuis in a race for the ball with Alan Wright on the right side of the Villa area. Perhaps fortunate not to concede a penalty for holding, the Villa full-back managed to scramble the ball clear.

Villa had by now eased off after their sprightly opening and when Peter Enckelman pushed the ball away from Olivier Monterrubio's head in the 14th minute, they were glad to see Cyril Yapi shoot wide from inside the box.

Relying on his relentless pace, Chapuis fashioned a shot from nothing to test Enckelman in the 21st minute and Monterrubio forced another good save from the Finn just moments later with a low header from Yapi's cross.

There was an anxious edge to the Holte End's exhortations by the time Dion Dublin partially cleared a 23rd minute cross, allowing Escude to volley over the bar.

Happy to shoot from distance, the visitors' enthusiasm was matched neither by their accuracy or power, but at short range, they were a different proposition, and Monterrubio saw the goal loom large from a right-wing cross after half an hour, only for a deflection to carry his shot out for a corner.

▶ David Ginola, whose cross set up the only goal of the game, slides in to dispossess Stephane Gregoire as Rennes seek an equaliser.

▶ **ASTON VILLA**
claret shirts with blue trim, white shorts

1	Peter ENCKELMAN (Gk)
2	Mark DELANEY
3	Alan WRIGHT
4	Gareth BARRY ❏
5	ALPAY Ozalan
6	George BOATENG
8	Hassan KACHLOUL
9	Dion DUBLIN g5
10	Paul MERSON (c) (57)
11	Lee HENDRIE (76)
14	David GINOLA (85)
	Substitutes
7	Steve STONE (11)
12	Darius VASSELL (14)
13	Boaz MYHILL (Gk)
15	Juan Pablo ANGEL
16	Jlloyd SAMUEL
17	Moustapha HADJI (10)
18	Steve STAUNTON

▶ **STADE RENNAIS**
black shirts with red sash, black shorts

16	Eric DURAND (Gk) (c)
3	Gregory PAISLEY
7	Yohann BIGNÉ
13	Lamine DIATTA
15	Stéphane GREGOIRE ❏
17	Julien ESCUDÉ
18	Olivier MONTERRUBIO (77)
25	Cyril YAPI ❏
26	Gaël DANIC
28	Cyril CHAPUIS (52)
29	Marques VANDERSON (58)
	Substitutes
1	Fabien DEBEC (Gk)
6	Dominique ARRIBAGÉ
8	Christophe LE ROUX (29)
9	Frederic PIQUIONNE (18)
10	Jocelyn GOURVENNEC
19	Severino LUCAS (28)
21	Anthony RÉVEILLÈRE

▶ Mark Delaney briefly wears the captain's armband after Paul Merson is substituted, before handing it to Dion Dublin

INTERTOTO CUP FINAL FIRST LEG — MATCH 05

Swiss rolled by Merson

▶ After moving within touching distance of a place in the UEFA Cup, Aston Villa may feel that their real InterToto Cup Final came in the previous round.

Full of sound and fury signifying little, FC Basel were a pale shadow of the dashing Stade Rennais side Villa had only just overcome in the semi-final, and Paul Merson's tap-in from a rebound after Hassan Kachloul's 59th minute shot threatened to turn the second leg into a formality.

Having given themselves a lifeline with late away goals in their previous ties, however, it was Villa's turn to be frustrated. Christian Gimenez put a slightly rosier look on his team's prospects when he also relied on a rebound to net the equaliser in the 76th minute, after substitute Carlos Varela broke down the right to fire a shot which keeper Peter Enckelman could only parry.

Varela's contribution merely added to the home fans' delight, for he had threatened to prompt the loudest noise of a tame contest even before his 59th-minute introduction, such was the crowd's insistence that he be brought on to enliven the hosts' performance.

Against a workmanlike display by their visitors, Basel's weaknesses were exposed in the first half. Prompted by playmaker Hakan Yakin and the surging runs of Gimenez and Ivan Ergic, the hosts lacked nothing in effort but much in execution as the lack of a final pass and aerial presence among their forwards revealed their limitations.

▶ *Lee Hendrie adopts a balletic pose in Switzerland to win this midfield challenge at St Jacob-Park.*

In seeing off those initial thrusts, Villa owed much to Enckelman, who got down well to save from Hakan Yakin after the latter got behind the defence in the second minute. The Turkish-born midfielder repeated the feat 42 minutes later with a burst of pace completely at odds with what had become a sluggish contest, but the Finn again acted quickly, keeping the shot out with his knees.

The keeper had previously been beaten by an angled drive from Gimenez, but the Argentinian saw his effort slip just past the far post, and team-mate Ergic was similarly off-target from the edge of the Villa area in the 37th minute after some promising build-up work by the hosts.

Already under the cosh from their supporters, who had to endure a faltering start to their club's domestic campaign, the half-time mood in the Basel changing room would have been grim indeed, had Moustapha Hadji been able to convert a Dion Dublin knock-down from just a few feet out.

Villa finally broke the deadlock shortly before the hour mark, when Hassan Kachloul tried a shot from the left that was too hot to handle for Pascal Zuberbühler. The keeper's block left Merson with a simple tap-in for arguably the easiest goal of his career.

Basel could have made an immediate response but were once again let down by poor finishing, when a deft back heel by Hakan Yakin set up Ergic. The Yugoslav U21 international saw his shot deflected by Alpay Ozalan, setting up an even better opening for Jean-Michel Tchouga, who blasted his effort well over the bar.

The home side looked a spent force, yet the game was transformed when Varela broke away to shoot at Enckelman, who blocked the effort only as far as Gimenez, who set up an intriguing second leg with his simple conversion.

Date: Tuesday 7 August 2001
Venue: St Jacob-Park, 7.30pm

FC BASEL (0) 1
ASTON VILLA (0) 1

Attendance 25,879
Referee Eric Romain
Assistants R. Van Nylen and L. Rems
Officials from Belgium

▶ **FC BASEL**
red and blue striped shirts, blue shorts

1 Pascal ZUBERBÜHLER (Gk)	
4 Alexandre QUENNOZ	
5 Oliver KREUZER	
7 Jean-Michel TCHOUGA	
10 Hakan YAKIN (72)	
13 Christian GIMENEZ	g76
15 Murat YAKIN	
16 Yao AZIAWONOU	
17 Mario CANTALUPPI (59)	
22 Ivan ERGIC	
26 Scott CHIPPERFIELD	
Substitutes	
6 Benjamin HUGGEL	
8 Carlos VARELA (17)	
11 Hervé TUM	
12 Sébastien BARBERIS (10)	
20 Ivan KNEZ	
18 Romain CREVOISIER (Gk)	
23 Philipp DEGEN	

▶ **ASTON VILLA**
platinum shirts, platinum shorts

1 Peter ENCKELMAN (Gk)	
2 Mark DELANEY	
3 Alan WRIGHT ❑	
4 Gareth BARRY	
5 ALPAY Ozalan	
6 George BOATENG	
8 Hassan KACHLOUL	
9 Dion DUBLIN (79)	
10 Paul MERSON (c) (64)	g59
11 Lee HENDRIE	
17 Moustapha HADJI	
Substitutes	
7 Steve STONE (9)	
12 Darius VASSELL (10) ❑	
13 Boaz MYHILL (Gk)	
14 David GINOLA	
15 Juan Pablo ANGEL	
16 Jlloyd SAMUEL	
18 Steve STAUNTON	

▶ *Another first for the club – Villa had not previously faced Swiss opponents in a competitive match*

FA BARCLAYCARD PREMIERSHIP

MATCH 06

Premiere a well-rehearsed routine

Date Saturday 18 August 2001
Venue White Hart Lane, 3.00pm

TOTTENHAM H. (0) **0**
ASTON VILLA (0) **0**

Attendance 36,059
Referee Dermot Gallagher
Assistants R. Burton and P. Barnes

▸ Villa's third goalless draw in four years on the opening day of the Premiership season was gratefully received, after a late scare threatened to hand the Londoners a fortuitous win.

Roared on by fans impatient for the Glenn Hoddle era to begin in style and in earnest, Spurs had snapped out of the indifference that hampered their game in the latter stages, to make serious inroads into their opponents' new-look defence as the clock wound down.

No-one perked up more than the diminutive Ukranian Sergiy Rebrov, whose cross in the 89th minute picked out Gary Doherty at the far post. The Republic of Ireland international swung at the ball first time and was denied a 'Goal of the Month' contender solely by the width of Peter Schmeichel's crossbar, with the Dane reduced to a spectator. A more favourable outcome for the Spurs striker would have been harsh on Villa, who had put an unremarkable first half behind them to produce most of the second period's highlights.

A new-look forward combination of Juan Pablo Angel and Darius Vassell were served with a series of crosses into the Spurs box, although it was Hassan Kachloul who came closest to dispatching one of them, when his looping far-post header struck an upright with Spurs keeper Neil Sullivan beaten.

Earlier, Vassell had worked an opening to get a clean header onto a 47th-minute Paul Merson corner, only for his effort to fly narrowly over the bar. He was unlucky soon afterwards when he fought off his marker's attentions to get a stab at a low cross from Mark Delaney, only to see his effort again clear the bar.

Alpay Ozalan was the next to go close, the Turkish defender heading another corner from the skipper wide of the post. There was at least some consolation from the big Turk who will have been delighted with the partnership struck up in the centre of Villa's defence with Olof Mellberg.

Restricted to fitness training and 70 minutes of action in the previous weekend's friendly against his former club, Santander, the Swede might have been expected to need some time to get used to the Premiership, yet he looked to the manner born in an impressive debut that had Villa fans drooling and their Tottenham counterparts lamenting an enforced reshuffle in their forward line.

Teddy Sheringham's long-awaited debut in the second instalment of his Tottenham career remained on ice, along with his Achilles tendon, and Les Ferdinand had to join him on the sidelines with the game just 11 minutes old, when he failed to run off the effects of an earlier challenge by Alan Wright.

This brought the not inconsiderable talents of Steffen Iversen into play but it was two of Spurs' summer signings who caught the eye. Ex-Chelsea man Gustavo Poyet slipped effortlessly into the same playmaker role he enjoyed at Stamford Bridge, linking well with wing-back Christian Ziege, newly-arrived from Liverpool.

Ziege almost broke the deadlock seven minutes before half-time, when his shot brought a good save out of Schmeichel before Poyet's effort was stopped by a Mellberg interception. The same Spurs duo linked well early in the second half but as Villa began to press, the hosts lost their impetus and the chance of a Villa away win to start the season began to grow.

▸ *Olof Mellberg, who enjoyed an outstanding debut at the heart of Villa's defence, nips in front of Gustavo Poyet to head clear.*

▸ **TOTTENHAM HOTSPUR**
white shirts, navy blue shorts

1	Neil SULLIVAN (Gk)
3	Mauricio TARICCO (81)
4	Steffen FREUND (67)
5	Goran BUNJEVCEVIC
9	Les FERDINAND (c) (21)
11	Sergiy REBROV
12	Gary DOHERTY ❑
14	Gustavo POYET
23	Christian ZIEGE ❑
25	Stephen CLEMENCE ❑
26	Ledley KING
	Substitutes
6	Chris PERRY (3)
7	Darren ANDERTON (4)
13	Kasey KELLER (Gk)
16	Steffen IVERSEN (9)
29	Simon DAVIES

▸ **ASTON VILLA**
claret shirts with blue trim, white shorts

1	Peter SCHMEICHEL (Gk)
2	Mark DELANEY ❑
3	Alan WRIGHT
4	Olof MELLBERG
5	ALPAY Ozalan
6	George BOATENG ❑
8	Juan Pablo ANGEL (62)
10	Paul MERSON (c)
17	Lee HENDRIE
22	Darius VASSELL (74)
30	Hassan KACHLOUL (81)
	Substitutes
12	Peter ENCKELMAN (Gk)
14	David GINOLA (8)
15	Gareth BARRY
18	Steve STONE (30)
20	Moustapha HADJI (22)

Before	P	W	D	L	F	A	pts
- Villa	0	0	0	0	0	0	0
- Spurs	0	0	0	0	0	0	0
After	P	W	D	L	F	A	pts
- Villa	1	0	1	0	0	0	1
- Spurs	1	0	1	0	0	0	1

▸ Goalless at White Hart Lane for the second consecutive season ▸ League debuts for Schmeichel, Mellberg, Kachloul and Hadji

INTERTOTO CUP FINAL SECOND LEG   MATCH 07

No mercy as Villa clinch UEFA spot

Date   Tuesday 21 August 2001
Venue   Villa Park 7.45pm

▶ For 14 minutes, Christian Gross looked set for revenge of sorts on English football, Australian Scott Chipperfield having wiped out Villa's away goal. At long last, the man who knew only brickbats in his time as Spurs manager, seemed on the brink of proving a point or two, only for one of his former players to blow a gale through his hopes.

ASTON VILLA (1) 4
FC BASEL (1) 1

Attendance 39,593
Referee   Claus Bo Larsen
Assistants J. Larsen and A.D. Nielsen
            Officials from Denmark

We will never know the answer, but it is interesting to speculate how differently the Worthington Cup semi-final and FA Cup Final of 2000 might have turned out had David Ginola been a Villa player at the time. Villa froze on both occasions, and as Chipperfield pounced on Christian Gimenez's cross to pick his spot in the 30th minute, those big-day nerves were encroaching once more.

But Ginola had emerged to hand Villa a lifeline in the previous two rounds of this competition, and his performance against Basel was just as telling.

A minute before half-time, he flicked on the pass that allowed the impressive Darius Vassell to power an equaliser past Pascal Zuberbühler, and with the visitors still looking dazed, Ginola swung a cross towards Zuberbühler's near post that set up the go-ahead goal.

At which point, enter The Executioner. If his goal against Coventry broke the ice and two against Santander turned up the heat, maybe history will recall this as the night when Juan Pablo Angel finally caught fire as a Villa player.

Any doubts that the Colombian might be in for another game of vague promise, rather than production, were dispelled 11 minutes into the second half. Angel and Ginola had become buddies off the field and their mutual understanding showed when only the Colombian was alert to Ginola's free kick, arriving at the near post to head the hosts ahead for good.

With his name ringing down from the Holte End, no-one in the claret and blue camp would have begrudged his slice of good fortune 22 minutes later, when his shot took a sizeable deflection to beat the Basel keeper.

Once Peter Schmeichel spread himself to deny a Chipperfield header, the Swiss side knew their foreign jaunts were over for the year. If the relationship between Ginola and Villa fans had cooled a little following his threat of legal action against manager John Gregory, this was 'kiss and make up' time in no uncertain terms.

Playing once again like a man to whom every game is his cv, the French winger had spent the evening sowing seeds of doubt throughout the Basel defence. Now that Vassell and Angel had cashed in, the chance for Ginola himself to reap a harvest finally arrived with just six minutes to go.

Head down, hair trailing, a burst of speed in from the left flank and a shot stroked into the corner. It was a classic finale to an outstanding display which ensured Villa of a piece of silverware just three days into the Premiership campaign.

▶ ASTON VILLA
claret shirts with blue trim, white shorts

1	Peter SCHMEICHEL (Gk) (c)
2	Mark DELANEY
3	Steve STAUNTON (67)
4	Gareth BARRY
5	ALPAY Ozalan
6	George BOATENG
7	Steve STONE
11	Lee HENDRIE (64)
12	Darius VASSELL g44
14	David GINOLA g84
15	Juan Pablo ANGEL (77) g55, 77
	Substitutes
8	Hassan KACHLOUL (11)
9	Dion DUBLIN (15)
10	Paul MERSON
13	Peter ENCKELMAN (Gk)
16	Jlloyd SAMUEL (3)
17	Moustapha HADJI
18	Jonathan BEWERS

▶ FC BASEL
white shirts, blue shorts

1	Pascal ZUBERBÜHLER (Gk)
2	Philippe CRAVERO
4	Alexandre QUENNOZ
5	Oliver KREUZER (c)
6	Benjamin HUGGEL
8	Carlos VARELA
9	George KOUMANTARAKIS
10	Hakan YAKIN
13	Christian GIMENEZ (82)
15	Murat YAKIN
26	Scott CHIPPERFIELD (67) g30
	Substitutes
7	Jean-Michel TCHOUGA
11	Hervé TUM (13)
12	Sébastien BARBERIS (26)
16	Yao AZIAWONOU
18	Romain CREVOISIER (Gk)
20	Ivan KNEZ
23	Philipp DEGEN

▶ *Villa's players celebrate their InterToto triumph, which secured qualification for the UEFA Cup.*

▶ A new trophy for the Villa Park cabinet   ▶ Victory ensures entry to the UEFA Cup

FA BARCLAYCARD PREMIERSHIP

Stoppage-time agony for Alpay

▶ But for an injury time equaliser, you might not be reading these words, for by the time Sir Alex Ferguson had finished his broadside at the media in his post-game press conference, those of us in the first few rows were inclined to speculate on our fate if United had lost.

Bristling with indignation at the amount of stoppage time decreed at the end of the second half, the United manager was unimpressed that those responsible for reporting the game to the nation weren't similarly seething.

His team's persistence was rather easier to admire, even if it did break Villa hearts that had been given all of 88 minutes to savour a first league win in six years over the reigning Premiership champions.

When Darius Vassell attached himself to a low cross of consummate precision by Hassan Kachloul in the fourth minute to give Villa the lead, there seemed every possibility of such an outcome. Paul Merson's pre-season prediction that this was the best time to be playing United looked shrewder by the minute as Villa went about their work with confidence.

The latest cog in their machine watched much of the game from the substitutes' bench before making a promising debut, and while his Dinamo Zagreb pedigree means that Bosko Balaban probably doesn't need the tuition, what followed Vassell's goal was an object lesson in how the tough get going when the going gets tough.

▶ *Juan Pablo Angel shields the ball from Mikael Silvestre as Villa apply some early pressure.*

Anyone inclined to decry United as beneficiaries of the Devil's luck when a corner was inadvertently deflected past Peter Schmeichel by Alpay Ozalan two minutes into stoppage time needs to consider this: from the moment Vassell put Villa ahead, not once did United panic.

They struggled, for sure. David Beckham wasn't quite at concert pitch and their back line didn't give new goalkeeper Roy Carroll, in for the injured Fabien Barthez, quite the scare-free Premiership debut he would have hoped for, yet United stuck patiently to their task, probing with the assuredness of men who know their collective class is irresistible against all but the very best opposition.

Yet Villa could have easily slipped into that category. Ozalan and Mellberg versus Van Nistelrooy was just as enthralling an encounter as its pre-match billing suggested, with Delaney v Giggs an unexpected supporting bout, and in both cases the Villa players came out ahead on points.

In midfield, Lee Hendrie and George Boateng gave Juan Veron & Co as good as they got, while up front, Vassell and Juan Pablo Angel worked more openings than a travelling salesman. But Villa rarely found a move to match the penetration of the one which led to their goal. Lee Hendrie's crossfield pass from deep in midfield was taken on by Kachloul and curled around a forest of United legs like the decisive wood on a bowling green for Vassell to open his domestic account.

Peter Schmeichel had a busy afternoon, blocking efforts from Van Nistelrooy, Scholes and Keane before he was finally beaten. When Ryan Giggs' last-ditch corner came over from the right, Ronnie Johnsen's header sent the ball cannoning off Alpay into the net to give Sir Alex some good cheer. Relatively speaking.

MATCH 08

Date   Sunday 26 August 2001
Venue   Villa Park, 2.00pm

ASTON VILLA (1) 1
MANCHESTER UTD (0) 1

Attendance   42,632
Referee   Graham Barber
Assistants   M. Tingey and J. Devine

▶ **ASTON VILLA**
claret shirts with blue trim, white shorts

1	Peter SCHMEICHEL (Gk)	
2	Mark DELANEY	
3	Alan WRIGHT	
4	Olof MELLBERG	
5	ALPAY Ozalan	og90
6	George BOATENG	
8	Juan Pablo ANGEL (78)	
10	Paul MERSON (c) (63)	
17	Lee HENDRIE	
22	Darius VASSELL	g4
30	Hassan KACHLOUL	
	Substitutes	
12	Peter ENCKELMAN (Gk)	
14	David GINOLA	
19	Bosko BALABAN (8)	
20	Moustapha HADJI (10)	
31	Jlloyd SAMUEL	

▶ **MANCHESTER UNITED**
white shirts, black shorts

13	Roy Carroll (Gk)	
2	Gary NEVILLE	
4	Juan VERON ❏	
5	Ronny JOHNSEN	
7	David BECKHAM (70)	
10	Ruud van NISTELROOY	
11	Ryan GIGGS	
16	Roy KEANE	
18	Paul SCHOLES ❏ (83)	
24	Wes BROWN	
27	Mikael SILVESTRE (45)	
	Substitutes	
9	Andy COLE (7)	
12	Phil NEVILLE (27)	
17	Raimond van der GOUW (Gk)	
19	Dwight YORKE	
20	Ole Gunnar SOLSKJAER (18)	

Before	P	W	D	L	F	A	pts
6 Man Utd	2	1	1	0	5	4	4
16 Villa	1	0	1	0	0	0	1
After	P	W	D	L	F	A	pts
7 Man Utd	3	1	2	0	6	5	5
15 Villa	2	0	2	0	1	1	2

▶ *Villa without a league win over United since the opening day of 1995-96*   ▶ *Vassell's first Premiership goal of the season*

FA BARCLAYCARD PREMIERSHIP   MATCH 09

Anfield of dreams

▶ Aston Villa victories at Anfield are something of a rarity, but there was particular reason to savour their latest success on Merseyside.

On this occasion, the assignment looked tougher than ever, given the fact that Liverpool players had scored all seven England goals as Sven Goran Eriksson's side had soared to the top of their World Cup qualifying group during the preceding seven days. It was also almost 12 months to the day since Villa had crumbled 3-1 in the face of Michael Owen's first half hat-trick in last season's corresponding fixture, so the signs were not particularly encouraging.

Manager John Gregory must have felt his side had a chance, though, when the Liverpool team-sheet indicated that Owen, despite his England hat-trick against Germany seven days earlier, would start the match on the substitutes bench.

The lethal 21-year-old was eventually introduced as a 59th minute substitute for Nick Barmby which meant Liverpool were spearheaded by a trio of England strikers - Owen, Emile Heskey and Robbie Fowler - for the final half hour.

By then, it hardly mattered. Even with three up front, the home side were unable to make any impression on a rock solid Villa back line in which Olof Mellberg and Alpay were outstanding.

If Owen's absence from the Reds' starting line-up was an unexpected bonus, Villa received a second boost when Stephen Gerrard, another of England's heroes, was sent off for his reckless 74th minute tackle on George Boateng, but even against 11 men, there was no question about the visitors' superiority.

▶ *Alan Wright lunges to block a powerful drive from Steven Gerrard before the Liverpool player was sent off.*

Having been agonisingly close to three points in their previous match against champions Manchester United, they were calm and composed throughout, knocking the ball around with all the confidence of a team who believe they are capable of challenging for honours during the coming months.

Villa's early play, to be fair, was pleasing on the eye rather than penetrating, although Paul Merson tested Liverpool's new Polish goalkeeper Jerzy Dudek with a fierce 28th minute left-foot drive after Hendrie had cut the ball back invitingly from the byline. Two minutes later, after Mark Delaney had been felled by Nick Barmby's crude challenge, Merson curled a superb free-kick into the danger zone, and Dion Dublin marked his first appearance of the campaign with a bullet header inside Dudek's left-hand post.

Gerrard's headed equaliser after just 54 seconds of the second half briefly threatened to throw the visitors out of their stride, but once Hendrie had restored the lead on 54 minutes, there was little doubt about the outcome.

Dublin was again involved, chesting down Wright's deep free-kick before flicking the ball past a defender to set himself up for a close-range shooting opportunity. His subsequent miskick might have been embarrassing, but Hendrie was on hand to lash an unstoppable shot into the far corner.

Gerrard's dismissal might have left Liverpool a man short, but they were already behind on points before Vassell delivered his knockout blow.

The England under-21 striker's speed enabled him to reach Mellberg's long clearance and although there seemed no immediate danger, he teased Sammy Hyypia before unleashing a right-foot shot which took a slight deflection off the Liverpool defender and looped over Dudek.

Date Saturday 8 September 2001
Venue Anfield, 3.00pm

LIVERPOOL (0) 1
ASTON VILLA (1) 3

Attendance 44,102
Referee Andy D'Urso
Assistants A.J. Martin and T. Massey

▶ **LIVERPOOL**
red shirts, red shorts

12	Jerzy DUDEK (Gk)	
2	Stephane HENCHOZ (76)	
4	Sami HYYYPIA	
8	Emile HESKEY	
9	Robbie FOWLER (c)	
16	Dietmar HAMANN	
17	Steven GERRARD ■	g46
18	John Arne RIISE (59)	
20	Nick BARMBY ❑ (59)	
21	Gary McALLISTER	
23	Jamie CARRAGHER ❑	
Substitutes		
10	Michael OWEN (20)	
13	Danny MURPHY (2)	
25	Igor BISCAN	
27	Gregory VIGNAL (18) ❑	
19	Pegguy ARPHEXAD (Gk)	

▶ **ASTON VILLA**
platinum shirts, navy blue shorts

1	Peter SCHMEICHEL (Gk)	
2	Mark DELANEY	
3	Alan WRIGHT	
4	Olof MELLBERG ❑	
5	ALPAY Ozalan ❑	
6	George BOATENG	
9	Dion DUBLIN	g31
10	Paul MERSON (c) (70)	
17	Lee HENDRIE (89)	g55
22	Darius VASSELL	g86
30	Hassan KACHLOUL	
Substitutes		
11	Steve STAUNTON (17)	
12	Peter ENCKELMAN (Gk)	
14	David GINOLA	
19	Bosko BALABAN	
20	Moustapha HADJI (10)	

Before	P	W	D	L	F	A	pts
12 Liverpool	2	1	0	1	3	3	3
15 Villa	2	0	2	0	1	1	2
After	P	W	D	L	F	A	pts
8 Villa	3	1	2	0	4	2	5
15 Liverpool	3	1	0	2	4	6	3

▶ *Villa win at Anfield for only the third time in 23 visits* ▶ *Hendrie, Dublin open their Premier accounts*

FA BARCLAYCARD PREMIERSHIP

Honours even on a sombre day

▶ As one newspaper columnist pointed out in the wake of the World Trade Centre disaster, it would be worrying if too many sportsmen were able to play out of their skins so soon after a horror story that put sport so firmly in its place. By this standard, Villa and Sunderland have nothing for which to reproach themselves after a game that stubbornly refused to move beyond the level of earnest endeavour.

If the sight of professional footballers each carrying a solitary flower onto the field initially seemed incongruous, it showed how the players had been as affected as the rest of us by events in New York, as they proceeded to hand them to fans behind each goal.

The minute's silence was conducted with both teams opting to stand with their arms around each other's shoulders, rather than spaced around the centre circle, as the American flag made a rare appearance at Villa Park, held aloft at various points in the crowd while silence descended on the stadium.

A diversion from the pain of real life was the only credible function of sport on this solemn weekend, and for 15 minutes, it looked as though Villa-Sunderland might just be able to take us out of ourselves for a while.

Villa, rampant from their upset of Liverpool eight days earlier, squared up to a well-drilled Wearside outfit and the game initially ebbed and flowed with promise in the autumnal sunshine.

As the afternoon wore on, however, forward and reverse eventually merged into neutral, as it became apparent that the two sides cancelled each other out; Kevin Kilbane and Julio Arca against Mark Delaney and Alan Wright on the flanks and Gavin McCann and Stefan Schwarz against Lee Hendrie and George Boateng in the middle.

And if openings still emerged in front of goal, skill and fortune intervened to ensure we would be denied a goal, which was harsh on man-of-the-match, Darius Vassell, whose snowballing confidence was evident in a series of quicksilver manoeuvres that left Sunderland defenders tackling thin air.

▶ *George Boateng is a picture of concentration as he wins the ball from Sunderland hot shot Niall Quinn.*

Twice within the first 10 minutes, he threatened to give Villa an early boost. His own confidence done no harm by his success at Anfield a week earlier, Dion Dublin flicked the ball into his team-mate's path with three minutes gone, only for a timely interception by George McCartney to send the ball out for a corner.

In the 10th minute, the Villa duo combined in similar fashion and this time Vassell managed to get his boot to the ball, Jurgen Macho saving alertly inside his near post.

Throughout the game, the England U21 international would show the eye-catching menace that is becoming a staple dish on the Villa menu. With two defenders transfixed in front of him later in the first half, Vassell fired a shot just wide of the post, and he went similarly close after the interval, having weaved his way through a cluster of defenders to bring Macho's goal within range.

Ultimately, all we were left with as the game lapsed into a fragmented affair, but there will be more appropriate afternoons for getting worked up about two points dropped at home.

MATCH 10

Date Sunday 16 September 2001
Venue Villa Park, 3.00pm

ASTON VILLA (0) 0
SUNDERLAND (0) 0

Attendance 31,688
Referee Uriah Rennie
Assistants M. L. Short and W. Jordan

▶ **ASTON VILLA**
claret shirts with blue trim, white shorts

1	Peter SCHMEICHEL (Gk)
2	Mark DELANEY
3	Alan WRIGHT
4	Olof MELLBERG
5	ALPAY Ozalan
6	George BOATENG
9	Dion DUBLIN (68)
10	Paul MERSON (c) (55)
17	Lee HENDRIE
22	Darius VASSELL
30	Hassan KACHLOUL
	Substitutes
12	Peter ENCKELMAN (Gk)
14	David GINOLA (10)
15	Gareth BARRY
19	Bosko BALABAN (9)
20	Moustapha HADJI

▶ **SUNDERLAND**
red and white striped shirts, black shorts

30	Jurgen MACHO (Gk)
2	Bernt HASS ❑
3	Michael GRAY (c)
8	Gavin McCANN ❑
9	Niall QUINN (82)
10	Kevin PHILLIPS ❑
11	Kevin KILBANE
17	Jody CRADDOCK
20	Stefan SCHWARZ ❑
24	George McCARTNEY
33	Julio ARCA
	Substitutes
7	Lilian LASLANDES (9)
13	Michael INGRAM (Gk)
15	David BELLION
18	Darren WILLIAMS
21	Paul THIRLWELL

Before	P	W	D	L	F	A	pts
6 S'land	4	2	1	1	3	3	7
9 Villa	3	1	2	0	4	2	5
After	P	W	D	L	F	A	pts
7 S'land	5	2	2	1	3	3	8
9 Villa	4	1	3	0	4	2	6

▶ *Goalless at home to Sunderland for the second consecutive season*

15

UEFA CUP FIRST ROUND FIRST LEG   MATCH 11

Angel keeps Euro hopes alive

Date Thursday 20 September 2001
Venue Villa Park 7.45pm

▶ For a team who have become adept at establishing strong positions after the first 90 minutes of European matches, Villa could hardly have made things more difficult for themselves as they hit the UEFA Cup trail.

As if defeat on home soil were not bad enough, John Gregory's side were penetrated three times by a Varteks outfit who became odds-on favourites to progress in the event of the tie being decided by the away goals rule.

Juan Pablo Angel's two second half goals underlined the point as Villa twice battled from behind, only for the home side's normally sound back line to suddenly creak alarmingly.

Commanding defensive work had been the cornerstone of an encouraging start which had seen Villa unbeaten in their opening four Premiership fixtures, and until a minute before half time the trend looked certain to continue.

Before striker Sasa Bjelanovic put Varteks ahead, it had merely seemed a question of whether Villa would be able to establish a lead. Once the deadlock had been broken, however, a goal looked likely every time either side moved forward. The outcome was a thrilling second half which culminated with goalkeeper and acting captain Peter Schmeichel racing upfield to get in a header and a shot during a desperate late onslaught. After a generally low-key opening period, it was dramatic fare, indeed, even if Holte Enders were ultimately left feeling bitterly disappointed.

If there was one positive to be taken from a depressing result, it was undoubtedly the predatory instincts of Angel, who specialises in playing against European opposition. Having scored twice in the InterToto Cup final triumph over Swiss club Basel, the former River Plate marksman was again in lethal form as he converted Steve Stone's low 53rd minute cross and then headed in Hassan Kachloul's deep 68th minute centre.

It was just a pity that each time Villa hauled themselves level, they failed to press home their advantage, a failing for which they paid heavily.

Varteks came up with a sucker punch just before half-time when Mumlek's piercing through ball evaded Alpay and Alan Wright. Although Bjelanovic's shot did not carry a great deal of power, it slipped through the advancing Schmeichel's legs and Villa were up against it.

Home hopes soared when Angel pounced eight minutes after the break. Kachloul's centre drifted beyond the Colombian, but when Stone whipped it back into the goalmouth, he reacted with a low shot which left Madaric helpless. The South American then had a drive deflected for a corner, but within five minutes of his equaliser, Varteks were back in front as Zoran Kastel surged through the middle and set up Veldin Karic for a left-foot which flew just inside the post.

Substitute David Ginola was instrumental in Villa's second, the French winger's clever backheel allowing Kachloul to deliver a deep cross which Angel met with a header which was too powerful for Madaric.

But just when it seemed Villa had done enough to start the second leg all square, Bjelanovic slid into the danger zone to meet Devis Mukaj's floated free-kick. The striker's deft volley was just enough to take the ball beyond Schmeichel and send Varteks' travelling contingent - all 30 of them - into celebration mode.

▶ *Alpay is at full stretch to flick the ball away from Varteks' striker Sasa Bjelanovic, scorer of two of the Croatian side's goals.*

ASTON VILLA (0) 2
NK VARTEKS (1) 3

Attendance 27,132
Referee Paulo Costa
Assistants P. Ribeiro and A. Da Silva
Officials from Portugal

▶ **ASTON VILLA**
claret shirts with blue trim, white shorts

1	Peter SCHMEICHEL (Gk) (c)
2	Mark DELANEY
3	Alan WRIGHT
4	Olof MELLBERG
5	ALPAY Ozalan
6	George BOATENG
8	Juan Pablo ANGEL ☐ g53, 68
18	Steve STONE (63)
20	Moustapha HADJI
22	Darius VASSELL
30	Hassan KACHLOUL (75)
	Substitutes
11	Steve STAUNTON
12	Peter ENCKELMAN (Gk)
14	David GINOLA (18)
15	Gareth BARRY (30)
19	Bosko BALABAN
23	Stefan MOORE
31	Jlloyd SAMUEL

▶ **NK VARTEKS**
blue and white shirts, blue shorts

1	Daniel MADARIC (Gk)
5	Danijel HRMAN (90)
6	Matija KRISTIC
7	Ian REZIC
8	Devis MUKAJ
9	Veldin KARIC g63
10	Miljenko MUMLEK (c)
11	Sasa BJELANOVIC g44, 85
14	Goran GRANIC
24	Silvestar SABOLCKI
25	Zoran KASTEL
	Substitutes
12	Antun ANDRICEVIC
3	Goran BOROVIC
12	Zeljko RUMBAK (Gk)
18	Andrija BALAJIC (5)
19	Hrvoje SKLEPIC
20	Nikola SAFARIC
26	Oscar DROBNE

▶ *Villa's second consecutive UEFA Cup home defeat – they lost by the same score to Celta Vigo in November, 1998*

FA BARCLAYCARD PREMIERSHIP

Quite contrary at St Mary's

▶ Well, well, well. One minute a game chugging quietly along - Villa tidy and restored; Southampton ragged and beleaguered - the next a Monday night hot-pot with three goals, two men sampling the early bath and tempers generally simmering on medium heat.

Picture Matthew Le Tissier being introduced into this little lot for the last 13 minutes amid a hero's welcome, and you realise why three points, which looked routine to Villa fans mid-way through the first half, had taken on the appearance of gold-dust by the final whistle.

That they belonged exclusively to the visitors, is due in no small part to Moustapha Hadji. If the home crowd's appreciation of Le Tissier was understandable, their perception wasn't always so spot on. For 69 minutes they had solidly booed another former favourite in Hassan Kachloul, only to find they had reserved their bile for the wrong Moroccan.

Just when the stage seemed set for Saints to be a source of bedevilment to Villa on the south coast for the third year running, Hadji's thumping header to Lee Hendrie's 79th minute cross put the game beyond Southampton's grasp at 3-1 and ensured that an impressive first half by the visitors was not in vain.

Villa had comfortably taken that opening period on points, as well as with a couple of seemingly knock-out punches scored by George Boateng and the burgeoning Juan Pablo Angel.

Marian Pahars had finally found his touch after several false starts to pull one back just before half-time and Villa still seemed to be clearing their heads when the dismissal of Rory Delap for a last-ditch foul on Kachloul in the 52nd minute was cancelled out by Dion Dublin's departure for what was assessed as a blow to Tahar El Khalej's head, five minutes later.

With the game's mood darkening and Le Tissier warming up, Villa had most to lose in the chaos and Hadji's strike was the most timely sedalive.

Villa's opening goal in the ninth minute had been the perfect antidote to the disappointment of their previous game. Showing good speed, Angel got the benefit of the doubt from the referee when tussling with El Khalej over a long ball from Alan Wright. The Colombian picked out Dion Dublin, who nudged the ball into the path of an overlapping George Boateng, and the midfielder opened his account for the season with a confident drive into the roof of the net from an awkward angle.

It came shortly after Saints tested Schmeichel's mettle with just two minutes gone, when Rory Delap's deep cross was met forcefully by the head of Kevin Davies, only for the Dane to claw the ball away.

▶ Saints 'keeper Paul Jones makes a vain attempt to keep out George Boateng's ninth minute opener.

It would be some time before he was similarly examined, and while Pahars' finishing fell short of its usual high standard, Villa made hay.

If the hosts' defence was exposed by the opening goal, it was stripped bare by the second just six minutes later, when some delightful inter-passing around the box by Hendrie and Dublin made spectators of their markers, allowing Angel room to score in the corner.

The atmosphere among home supporters lightened when Pahars diverted Beattie's 45th-minute centre inside Schmeichel's' far post to set up a jittery final minute for the visitors, with Mark Delaney heading off the line.

MATCH 12

Date: Monday 24 September 2001
Venue: St Mary's Stadium, 8.00pm

SOUTHAMPTON (1) 1
ASTON VILLA (2) 3

Attendance 26,794
Referee Steve Dunn
Assistants S. Gagen and T. Kettle

▶ **SOUTHAMPTON**
red and white striped shirts, black shorts

1 Paul JONES (Gk)	
3 Wayne BRIDGE	
5 Claus LUNDEKVAM (c)	
8 Matthew OAKLEY	
9 James BEATTIE	
10 Kevin DAVIES (77)	
12 Anders SVENSSON	
17 Marian PAHARS (77)	g45
18 Rory DELAP ■	
20 Tahar EL KHALEJ	
21 Jo TESSEM (66)	
Substitutes	
4 Chris MARSDEN	
7 Matt LE TISSIER (17)	
13 Neil MOSS (Gk)	
15 Francis BENALI (21)	
30 Scott McDONALD (10)	

▶ **ASTON VILLA**
claret shirts with blue trim, white shorts

1 Peter SCHMEICHEL (Gk) (c)	
2 Mark DELANEY	
3 Alan WRIGHT	
4 Olof MELLBERG	
5 ALPAY Ozalan	
6 George BOATENG	g9
8 Juan Pablo ANGEL (74)	g15
9 Dion DUBLIN ■	
17 Lee HENDRIE ❑ (87)	
20 Moustapha HADJI	g78
30 Hassan KACHLOUL ❑ (69)	
Substitutes	
11 Steve STAUNTON (30)	
12 Peter ENCKELMAN (Gk)	
14 David GINOLA	
18 Steve STONE (17)	
19 Bosko BALABAN (8)	

Before	P	W	D	L	F	A	pts
13 Villa	4	1	3	0	4	2	6
20 Saints	4	1	0	3	1	6	3
After	P	W	D	L	F	A	pts
5 Villa	5	2	3	0	7	3	9
20 Saints	5	1	0	4	2	9	3

▶ Villa's first away win against the Saints since 1998 ▶ Dublin's red card later rescinded to a yellow

17

UEFA CUP FIRST ROUND SECOND LEG

MATCH 13

Too little, too late, as Villa bow out

Date	Thursday 27 September 2001
Venue	Varazdin Stadium, 9pm

NK VARTEKS (0) 0
ASTON VILLA (0) 1

Attendance 9,000
Referee Nicolai Vollquartz
Assistants B. Pedersen and F. Rasmussen
Officials from Denmark

▶ The game in a nutshell. 37th minute; Varteks striker Veldin Karic, far from home in the deeper reaches of his team's half, receives the ball on the left flank facing his own goal and with Alan Wright snapping at his heels.

You'd put money on a hurried lay-off, yet Karic, despite being in the one area of the field where his team have looked vulnerable, holds the ball like he's in a training session, fending off Wright and biding his time until the most appropriate pass presents itself.

It was further confirmation that anyone who still bandies around the term 'East European minnows' needs to redefine his footballing atlas. For a few shaky minutes at 1-1 in the first leg of this tie, Varteks looked rattled; for the rest, they have matched their opponents with aplomb and given as good as they got; good enough to send Villa out of the UEFA Cup at the first time of asking.

The visitors' 12 hours of European football this season came to nothing at the hands of the away goals rule, as a jittery first-half defensive performance eroded the confidence they brought into the game, despite being stung by a 3-2 first leg defeat, while their inability to look after the ball played straight into the hands of a Croatian side who are lethal on the counter-attack.

A 20-yard Moustapha Hadji goal out of nothing in injury-time gave Villa a flicker of hope, but the two goal margin they needed to wipe out the woes of a week ago never looked within their reach once the relentless harassment by their opponents had blunted their edge, midway through the second half.

If Villa appeared to be caught off-balance by the calibre of the opposition in the first leg, there was no such mistake this time. Employing the flair of David Ginola and the local knowledge of Bosko Balaban in their starting line-up, they set about the home side with purpose but while their attack boded well, problems at the other end of the field hinted at a long night ahead. Varteks' exuberance led to them repeatedly outnumbering Villa's defence when sweeping forward, and the visitors' problems only increased when Olof Mellberg was stretchered off with a twisted ankle, following a collision in the final throes of the first half. He made way for substitute Steve Stone, who renewed his acquaintance with the right back slot while Mark Delaney moved across to deputise for the injured Swede.

While Villa repeatedly made good progress down the left wing, the hosts had an early chance to put the tie beyond their opponents, when Veldin Karic broke down the right but ignored the calls of two wide-open team-mates inside and eventually ran into a dead end.

His team's principal danger throughout, Karic almost redeemed himself in the 13th minute when he was sent away down the left and nimbly skipped past Alpay Ozalan, only to overrun himself again, on his way into the Villa box.

Villa, in fact, had little of their customary assuredness at the back, and when Schmeichel sold Ozalan short with a 21st minute pass, Devis Mukaj nipped in to send over a cross that was just inches away from Sasa Bjelanovic.

Hendrie managed to drive the ball home after 35 minutes, only for an offside flag following a Villa free-kick to negate his efforts and the visitors ultimately had to settle for Hadji's opportunistic strike from distance in stoppage time. It was, however, a hollow victory.

▶ Moustapha Hadji grabbed Villa's last minute winner, but there was no way through on this occasion.

▶ **NK VARTEKS**
blue shirts, white shorts

1	Danijel MADARIC (Gk)
5	Danijel HRMAN (89)
6	Matija KRISTIC
7	Ivan REZIC
8	Devis MUKAJ
9	Veldin KARIC ❑ (89)
10	Miljenko MUMLEK (c) (57)
11	Sasa BJELANOVIC
14	Goran GRANIC
24	Silvester SABOLCKI
25	Zoran KASTEL
	Substitutes
2	Antun ANDRIVICEVIC (5)
3	Goran BOROVIC
12	Zeljko RUMBAK (Gk)
18	Andrija BALAJIC (10)
19	Hrvoje SKLEPIC
20	Nikola SAFARIC
26	Oskar DROBNE (9)

▶ **ASTON VILLA**
claret shirts with blue trim, claret shorts

1	Peter SCHMEICHEL (Gk) (c)	
2	Mark DELANEY	
3	Alan WRIGHT	
4	Olof MELLBERG (45)	
5	ALPAY Ozalan	
6	George BOATENG ❑	
14	David GINOLA ❑	
17	Lee HENDRIE	
19	Bosko BALABAN (46)	
20	Moustapha HADJI	g90
30	Hassan KACHLOUL (63)	
	Substitutes	
8	Juan Pablo ANGEL (19)	
9	Dion DUBLIN (30)	
11	Steve STAUNTON	
12	Peter ENCKELMAN (Gk)	
15	Gareth BARRY	
18	Steve STONE (4)	
31	Jlloyd SAMUEL	

▶ Mellberg starts a lengthy lay-off after being stretchered off with an ankle injury

FA BARCLAYCARD PREMIERSHIP

Six of the best for Juan Pablo

▶ Six starts, six goals – this Angel is turning out to be heaven sent after all. It's no secret that Villa's £9.5million record signing did not really justify his price tag during his first few months in claret-and-blue, but manager John Gregory's faith in the Colombian striker was clearly justified.

We might have waited from January until May for his first goal, but Juan Pablo Angel suddenly looks capable of scoring every time he ventures into the opposition penalty area. He was once again the outstanding individual as Villa dug out victory against Premiership new boys Blackburn, crowning an excellent display by scoring the crucial opening goal and then having a hand in the second.

This wasn't vintage Villa by any means, but their commitment and resilience were beyond question, and Angel's second half delights enabled them to climb to fourth in the table.

The former River Plate marksman claimed his sixth goal of the campaign with a 46th minute finish which was as clinical as you could wish to see, and then combined superbly with Lee Hendrie to pave the way for Darius Vassell to secure the points on 71 minutes.

Blackburn, who had won convincingly on their two previous visits to Villa Park, proved formidable opponents, with Matt Jansen always a threat up front.

But with Steve Staunton proving an able deputy for the injured Olof Mellberg, Villa's defence maintained the solid look which had been an integral feature of the team's six-match unbeaten start to the league campaign.

It wasn't until five minutes before the interval, though, that they started to produce anything like the penetrating football which had cut Southampton to shreds in their previous Premiership match. When Mark Delaney's 40th minute header flashed wide following a Moustapha Hadji corner it was the home side's first serious goal attempt, and served to spark them into more positive action.

On the stroke of half-time, the deadlock was almost broken when Hendrie's pass set up Moustapha Hadji for a deep centre which was headed back across the face of goal by Vassell. There was panic in the Blackburn defence, but the ball bounced unkindly for Angel as he attempted to hook in at close-range.

The Colombian striker then met Hadji's free-kick with a header which flashed just too high, although the visitors generally had the better of the opening period, David Dunn forcing Peter Schmeichel into a smart save after only three minutes and Alan Mahon sent a worrying low drive across the face of goal.

If Villa were generally lethargic before the break, though, they could hardly have resumed in more emphatic fashion. With barely 30 seconds on the clock, Angel took Hendrie's piercing pass in his stride as he surged into the penalty area before beating the advancing Brad Friedel with a beautifully-stroked right footer into the bottom corner.

The clinching second goal followed a let-off at the other end of the pitch. Blackburn were a touch unfortunate when Gary Flitcroft's speculative effort came back off the bar before Delaney completed the clearance, but Villa immediately swept upfield to effect a textbook counter attack.

Angel's delightful little scoop enabled Hendie to deliver a volleyed centre, and Vassell slid in to add the finishing touch.

▶ It's a towering Turk as Alpay climbs to head clear from Blackburn striker Matt Jansen.

MATCH 14

Date Sunday 30 September 2001
Venue Villa Park, 3.00pm

ASTON VILLA (0) 2
BLACKBURN RVRS. (0) 0

Attendance 28,623
Referee Mark Halsey
Assistants P. Barston and N. Bannister

▶ **ASTON VILLA**
claret shirts with blue trim, white shorts

1 Peter SCHMEICHEL (Gk) (c)	
2 Mark DELANEY	
3 Alan WRIGHT	
5 ALPAY Ozalan	
6 George BOATENG	
8 Juan Pablo ANGEL ❏ (84)	g46
11 Steve STAUNTON	
17 Lee HENDRIE	
20 Moustapha HADJI	
22 Darius VASSELL ❏	g71
30 Hassan KACHLOUL (84)	
Substitutes	
9 Dion DUBLIN (8)	
12 Peter ENCKELMAN (Gk)	
14 David GINOLA	
19 Bosko BALABAN	
31 Jlloyd SAMUEL (30)	

▶ **BLACKBURN ROVERS**
blue and white halved shirts, blue shorts

1 Brad FRIEDEL (Gk)
3 TUGAY Kerimoglu
4 Henning BERG
5 Stig-Inge BJORNEBYE
7 Garry FLITCROFT (c) ❏
8 David DUNN (81)
10 Matt JANSEN
12 Mark HUGHES (60)
16 Alan MAHON ❏
19 Damien JOHNSON (68)
31 Lucas NEILL
Substitutes
13 John FILAN (Gk)
15 Craig HIGNETT (8)
17 Jason McATEER (19)
20 Egil OSTENSTAD (12)
30 Gordon GREER

Before	P	W	D	L	F	A	pts
6 Villa	5	2	3	0	7	3	9
9 Blackburn	7	2	3	2	8	8	9
After	P	W	D	L	F	A	pts
4 Villa	6	3	3	0	9	3	12
11 Blackburn	8	2	3	3	8	10	9

▶ Villa's first Premiership home win of the season ▶ Blackburn beaten for the first time in three visits

WORTHINGTON CUP THIRD ROUND

MATCH 15

Brave Royals take Villa to the wire

Date   Wednesday 10 October, 2001
Venue   Villa Park, 7.45pm

▶ If only Reading had the element of surprise at their disposal, their first meeting in 13 years with Villa might at the very least have gone to extra time.

Unfortunately for the valiant Berkshire club, if there's one thing Villa are ready for these days, it's cup heroics from underdogs in blue and white.

After their UEFA Cup exit to Varteks, Villa's line-up and performance took no chances against their Second Division opponents and while the Royals put their hosts under some pressure, Villa too might have had more to show for their efforts than a decider from Dion Dublin.

In an ironic moment, the striker replaced Mark Delaney after the Welsh international sustained a neck injury reminiscent of that which removed Dublin from a large part of the 1999-00 season. Almost as if to prove to his departed colleague that these things can be overcome, Dublin stooped low to head home the game's only goal on the stroke of half-time, after Hassan Kachloul had stabbed a deep David Ginola corner-kick back into the goalmouth.

It was a good time to score, yet while the last lower division side to visit Villa Park in this competition, Chester City, went down like a pack of cards at the first hint of a chilly draught, Reading merely redoubled their efforts after the setback, and what looked plain one-sided fare on paper before the kick-off, brewed up into a most entertaining cup-tie.

Three times, Villa fans were entitled to hold their breath with the ball in their team's penalty area, as two borderline challenges on Reading players were adjudged fair not foul by the referee, and what looked like contact between Steve Staunton's hand and the ball was deemed accidental.

Then again, it was Staunton's night in many respects, the Irish international doing a sterling job of cleaning up on more than one occasion as Villa's defence teetered against bursts of pace from the Reading forward line.

Moustapha Hadji was lost to Villa's attack as he moved to the right-back slot vacated by Mark Delaney, with the Welshman stretchered off in a head brace after being accidentally caught in the neck by Tony Rougier after six minutes, but the slack was ably taken up by Juan Pablo Angel, David Ginola and Lee Hendrie.

Hendrie broke out of midfield in the 42nd minute, only to shoot straight at keeper Phil Whitehead and Ginola was desperately unlucky when a defender's late lunge deflected what looked a promising shot as the Frenchman rounded off a mazy run past two opponents with the first half slipping into stoppage time.

Lovely skill by Angel just after the restart saw him similarly take out two markers before his shot was intercepted and Villa looked even more likely to score soon afterwards, when Hendrie and Angel combined down the left, the Colombian sending over a cross which Hassan Kachloul was unable to capitalise on before the defence cleared.

Just after the hour mark, Ginola's trademark back-heel down the flank allowed Hendrie to set up Angel to fire into the net, but an offside flag marred a delightful move.

Villa's defensive wobbles continued when Schmeichel misjudged a clearance under the attention of Butler, leaving Staunton to clear off the line.

In what was now an exciting end-to-end affair, Villa fashioned another lightning-quick move in the 80th minute, Ginola and Hendrie working in unison once more to leave Dublin through for a shot on goal, which the goalkeeper spread himself to save.

ASTON VILLA (1) 1
READING (0) 0

Attendance   23,431
Referee   Matt Messias
Assistants   K. Hawkes and M. Short

▶ **ASTON VILLA**
claret shirts with blue trim, white shorts

1	Peter SCHMEICHEL (Gk) (c)	
2	Mark DELANEY (27)	
3	Alan WRIGHT ❑	
5	ALPAY Ozalan	
6	George BOATENG ❑	
8	Juan Pablo ANGEL (87)	
11	Steve STAUNTON	
14	David GINOLA	
17	Lee HENDRIE	
20	Moustapha HADJI ❑	
30	Hassan KACHLOUL	
	Substitutes	
9	Dion DUBLIN (2)	g45
12	Peter ENCKELMAN (Gk)	
15	Gareth BARRY	
19	Bosko BALABAN (8)	
29	Stephen COOKE	

▶ **READING**
blue and white hooped shirts, blue shorts

1	Phil WHITEHEAD (Gk)
5	Adi Viveash
7	Anthony ROUGIER (80)
8	Adie WILLIAMS
9	Martin BUTLER
10	Nicky FORSTER
15	James HARPER
16	Phil PARKINSON (c) ❑ (70)
17	Neil SMITH
18	Adi WHITBREAD (80)
28	Nicky SHOREY
	Substitutes
3	Matt ROBINSON (18)
12	Jamie CURETON (7)
19	Joe GAMBLE
21	Jamie ASHDOWN (Gk)
24	Darius HENDERSON (16)

▶ *Juan Pablo Angel almost appears to be asking permission to leave as he raises his arm.*

▶ *Villa's third League Cup meeting with Reading is again successful*

FA BARCLAYCARD PREMIERSHIP

Taylor-made comeback

▶ Three more points, Villa unbeaten after seven league matches and back up to fourth in the table, a sixth goal of the season for Darius Vassell. There was no shortage of reasons to celebrate as Premiership new boys Fulham were beaten on a misty afternoon at Villa Park.

More than anything, though, this match was special for a player who was surprised to find himself involved, let alone scoring the clinching second goal.

Ian Taylor's introduction as a 15th minute substitute after Hassan Kachloul limped off with a hamstring injury was the hard-tackling midfielder's first taste of competitive action since he was sent off at Newcastle on the final day of last season.

That red card at St James' Park, brandished for a tete-a-tete with Gary Speed, was subsequently reduced to a yellow, but it was scant consolation for Taylor as he spent his summer resting a knee problem which ultimately needed surgery.

Having come through a practice game and an hour of a reserve match, however, the Birmingham-born 33-year-old was offered a place on the bench against the Cottagers, and finished the afternoon a hero.

Adoring Holte Enders, with whom he has always had a special affinity, were happy enough to see Taylor back at his biting best in midfield, breaking up opposition moves and setting Villa in motion, but it was a real bonus when he marked his comeback with a well-taken 61st minute goal.

▶ *Dutch midfielder George Boateng goes in where it hurts to put Fulham under pressure in the first half.*

It was created by Juan Pablo Angel, the six-goal striker who is rapidly establishing himself as a creator as well as a predator. After controlling a headed clearance on his chest, the Colombian timed his through ball to perfection and Taylor did the rest, never breaking his stride as he drove hard and low inside the left-hand post.

Villa's opening goal, 11 minutes earlier, had been equally well executed, Alan Wright collecting a Fulham clearance out on the left and playing the ball to Lee Hendrie, who exchanged passes with Angel before passing wide to Moustapha Hadji on the opposite flank.

The Moroccan midfielder's teasing low cross was a nightmare for defenders on a greasy surface and Vassell, back after a knee injury, slid into the six-yard box to divert the ball past Dutch goalkeeper Edwin Van Der Sar.

Villa's two-goal blast capped a result and performance which were almost a mirror image of their home victory over Blackburn two weeks earlier, although this match was considerably more enjoyable.

The first half may have been unproductive in terms of goals, but there was no shortage of intrigue for the Villa Park crowd and Sky TV audience as Villa's short-passing style contrasted with Fulham's ploy of launching long balls for their pacey front runners.

When Taylor pounced with the second goal, Villa looked capable of scoring three or four, although it was Fulham who finished the stronger, the visitors squandering a chance to reduce the deficit when Louis Saha shot wide from an 86th minute penalty.

MATCH 16

Date Sunday 14 October 2001
Venue Villa Park, 4.00pm

ASTON VILLA (0) 2
FULHAM (0) 0

Attendance 28,597
Referee Paul Durkin
Assistants A. Butler and L. Mason

▶ **ASTON VILLA**
claret shirts with blue trim, white shorts

1	Peter SCHMEICHEL (Gk) (c)	
3	Alan WRIGHT	
5	ALPAY Ozalan	
6	George BOATENG	
8	Juan Pablo ANGEL (62)	
11	Steve STAUNTON	
17	Lee HENDRIE	
18	Steve STONE	
20	Moustapha HADJI ❏	
22	Darius VASSELL	g50
30	Hassan KACHLOUL (15)	
	Substitutes	
7	Ian TAYLOR (30)	g61
12	Peter ENCKELMAN (Gk)	
14	David GINOLA	
15	Gareth BARRY	
19	Bosko BALABAN (8)	

▶ **FULHAM**
white shirts, black shorts

1	Edwin VAN DER SAR (Gk)
2	Steve FINNAN
3	Rufus BREVETT
4	Andy MELVILLE (c)
9	Steve MARLET (65)
10	John COLLINS
14	Steed MALLBRANQUE
16	Zat KNIGHT (65)
18	Sylvain LEGWINSKI
20	Louis SAHA
23	Sean DAVIS (65) ❏
	Substitutes
8	Lee CLARK
12	Maik TAYLOR (Gk)
15	Barry HAYLES (9)
22	Luis BOA MORTE (23)
24	Alain GOMA (16)

Before	P	W	D	L	F	A	pts
7 Villa	6	3	3	0	9	3	12
15 Fulham	7	1	4	2	7	8	7
After	P	W	D	L	F	A	pts
4 Villa	7	4	3	0	11	3	15
15 Fulham	8	1	4	3	7	10	7

▶ *Fulham's first visit to Villa Park in the top flight since 1966-67* ▶ *Ian Taylor scores on his first appearance of the season*

21

Peter the Great is just too late

▶ The sight of Peter Schmeichel smashing home the ball at close range was one to savour for Villa supporters who made the trip to Goodison Park. Sadly, the travelling band also witnessed their team's first Premiership setback of the season.

Even with defeat looming, though, it was typical of the Danish goalkeeper that he should have the final say in a match which was never short on entertainment despite its disappointing outcome.

It's not the first time Schmeichel has gone charging upfield, of course. He once scored with a header for Manchester United in a European tie, and the Villa faithful had already seen him venture into the opposition penalty area during the recent UEFA Cup clash against NK Varteks.

His long run was unproductive on that occasion, but this time he displayed all the qualities of a lethal striker as he unleashed an unstoppable right-foot shot after Darius Vassell had flicked on Steve Staunton's stoppage time corner.

It was just a pity that the rarity came too late to alter the course of the match. Moustapha Hadji had also scored with a fine 69th minute header, but by then John Gregory's side were three-down on an afternoon when their defence conceded as many goals as they had in the previous seven league matches.

Yet there had been no early indications that Villa's 11-match unbeaten sequence against the Toffees was about to come to a sticky end.

As the first half progressed, however, Everton's confidence increased and on the half hour mark Villa found themselves on the slippery slope to defeat, Naysmith nodding down Alexandersson's deep cross for Watson to score with a lunging far post header which drifted across Schmeichel.

Villa's response came in the form of a fine Angel run which ended with a shot which was well held by Gerrard, but it could easily have been 2-0 in first half stoppage time. With Villa pressing, Everton launched a swift counter attack which saw Radzinski racing down the left to hit a cross which the unmarked Kevin Campbell fired wide when a goal looked certain.

The home side were more forceful after the interval, increasing their lead in the 59th minute. Delaney stumbled as he attempted to collect Alpay's misplaced clearance, and Naysmith cashed in on that uncharacteristic defensive hesitancy with a cross which presented an open goal for Radzinski.

Villa had barely recovered from that setback when Gravesen smashed home Scot Gemmill's short free-kick inside the penalty area after Delaney had been punished for having his boot too high.

The situation looked pretty grim, but Villa kept battling. Vassell's skills instigated the move which led to their first goal, the young striker striker wriggling through the middle before substitute Dion Dublin played the ball wide to Alan Wright, whose cross was headed home firmly by Hadji. And after Dublin had been just off target with both a header and a shot, along came Schmeichel with that memorable last-gasp strike. What a pity it counted for nothing.

▶ *George Boateng comes away with the ball from this challenge, but Villa were three-down before they staged a spirited revival.*

MATCH 17

Date Saturday 20 October 2001
Venue Goodison Park, 3.00pm

EVERTON (0) 3
ASTON VILLA (0) 2

Attendance 33,352
Referee Rob Styles
Assistants D. Drysdale and M. Tingey

▶ **EVERTON**
blue shirts, white shorts

1	Paul GERRARD (Gk)	
2	Steve WATSON	g30
3	Alessandro PISTONE	
5	David WEIR	
7	Niclas ALEXANDERSSON	
8	Tomasz RADZINKSI (77)	g59
9	Kevin CAMPBELL (c)	
11	Mark PEMBRIDGE (42)	
15	Gary NAYSMITH ❏	
16	Thomas GRAVESEN (80)	g62
24	Abel XAVIER	
	Substitutes	
6	David UNSWORTH	
10	Duncan FERGUSON (8)	
13	Steve SIMONSEN (Gk)	
17	Scot GEMMILL (11)	
18	Paul GASCOIGNE (16)	

▶ **ASTON VILLA**
platinum shirts, navy blue shorts

1	Peter SCHMEICHEL (Gk) (c)	g90
2	Mark DELANEY	
3	Alan WRIGHT	
5	ALPAY Ozalan (63)	
6	George BOATENG	
8	Juan Pablo ANGEL (63)	
11	Steve STAUNTON	
17	Lee HENDRIE (77)	
18	Steve STONE	
20	Moustapha HADJI	g69
22	Darius VASSEL	
	Substitutes	
9	Dion DUBLIN (8) ❏	
12	Peter ENCKELMAN (Gk)	
14	David GINOLA (17)	
15	Gareth BARRY	
19	Jlloyd SAMUEL (5)	

Before	P	W	D	L	F	A	pts
4 Villa	7	4	3	0	11	3	15
11 Everton	8	3	2	3	12	10	11
After	P	W	D	L	F	A	pts
5 Villa	8	4	3	1	13	6	15
8 Everton	9	4	2	3	15	12	14

▶ *Villa's first competitive goal from a goalkeeper* ▶ *Lee Hendrie signs new four-year contract*

FA BARCLAYCARD PREMIERSHIP

Kach opens account

▶ Three or four hundred years ago, the equivalent form of entertainment would have been to lock Dean Kiely in the stocks and throw rotten fruit at him.

This being a more sophisticated age, we now make do with putting the Charlton goalkeeper in a beleaguered goalmouth and watching while a succession of unconvincing back-passes on a drenched pitch threaten to shred his nerves in front of a wholly unsympathetic Holte End.

All right, so it's hardly the beautiful game, but it was a welcome sideshow on a night when the main event meekly followed the form book.

Place these two teams alongside each other on paper and it is an unavoidable fact that the star quality is confined to one side of the page.

Charlton looked like a team who had learned well at the Premiership's School of Hard Knocks. They harassed and harried, they refused to go under despite leaking a goal as early as the ninth minute.

What they did not offer, however, was a game-breaker; the individual wizard, mandatory at this level, who can fashion something out of nothing. Villa may have spent the whole game with a wary eye on the Addicks' jab but they never had to worry about a lurking haymaker.

The only loose end left untied once Hassan Kachloul hammered in his first goal for the club from close range after a Darius Vassell header was blocked on the line, was whether Villa's inability to ram home their clear superiority would cost them dear.

Charlton simply had no answer to Villa's twin-pronged Moroccan assault that saw Kachloul and then Moustapha Hadji run them ragged in the second half.

Kiely had done well to catch a well-struck Lee Hendrie shot from 20 yards even before the goal but could only watch when Darius Vassell leapt like a salmon to head a Hadji cross past the far post in the 14th minute.

It took the Londoners 17 minutes to make inroads into their opponents' defence, Jonatan Johansson's diagonal shot from the right hand side of the penalty area passing over Peter Schmeichel's crossbar, but any genuine menace was almost exclusively Villa's.

Repeatedly probing the gaps in Charlton's defence, Hendrie volleyed over in the 26th minute

▶ *Villa had to settle for a single goal, although darius Vassell was not far off target with this header.*

and Vassell forced another fine save from Kiely soon afterwards, rounding off a series of quick-fire Villa passes with a low shot that was headed for the bottom corner until the keeper intervened.

It was one of the more orthodox moments in a hectic evening for Republic of Ireland international Kiely, whose attempted clearance 10 minutes before the interval came off back off Dion Dublin's head before the Villa striker knew much about it, and rolled just past the wide-open goal.

The game returned to Keystone Cops mode when a misplaced back-pass by Charlton defender Paul Konchesky forced his goalkeeper into a hurried clearance down the left flank. While Kiely was still returning to base, an accurate shot from all of 50 yards by Hadji was on target but Kiely had made just enough ground to catch the ball on the line.

MATCH 18

Date Wednesday 24 October 2001
Venue Villa Park, 7.45pm

ASTON VILLA (1) 1
CHARLTON ATH. (0) 0

Attendance 27,701
Referee David Pugh
Assistants S. Gagen and R. Bone

▶ **ASTON VILLA**
claret shirts with blue trim, white shorts

1	Peter SCHMEICHEL (Gk) (c)	
2	Mark DELANEY	
3	Alan WRIGHT	
5	ALPAY Ozalan	
6	George BOATENG	
9	Dion DUBLIN	
11	Steve STAUNTON	
17	Lee HENDRIE (70)	
20	Moustapha HADJI	
22	Darius VASSELL	
30	Hassan KACHLOUL	g9
	Substitutes	
7	Ian TAYLOR (17)	
10	Paul MERSON	
12	Peter ENCKELMAN (Gk)	
14	David GINOLA	
19	Bosko BALABAN	

▶ **CHARLTON ATHLETIC**
white shirts, red shorts

1	Dean KIELY (Gk)
3	Chris POWELL (85)
8	Mark KINSELLA (c)
12	Steve BROWN
17	Scott PARKER
18	Paul KONCHESKY
19	Luke YOUNG
20	Claus JENSEN (70)
21	Jonatan JOHANSSON
36	Mark FISH
37	Shaun BARTLETT (45)
	Substitutes
9	Jason EUELL (37)
11	John ROBINSON (20)
22	Ben ROBERTS (Gk)
23	Gavin PEACOCK (3)
24	Jonathan FORTUNE

Before	P	W	D	L	F	A	pts
5 Villa	8	4	3	1	13	6	15
14 Charlton	8	2	4	2	8	8	10
After	P	W	D	L	F	A	pts
3 Villa	9	5	3	1	14	6	18
15 Charlton	9	2	4	3	8	9	10

▶ *Hassan Kachloul's first Villa goal since his summer transfer from Southampton*

23

Angel soars as Villa go top

▶ It was the final weekend of October before Villa sampled what is regarded as the traditional 3pm Saturday kick-off, but when it finally came along they were well prepared.

Victory over battling Bolton took them to the head of the table for the first time since January, 1999. "We are top of the league" chanted ecstatic Holte Enders, and their delight was understandable.

Juan Pablo Angel and Darius Vassell took their respective goal hauls to eight and seven respectively – and neither player was even on the pitch at the end.

It was almost a pity the game had to finish, for this was a superb piece of entertainment, almost old fashioned in the way the action swung from one end to the other with barely a moment to come up for breath.

Bolton played their part in an absorbing contest and when former Walsall striker Michael Ricketts fired them ahead in the second minute, there was every prospect of them repeating their shock victory over Manchester United seven days earlier.

They certainly earned a few new admirers among the Villa faithful for the positive manner in which they approached this match.

Fortunately for Villa, the visitors were unable to build on their early advantage, and by the 13th minute the scores were level. Moustapha Hadji unleashed a tremendous shot which was diverted for corner, and when Steve Staunton delivered the flag kick, Angel soared in a crowded six yard box to score with a downward header.

▶ *Moustapha Hadji goes down under Riccardo Gardner's challenge – and Juan Pablo Angel did the rest from the penalty spot.*

That should have been followed by further goals as Hadji teased and tormented full-back Simon Charlton while the likes of Staunton and Lee Hendrie displayed a willingness to shoot at any opportunity, but Villa had to wait until three minutes before half-time to take the lead.

Angel was again involved, his flick releasing Vassell for a finish as clinical as you could wish to see, the England under-21 international shrugging off his marker to send a low 15-yard shot just inside the right hand post.

The visitors could easily have been back on level terms in first half stoppage time when Riccardo Gardner shot tamely at Peter Schmeichel from eight yards, but within a minute of the re-start Villa had increased their advantage when they were awarded their first penalty for more than a year.

Gardner was adjudged to have pushed Hadji as they contested Alan Wright's cross and although Bolton protested strongly, Wolstenholme had no hesitation in pointing to the spot.

Angel was equal to the task, calmly firing low to Banks's right and four minutes later, the crowd rose in anticipation of a hat-trick when the striker's magnificent control on the edge of the area was followed by a rising drive which was destined for the top corner until Banks stretched to tip it away.

But the Colombian was withdrawn on 72 minutes and when Ricketts reduced the deficit three minutes later, there were a few anxious moments before pole position was confirmed.

▶ Villa top for the first time in 34 months ▶ Angel converts the club's first penalty for more than a year

---

MATCH 19

Date: Saturday 27 October 2001
Venue: Villa Park, 3.00pm

ASTON VILLA (2) 3
BOLTON WDRS. (1) 2

Attendance 33,599
Referee Eddie Wolstenholme
Assistants R. Gould and N. Miller

▶ **ASTON VILLA**
claret shirts with blue trim, white shorts

1	Peter SCHMEICHEL (Gk) (c)
2	Mark DELANEY
3	Alan WRIGHT
5	ALPAY Ozalan ❏
6	George BOATENG
8	Juan Pablo ANGEL (72) g13, 46(p)
11	Steve STAUNTON
17	Lee HENDRIE (86)
20	Moustapha HADJI
22	Darius VASSELL (73) g42
30	Hassan KACHLOUL ❏
	Substitutes
7	Ian TAYLOR (17)
9	Dion DUBLIN (8)
10	Paul MERSON (22)
12	Peter ENCKELMAN (Gk)
14	David GINOLA

▶ **BOLTON WANDERERS**
white shirts, navy blue shorts

1	Steve BANKS (Gk)
2	Bruno N'GOTTY (90)
4	Gudni BERGSSON
7	Bo HANSEN (45)
8	Per FRANDSEN
11	Riccardo GARDNER (72)
14	Gareth FARRELLY
15	Kevin NOLAN
17	Michael RICKETTS ❏ g2, 75
23	Djibril DIAWARA ❏
25	Simon CHARLTON ❏
	Substitutes
5	Colin HENDRY
10	Dean HOLDSWORTH (11)
21	Rod WALLACE (7)
24	Anthony BARNESS (2)
30	Kevin POOLE (Gk)

Before	P	W	D	L	F	A	pts
3 Villa	9	5	3	1	14	6	18
6 Bolton	10	4	3	3	12	11	15
After	P	W	D	L	F	A	pts
1 Villa	10	6	3	1	17	8	21
9 Bolton	11	4	3	4	14	14	15

FA BARCLAYCARD PREMIERSHIP

No answer to hot-shot Bellamy

▶ It might be the number nine shirt that carries all the tradition at St James' Park but much more of this from Craig Bellamy and Geordie folklore may soon have to make room for number 17.

On a day when the stage looked all set for Alan Shearer, making his 400th league appearance, understudy Bellamy stole the headlines with two goals.

The visitors' studied avoidance of euphoria after reaching the Premiership summit seven days earlier looked almost prophetic, as they turned in a lacklustre away performance and were always a step behind their opponents.

But for another obstructive performance by Peter Schmeichel, Villa might easily have been looking at a pummelling, and the Dane deserved a more dignified ending than to have Bellamy's second goal scored between his legs with nine minutes left.

Ironically, it came after Villa's most promising segment of the game, although that was more a matter of industry and territorial advantage than cutting-edge.

The pace of Darius Vassell and the finishing of Juan Pablo Angel had been major themes of Villa's season so far but both were forced to abdicate the limelight at St James' Park in favour of Bellamy and Shearer.

Newcastle's simple ploy of depositing the ball in space for Bellamy to hare after worked to telling effect, as a succession of lofted passes from midfield took Villa's defence out of the game, before being seized upon by Bellamy.

If his second goal was highlighted by Schmeichel's discomfiture, his first was an exclusively black-and-white scenario.

The game was 38 minutes old when Robbie Elliott scooped a delightful pass over Villa's back line as the hosts pressed. Bellamy saw the move well before his markers and let the ball drop over his shoulder in the Villa box before smashing a fierce half volley into the roof of the net.

Though far from convincing, Villa had not lacked for chances of their own in the opening period and would not have been overly dismayed by this setback. But events shortly after the interval left the writing squarely on the wall for John Gregory's table-toppers.

Shearer had headed a deflected cross narrowly over the bar early in the game, before seeing a header graze the post just after half-time, but these were merely sighters for the finest goal of the game. As United built an attack down the left, the former England striker was allowed to advance on the opposite flank, warranting barely a backward glance from the Villa defence.

By the time Robert Lee arrowed a magnificent diagonal ball to the far post, Alan Wright had too much ground to make up between himself and Shearer, who struck a volley with supreme confidence into the far corner.

Villa, sadly, made little impression with what openings they found.

Goalkeeper Shay Given did, admittedly, have a lucky escape when Juan Pablo Angel intercepted his attempted pass to a defender and set up Hassan Kachloul for a shot that the United keeper did well to swat away for a corner.

▶ *A rare moment of Villa danger at St. James' Park, but Hassan Kachloul is unable to find a way past the Geordies' defence.*

MATCH 20

Date Saturday 3 November 2001
Venue St James' Park, 3.00pm

**NEWCASTLE UTD. (1) 3
ASTON VILLA (0) 0**

Attendance 51,057
Referee Clive Wilkes
Assistants C. Boyeson and A. Green

▶ **NEWCASTLE UNITED**
black and white striped shirts, black shorts

1	Shay GIVEN (Gk)	
3	Robbie ELLIOTT	
4	Nolberto SOLANO	
5	Andrew O'BRIEN	
7	Robert LEE	
9	Alan SHEARER (c)	g49
11	Gary SPEED	
17	Craig BELLAMY	g38, 81
18	Aaron HUGHES	
32	Laurent ROBERT (85)	
34	Nikolas DABIZAS	
	Substitutes	
6	Clarence ACUNA	
13	Steve HARPER (Gk)	
20	Lomana LUALUA	
24	Sylvain DISTIN	
35	Olivier BERNARD (32)	

▶ **ASTON VILLA**
claret shirts with blue trim, white shorts

1	Peter SCHMEICHEL (Gk) (c)
2	Mark DELANEY ❑
3	Alan WRIGHT
5	ALPAY Ozalan ❑
6	George BOATENG
8	Juan Pablo ANGEL (59)
11	Steve STAUNTON
17	Lee HENDRIE (59)
20	Moustapha HADJI
22	Darius VASSELL
30	Hassan KACHLOUL ❑
	Substitutes
7	Ian TAYLOR (17)
9	Dion DUBLIN (8)
12	Peter ENCKELMAN (Gk)
15	Gareth BARRY
19	Bosko BALABAN

Before	P	W	D	L	F	A	pts
1 Villa	10	6	3	1	17	8	21
6 United	10	5	2	3	18	14	17
After	P	W	D	L	F	A	pts
3 Villa	11	6	3	2	17	11	21
5 United	11	6	2	3	21	14	20

▶ *Alan Wright's 300th starting appearance* ▶ *A 3-0 defeat on Tyneside for the second consecutive season*

FA BARCLAYCARD PREMIERSHIP

Old boys blunt Villa's cutting edge

▶ After treating Gareth Southgate and Ugo Ehiogu to a hostile welcome, Villa fans were given a 90 minute demonstration of the very qualities for which they once cheered the duo to the rafters.

On another afternoon in which Villa ran the show yet had to settle for half the proceeds, it meant a win on points for the returning antiheroes, as Boro's solid recovery from a woeful start to the season passed another milestone.

They may have one of the most highly-regarded coaches in the English game at their helm but it was safety first as Boro looked to stabilise after the disappointments of recent seasons and Steve McLaren made no bones about his men's limited brief, after the visitors had spent 90 minutes parrying every thrust from their opponents while trying to steal the game on the break.

Holding it all together in the centre of defence were the two men at the eye of a relentless storm of disapproval that rained down from the Holte End – Ehiogu dominant in the air and Southgate as ever the tidy shepherd on the floor.

Their team needed nothing less on a day in which Villa spent lengthy periods camped in the Boro half of the pitch, probing at their opponents.

The closest they came to tripping the latch, was in the 11th minute, Juan Pablo Angel dealing effortlessly with Lee Hendrie's lobbed pass over the defence, chesting the ball into space and then dragging it past Ehiogu before rifling a shot against the crossbar.

While goalscoring seemed rather more of an unwanted optional extra where Middlesbrough were concerned, with Alen Boksic mercifully indifferent against Villa's defence, they made several chances and had their own what-might-have-been moment when Frank Querdrue landed a header on top of the crossbar.

It was a rare sortie forward for a Boro team that spent much of game back-pedalling, as Villa adapted well to losing Mark Delaney with a gashed thigh.

Angel was presented with another golden opportunity in the 17th minute when he escaped his marker unnoticed to enjoy a wide open header from a Vassell cross, only to put it wide.

That these were two teams with ample potential for cancelling each other out became all too apparent as the game began to stagnate midway through the first half, and two nice moves worked between Hassan Kachloul and Lee Hendrie were welcome, although the resultant shots were smothered in characteristic fashion by Boro's blanket defence.

▶ Villa midfielder Steve Stone controls the ball neatly on his chest, despite the close aattentions of Boro's Jonthan Greening.

The visitors hit back straight away, however. With Olof Mellberg returning to first team action for the first time since his injury in Varazdin in September, Villa's defence had barely missed a beat, yet it was dragged apart like the Red Sea by decoy runners as Szilard Nemeth advanced unchecked from midfield, only to send his shot high and wide.

Kachloul turned well in the 56th minute to hook a knock-down from Angel over the bar and Steve Stone – deputising for the injured Moustapha Hadji – seemed to have made the decisive breach when turning on a sixpence to beat his marker to the by-line in the 64th minute, only to overhit his cross.

MATCH 21

Date: Saturday 17 November 2001
Venue: Villa Park, 3.00pm

ASTON VILLA (0) 0
MIDDLESBROUGH (0) 0

Attendance 35,424
Referee Peter Jones
Assistants P. Barnes and D. Bryan

▶ **ASTON VILLA**
claret shirts with blue trim, white shorts

1	Peter SCHMEICHEL (Gk) (c)
2	Mark DELANEY (14)
3	Alan WRIGHT
4	Olof MELLBERG
5	ALPAY Ozalan
6	George BOATENG
8	Juan Pablo ANGEL
17	Lee HENDRIE
18	Steve STONE
22	Darius VASSELL ❏
30	Hassan KACHLOUL (71)
	Substitutes
7	Ian TAYLOR (2)
9	Dion DUBLIN
12	Peter ENCKELMAN (Gk)
14	David GINOLA (30)
19	Gareth BARRY

▶ **MIDDLESBROUGH**
black and blue striped shirts, black shorts

25	Mark CROSSLEY (Gk)
6	Gareth SOUTHGATE (c)
7	Robbie MUSTOE
8	Szilard NEMETH (81)
11	Alen BOKSIC ❏
12	Jonathan GREENING ❏
17	Ugo EHIOGU
23	Carlos MARINELLI (71)
27	Robbie STOCKDALE
32	Allan JOHNSTON
37	Frank QUERDRUE ❏ (45)
	Substitutes
15	Marlon BERESFORD (Gk)
20	Dean WINDASS (8)
21	Mark WILSON
24	Phil STAMP (23)
28	Colin COOPER (37)

Before	P	W	D	L	F	A	pts
3 Villa	11	6	3	2	17	11	21
13 Boro	12	4	2	6	16	20	14
After	P	W	D	L	F	A	pts
3 Villa	12	6	4	2	17	11	22
13 Boro	13	4	3	6	16	20	15

▶ Villa denied victory by Boro for the second season running ▶ Mellberg's first match for nearly two months

Kachloul classic earns a point

MATCH 22

Date: Sunday 25 November 2001
Venue: Elland Road, 3.00pm

LEEDS UNITED (1) 1
ASTON VILLA (1) 1

Attendance 40,159
Referee Neale Barry
Assistants A. Butler and R. Martin

▸ A point from Elland Road would normally be considered a satisfactory return, but Villa were not exactly celebrating as they headed back down the M1.

John Gregory's side were acutely aware that they had squandered a glorious opportunity of winning at Leeds for the third consecutive season after the home side had been reduced to 10 men by striker Alan Smith's sending off just past the half hour mark.

It wasn't just that the Yorkshire outfit were left a man short, they lost a player who had provided their greatest threat. Apart from firing his team into a 19th minute lead, Smith had provided a constant source of menace for Villa.

Unfortunately, the striker's menace also manifested itself in a physical manner and when he elbowed Alpay Ozalan in the 32nd minute, referee Neale Barry had no option but to brandish his red card.

Villa cashed in on Smith's departure by claiming a superb equaliser from Moroccan midfielder Hassan Kachloul four minutes later, and for a while, visiting fans were rubbing their hands at the prospect of an invaluable away win.

It didn't materialise because Villa were never able to make the most of their numerical superiority, and a niggling, untidy contest might easily have gone Leeds' way when England defender Rio Ferdinand hit the post with a late header.

Having survived an early scare when Robbie Keane miskicked in front of goal after Peter Schmeichel had failed to gather Smith's deep centre, Villa's early play was encouraging.

George Boateng had a shot charged down on the edge of the penalty area, while Alan Wright's skidding 30-yarder, after Paul Merson had touched a short free-kick to him, was tipped away by the diving Nigel Martyn.

Once Leeds had settled, however, most of the first half close calls were at the other end before Alan Wright's error paved the way for Leeds to go ahead.

The full-back's dreadful back pass left Schmeichel stranded on the left hand edge of the penalty area, and although Villa's other defenders retreated hastily to cover the danger, Smith's angled shot found its target with Steve Stone able only to help it over the line. It could have got worse, too, the unmarked Smith heading straight at Schmeichel from Ian Harte's corner before Keane headed against the 'keeper from Smith's dipping centre with Villa's defence in disarray.

That proved to be Smith's final contribution before his dismissal, which at least offered the visitors a way back into the game.

Kachloul's falling volley from Merson's curling free-kick was finishing of the highest order, and with Merson and Juan Pablo Angel both testing Martyn before the break, the stage was set for a second half Villa onslaught.

Unfortunately, it never materialised, and on more than one occasion, Gregory turned away in sheer frustration as passes continually went astray. Despite being a man short, in fact, it was Leeds who had the better opportunities. Villa's hearts were certainly in their mouths when Ferdinand met Harte's stoppage time free-kick with a header which beat Schmeichel and smacked against the foot of a post.

▸ It's a hair-raising experience for Juan Pablo Angel in this Elland Road tussle with Leeds full-back Danny Mills.

▸ **LEEDS UNITED**
white shirts, white shorts

1	Nigel MARTYN (Gk)
3	Ian HARTE
7	Robbie KEANE
16	Jason WILCOX
17	Alan SMITH ■ g17
18	Danny MILLS ❑
19	Eirik BAKKE
20	Seth JOHNSON ❑
21	Dominic MATTEO
23	David BATTY
29	Rio FERDINAND(c)
	Substitutes
2	Gary KELLY
4	Olivier DACOURT
13	Paul ROBINSON (Gk)
14	Stephen McPHAIL
22	Michael DUBERRY

▸ **ASTON VILLA**
claret shirts with blue trim, claret shorts

1	Peter SCHMEICHEL (Gk)
3	Alan WRIGHT ❑
4	Olof MELLBERG
5	ALPAY Ozalan
6	George BOATENG
8	Juan Pablo ANGEL (61)
10	Paul MERSON(c)
17	Lee HENDRIE ❑ (50)
18	Steve STONE
22	Darius VASSELL
30	Hassan KACHLOUL g34
	Substitutes
7	Ian TAYLOR (17)
9	Dion DUBLIN (8)
11	Steve STAUNTON
12	Peter ENCKELMAN (Gk)
14	David GINOLA

Before	P	W	D	L	F	A	pts
2 Leeds	12	6	5	1	15	7	23
4 Villa	12	6	4	2	17	11	22
After	P	W	D	L	F	A	pts
2 Leeds	13	6	6	1	16	8	24
5 Villa	13	6	5	2	18	12	23

▸ Villa unbeaten in eight visits to Leeds ▸ Kachloul's second goal for the club

WORTHINGTON CUP FOURTH ROUND   MATCH 23

Efan agony as Villa go out

Date	Wednesday 28 November 2001
Venue	Villa Park, 7.45pm

ASTON VILLA (0) 0
SHEFFIELD WED. (1) 1

Attendance	26,526
Referee	Clive Wilkes
Assistants	D. Richards and K. Woolmer

▶ Cup upsets are part and parcel of football's rich tapestry, we are told. Which is all very well as long as someone else is on the receiving end of the upset.

Villa supporters found nothing even remotely charming about 90 minutes of toil and sweat against Sheffield Wednesday, only to be on the receiving end of an inglorious defeat by a team struggling at the wrong end of the First Division.

The teams may have been separated by 34 league positions before kick-off, but that counted for nothing as substitute Efan Ekoku plundered the 40th minute goal which signalled Villa's exit from the competition just one stage down the line from where they alighted last season.

Even allowing for the Yorkshire club's vast improvement under new manager Terry Yorath, Villa were widely expected to make comfortable progress to the quarter-finals.

It quickly became evident, though, that there was to be no easy passage, and Ekoku's killer blow ensured a night of misery for home supporters.

Villa totally dominated the second half as they went in search of the equaliser which would at least have taken the tie to extra-time, but Dion Dublin, in particular was wasteful with at least two chances he might reasonably have been expected to convert.

This was one of those occasions when absolutely nothing went to plan, and as Villa fans trooped off disconsolately into the night, Wednesday's travelling band of 3,000 added the final movement to what had been a match-long concern to from the Witton end of Villa Park.

Bosko Balaban, making his first start on English soil, was soon in the thick of the action, rising to meet Steve Staunton's inswinging corner with a far post header which flew over.

But Wednesday, so impressive in their recent televised match against Wolves at Molineux, clearly had no intention of being overawed by their Premiership opponents, settling into a rhythm which accompanied the tuneful strains of their famous supporters' band.

It didn't help the Owls' cause when Alan Quinn was stretchered off in the 26th minute, the midfielder damaging his shoulder when he fell awkwardly after getting in a far post header, but that misfortune ultimately proved to be a blessing in disguise for the Owls.

Although Villa created by far the greater number of first half chances, with Balaban's powerful header forcing goalkeeper Kevin Pressman into a fine save and Staunton's probing crosses always posing problems, it was Quinn's replacement who made the vital breakthrough five minutes before the interval.

Much of Wednesday's early promise had subsided in the face of home pressure which saw Hadji twice go close before he limped off with a knee injury. But when Simon Donnelly produced a superb through ball out of nothing, Ekoku showed how it should be done by getting ahead of Alpay before beating the advancing Schmeichel.

▶ *Croatian striker Bosko Balaban, making a rare appearance for Villa's first team, shields the ball from Danny Maddix.*

▶ **ASTON VILLA**
claret shirts with blue trim, white shorts

1	Peter SCHMEICHEL (Gk)
4	Olof MELLBERG
5	ALPAY Ozalan
7	Ian TAYLOR (45)
9	Dion DUBLIN
11	Steve STAUNTON
17	Lee HENDRIE
18	Steve STONE
19	Bosko BALABAN (63)
20	Moustapha HADJI (40)
30	Hassan KACHLOUL
	Substitutes
6	George BOATENG (20)
12	Peter ENCKELMAN (Gk)
14	David GINOLA (7)
15	Gareth BARRY
22	Darius VASSELL (19)

▶ **SHEFFIELD WEDNESDAY**
blue and white striped shirts, black shorts

1	Kevin PRESSMAN (Gk)	
5	Leigh BROMBY ❏	
6	Trond SOLTVEDT	
7	Alan QUINN (28)	
8	Gerald SIBON (81)	
11	Owen MORRISON (54)	
12	Steven HASLAM	
18	Simon DONNELLY	
22	Derek GEARY ❏	
24	Phil O'DONNELL	
25	Danny MADDIX	
	Substitutes	
4	Paul McLAREN (11) ❏	
9	Efan EKOKU (7)	g40
10	Pablo BONVIN	
13	Chris STRINGER (Gk)	
21	Ashley WESTWOOD (8)	

▶ *Bosko Balaban's first starting appearance at Villa Park* ▶ *Villa bow out 1-0 at home for the second year running*

28

FA BARCLAYCARD PREMIERSHIP

Insult and injury on day of misery

▶ David Ginola sent off, Alpay stretchered off and an unbeaten Premiership home record surrendered. The first Saturday of December was one which will be remembered at Villa Park for all the wrong reasons.

It was bad enough that Leicester City should resume their stranglehold on this fixture, but the Turk's injury and the Frenchman's act of petulance undoubtedly compounded Villa's bitter sense of dejection.

Alpay's departure with damaged ankle ligaments early in the second half was bad enough, but when Ginola kicked out at Dennis Wise after being floored by the midfielder's rash 84th minute challenge, it just about summed up an afternoon of sheer misery.

Villa enjoyed vast territorial superiority but were unable to conjure up a goal against a goal against a side whose pre-match ambition had surely extended no further than a draw. Even that would have been preferable to a first league home defeat in a match which started tamely but ended in fury as Ginola shouted angrily at the fourth official following his sending-off.

The opening goal was also surrounded by controversy, Peter Schmeichel claiming he was pushed by Trevor Sinclair as Leicester skipper Matt Elliott flicked on Wise's corner for Ade Akinbiyi to head in at the far post.

The goalkeeper forcibly made his point as he chased referee Steve Bennett back to the halfway line, and Sinclair later admitted that he had given the Dane a crafty nudge.

Villa had accepted before kick-off that they were likely to face a frustrating time, and with the advantage of a lead, the visitors were only too content to get bodies behind the ball at every opportunity.

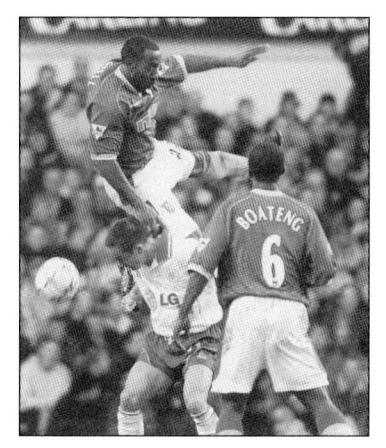

▶ *Darius Vassell climbs above Dennis Wise, with George Boateng hoping the loose ball will bounce his way.*

George Boateng raised hopes of an equaliser with a low shot which was blocked before Darius Vassell suffered the same fate after collecting the loose ball and flicking it up neatly, but those efforts merely set the tone for what was to deteriorate into a miserable afternoon.

As Villa pressed forward, Boateng drove wide and a well-struck Mark Delaney effort cannoned off Sinclair before Walker thwarted Villa's best chance.

Juan Pablo Angel was ready to celebrate when he turned and fired towards the bottom corner after Darius Vassell had headed down to him, only for the 'keeper to stretch and tip it away for a corner.

It wasn't all Villa, to be fair, and when James Scowcroft moved on to Wise's perfectly weighted free-kick, Delaney reacted with a crucial tackle just as the former Ipswich striker was about to pull the trigger.

But after Angel had seen another shot charged down in the 51st minute, the visitors swept straight to the other end to claim to killer second goal.

Akinbiyi was again involved, his challenge forcing Schmeichel to drop a looping Lee Marshall cross which appeared to be delivered more in hope than expectation. Even then, the danger may have been averted, but the 'keeper found Olof Mellberg in his way, an unfortunate obstruction which allowed Scowcroft to tap in a simple goal from six yards.

▶ *Villa's first Premiership home defeat of the season*

MATCH 24

Date   Saturday 1 December 2001
Venue Villa Park, 3.00pm

ASTON VILLA (0) 0
LEICESTER CITY (1) 2

Attendance 30,711
Referee   Steve Bennett
Assistants B. Baker and D. Babski

▶ **ASTON VILLA**
claret shirts with blue trim, white shorts

1	Peter SCHMEICHEL (Gk)
2	Mark DELANEY
3	Alan WRIGHT
4	Olof MELLBERG
5	ALPAY Ozalan (59)
6	George BOATENG
8	Juan Pablo ANGEL
10	Paul MERSON (c)
17	Lee HENDRIE (61)
18	Steve STONE
22	Darius VASSELL (68)
	Substitutes
9	Dion DUBLIN (22)
11	Steve STAUNTON (5)
12	Peter ENCKELMAN (Gk)
14	David GINOLA (17) ■
19	Bosko BALABAN

▶ **LEICESTER CITY**
white shirts, blue shorts

1	Ian WALKER (Gk)	
3	Frank SINCLAIR	
5	Alan ROGERS ❏ (76)	
8	Robbie SAVAGE ❏	
10	James SCOWCROFT	g51
11	Dennis WISE ❏	
14	Callum DAVIDSON	
18	Matt ELLIOTT (c)	
22	Ade AKINBIYI ❏ (90)	g12
24	Andrew IMPEY	
26	Lee MARSHALL	
	Substitutes	
7	Matthew JONES	
12	Simon ROYCE (Gk)	
17	Stefan OAKES	
20	Trevor BENJAMIN (22)	
23	Jordan STEWART (5)	

Before	P	W	D	L	F	A	pts
5 Villa	13	6	5	2	18	12	23
19 Leicester	14	2	4	8	7	25	10
After	P	W	D	L	F	A	pts
6 Villa	14	6	5	3	18	14	23
17 Leicester	15	3	4	8	9	25	13

Dion delight but it's only a point

▶ Just when they were ready to celebrate their first win in six matches, Villa paid a heavy price for a single lapse of concentration.

The match at Upton Park was in the second minute of stoppage time when Jermain Defoe found space on the right hand edge of the penalty area and delivered a stunning angled drive into the far corner of the net.

It was rough justice on goalkeeper Peter Enckelman, who had performed superbly as a stand-in for the injured Peter Schmeichel, but Villa could really have no complaints.

Having led from the first minute, when Dion Dublin headed home Steve Stone's right-wing centre, the visitors had dominated the first half and should really have been more than one goal to the good at the interval.

But it was very much a rearguard action from then on, and only some resolute defending and some fine Enckelman saves — including one from a tamely-hit Paulo Di Canio penalty — kept their lead intact for so long.

If Defoe's leveller was no more than West Ham deserved, though, Villa's performance was a vast improvement on their previous two matches.

Despite the absence of several key players, Villa were enterprising in the first half and dogged in the second with both Enckelman and Gareth Barry enjoying excellent first Premiership starts of the season.

Villa's injuries, in fact, necessitated the use of Barry on the left of midfield, rather than his usual central defensive role, but he acquitted himself well and was instrumental in several of the team's better moves.

Villa had rarely been in greater need of a tonic than after the previous Saturday's feeble offering against Leicester, and it arrived on just 49 seconds.

Stone capitalised on David James's poor clearance by cutting back inside Nigel Winterburn for a cross with his left foot, and Dublin climbed majestically in the goalmouth to head in firmly from close range.

▶ *Olof Mellberg keeps a close watch on Jermain Defoe, although the Hammers striker had the final word.*

Such an early boost could not have been more welcome after two games without a goal, and Villa could easily have doubled their lead during an intense spell of pressure from the 38th minute.

Merson's well-struck free-kick took a deflection for a corner while Dublin produced one header which was blocked and another which James scooped away — with some Villa players convinced the ball had crossed the line.

If Villa enjoyed the better of the opening period, though, they were very much on the back foot as Enckelman made two crucial saves from Di Canio. He kept out the striker's low 63rd minute shot with his right foot after Don Hutchison had set up the opening with an incisive pass which threw Villa's defence off balance and guessed right when Di Canio tried to outwit him from the penalty spot after Mellberg's foul on Defoe.

Dublin should really have put the issue beyond doubt two minutes from time, only to miscue his close-range shot after substitute Jlloyd Samuel's pass and George Boateng's cross had opened up the home defence. But just when the points looked secure, Defoe's right-foot drive arrowed beyond Enckelman.

MATCH 25

Date: Wednesday 5 December 2001
Venue: Upton Park, 7.45pm

WEST HAM UNITED (0) 1
ASTON VILLA (1) 1

Attendance 28,377
Referee Mike Dean
Assistants A. Garratt and R. Lewis

▶ **WEST HAM UNITED**
claret shirts with blue trim, white shorts

1	David JAMES (Gk)
2	Tomas REPKA
3	Nigel WINTERBURN
7	Christian DAILLY
4	Don HUTCHISON
8	Trevor SINCLAIR
10	Paolo DI CANIO (c) ❏
21	Michael CARRICK
25	Jermain DEFOE g90
26	Joe COLE
30	Sebastien SCHEMMEL
	Substitutes
17	Shaka HISLOP (Gk)
18	Svetoslav TODOROV
20	Scott MINTO
23	Steve POTTS
28	Laurent COURTOIS

▶ **ASTON VILLA**
platinum shirts, navy blue shorts

12	Peter ENCKELMAN (Gk)
2	Mark DELANEY (45)
3	Alan WRIGHT
4	Olof MELLBERG
6	George BOATENG
9	Dion DUBLIN g1
10	Paul MERSON (c) (67)
11	Steve STAUNTON
15	Gareth BARRY
17	Lee HENDRIE
18	Steve STONE ❏
	Substitutes
8	Juan Pablo ANGEL
13	Boaz MYHILL (Gk)
14	David GINOLA
22	Darius VASSELL (10)
31	Jlloyd SAMUEL (2)

Before	P	W	D	L	F	A	pts
7 Villa	14	6	5	3	18	14	23
16 W. Ham	14	4	3	7	16	27	15
After	P	W	D	L	F	A	pts
6 Villa	15	6	6	3	19	15	24
16 W. Ham	15	4	4	7	17	28	16

▶ *The seventh consecutive Premiership draw between the sides* ▶ *First league starts of the season for Enckelman and Barry*

FA BARCLAYCARD PREMIERSHIP

Stoppage time agony

▶ It was a valiant effort, no question about that, but Villa headed home from London for the second time in five days cursing a costly stoppage time lapse of concentration.

Conceding a last-gasp equaliser had been bad enough, but the disappointment at Upton Park was nothing compared with the dejection they experienced at Highbury, where Thierry Henry's late stunner condemned them to defeat in a match which had appeared to be theirs for the taking.

The French striker capitalised on errors by two Villa players who had otherwise performed admirably throughout an absorbing if sometimes ill-tempered contest in which Arsenal had four players cautioned.

Peter Enckelman's sliced clearance was out of character with everything he had done earlier and when Ashley Cole knocked the ball forward, the combative George Boateng was for once beaten in his challenge for the ball.

Robert Pires got the better of the Dutchman to thread a telling pass through the visitors' overworked defence, and Henry calmly slotted a low shot beyond Enckelman to give Arsenal victory.

It was a cruel blow to Gregory's men, who had performed brightly throughout the first half to deservedly hold a two-goal lead through former Highbury favourite Paul Merson and Steve Stone.

But Villa were under pressure from the moment substitute Sylvain Wiltord reduced the deficit within a minute of the re-start and it was no great surprise when Henry equalised on 72 minutes.

Yet the early signs were good. Enckelman had to make three excellent first half saves, but Villa knocked the ball around with the air of a team confident they could spring a surprise.

Their goals were of the highest quality, too. On 21 minutes, Enckelman's long goal kick was headed on by Dion Dublin, and Merson got away from Matthew Upson before lifting a delicate lob over advancing goalkeeper Stuart Taylor.

The build-up to the second, in the 34th minute, was even more impressive, featuring an Alan Wright pass and a neat exchange between Lee Hendrie and Dublin before Stone set himself up for a low left foot shot from 12 yards.

But the complexion of the game changed dramatically within a minute of the resumption. Wiltord's left foot volley was superbly executed, the ball had defelected off both Wright and Gareth Barry to present the former Bordeaux marksman with his inviting shooting opportunity.

The Gunners stepped up a gear after the boost of that goal yet Villa still had chances, with Steve Staunton, Jlloyd Samuel and Dublin all going close before Arsenal equalised on 72 minutes.

Having dispossessed Samuel, Viera delivered a low cross which left Henry with simple tap-in from close range.

When Keown's downward header was saved by Enckelman and Wiltord had an effort disallowed for offside, it looked like Villa would at least take something from a gruelling afternoon. Sadly, Henry had other ideas.

▶ *Paul Merson celebrates his goal against his former club, together with Lee Hendrie and Gareth Barry.*

MATCH 26

Date Sunday 9 December 2001
Venue Highbury, 4.00pm

ARSENAL (0) 3
ASTON VILLA (2) 2

Attendance 38,074
Referee Alan Wiley
Assistants A. Green and N. Bannister

▶ **ARSENAL**
red and white shirts, white shorts

13 Stuart TAYLOR (Gk)	
3 Ashley COLE	
4 Patrick VIEIRA (c) ❏	
7 Robert PIRES	
8 Frederic LJUNGBERG (45)	
10 Dennis BERGKAMP ❏ (68)	
12 LAUREN ❏	
14 Thierry HENRY ❏	g72, 90
15 Ray PARLOUR	
20 Matthew UPSON (45)	
23 Sol CAMPBELL	
Substitutes	
5 Martin KEOWN (20)	
11 Sylvain WILTORD (8)	g46
18 Gilles GRIMANDI	
25 KANU (10)	
43 Graham STACK (Gk)	

▶ **ASTON VILLA**
platinum shirts, navy blue Shorts

12 Peter ENCKELMAN (Gk)	
3 Alan WRIGHT	
4 Olof MELLBERG	
6 George BOATENG	
9 Dion DUBLIN	
10 Paul MERSON (c)	g21
11 Steve STAUNTON	
15 Gareth BARRY (78)	
17 Lee HENDRIE	
18 Steve STONE	g34
31 Jlloyd SAMUEL	
Substitutes	
8 Juan Pablo ANGEL	
13 Boaz MYHILL (Gk)	
14 David GINOLA	
22 Darius VASSELL (15)	
25 Jon BEWERS	

Before	P	W	D	L	F	A	pts
3 Arsenal	14	7	5	2	30	9	26
5 Villa	15	6	6	3	19	15	24
After	P	W	D	L	F	A	pts
2 Arsenal	15	8	5	2	33	11	29
5 Villa	16	6	6	4	21	18	24

▶ *First Premiership goals of the season for Merson and Stone* ▶ *Samuel's first start of the campaign*

FA BARCLAYCARD PREMIERSHIP

Colombian blend, with a sweetener

▶ An Angel isn't just for Christmas, but Juan Pablo's return to the Aston Villa line-up could not have been more timely.

Indeed, Holte Enders might argue it was heaven sent as the Colombian striker claimed the goals to end his team's depressing run of seven matches without a win.

Angel took his seasonal haul into double figures with his first goals since he netted twice in Villa's previous success, the 3-2 home victory over Bolton.

This time it was more a case of steadying a ship which had taken quite a bashing throughout the turbulent days of November and early December, and which was in danger of straying further off course when Nigerian Finidi George fired bottom-of-the-table Ipswich Town into a 17th minute lead.

Angel, thankfully, was hungry for goals after waiting patiently on the touchline for 180 minutes. His header from Steve Staunton's cross brought the scores level as half-time approached, and his 70th minute winner, which deflected in off Ipswich defender John McGreal, secured victory.

Villa's early play was littered with errors, but at least they attempted to drive the game, creating a number of openings which, unfortunately, promised more than they delivered. It wasn't exactly penetrative football, but at least things seemed to be moving in the right direction – until the 17th minute, that was.

Then, having surrendered possession, Villa were caught napping as Ipswich quickly worked the ball to the unmarked Finidi George, who rifled a low 25-yard drive inside the right-hand post as the unsighted Peter Schmeichel dived too late.

Villa's confidence then drained to the point where Merson found himself staging what was almost a one-man crusade. His endeavours finally paid dividends a minute before the break when he produced the latest of his superb passes to send Steve Stone haring down the right.

The midfielder's attempted cross was charged down for a corner, and although Steve Staunton's inswinging flag kick was dropped by goalkeeper Matteo Sereni, the chance appeared to have been lost as Ipswich scrambled the ball clear.

It only went as far as Staunton, though, and when the Republic of Ireland international delivered a fine cross, Angel climbed above McGreal and hung in the air to direct an angled header beyond Sereni and into the corner of the net.

Five minutes into the second half, it was almost 2-0 as Villa conjured up their best move so far and were agonisingly close to a brilliant goal.

Stone's neat pass found George Boateng in space down the right, and when the Dutch midfielder laid the ball back to Merson, the skipper responded with an exquisite first time chip which eluded Sereni and bounced off the top of the bar. But Villa forced their way in front with a superb piece of football, even if the finish was slightly fortuitous.

Angel accepted Stone's pass with a deft first touch which took him away from Venus and his powerful right foot shot might have gone in anyway. As it was, McGreal's challenge sent the ball looping over Sereni and into the net.

▶ *Steve Stone finds himself unbalanced by a forceful Ipswich challenge.*

MATCH 27

Date Monday 17 December 2001
Venue Villa Park, 8.00pm

ASTON VILLA (1) 2
IPSWICH TOWN (1) 1

Attendance 29,320
Referee Mike Dean
Assistants R. Pashley and P. Vosper

▶ **ASTON VILLA**
claret shirts with blue trim, white shorts

1	Peter SCHMEICHEL (Gk)	
3	Alan WRIGHT	
4	Olof MELLBERG	
6	George BOATENG	
8	Juan Pablo ANGEL (84)	g44, 70
10	Paul MERSON (c)	
11	Steve STAUNTON	
15	Gareth BARRY	
17	Lee HENDRIE (67)	
18	Steve STONE	
31	Jlloyd SAMUEL	
	Substitutes	
9	Dion DUBLIN (17)	
12	Peter ENCKELMAN (Gk)	
19	Bosko BALABAN	
22	Darius VASSELL (8)	
25	Jonathan BEWERS	

▶ **IPSWICH TOWN**
white shirts, black shorts

34	Matteo SERENI (Gk)	
4	John McGREAL	
5	Hermann HREIDARSSON	
6	Mark VENUS	
7	Jim MAGILTON	
8	Matt HOLLAND (c)	
10	Alun ARMSTRONG (80)	
12	Richard NAYLOR ❏	
14	Jermaine WRIGHT	
15	Chris MAKIN	
33	Finidi GEORGE (65)	g17
	Substitutes	
3	Jamie CLAPHAM (33)	
9	Pablo COUNAGO	
19	Titus BRAMBLE	
21	Keith BRANAGAN (Gk)	
38	Marcus BENT (10)	

Before	P	W	D	L	F	A	pts
8 Villa	16	6	6	4	21	18	24
20 Ipswich	16	1	6	9	14	25	9
After	P	W	D	L	F	A	pts
8 Villa	17	7	6	4	23	19	27
20 Ipswich	17	1	6	10	15	27	9

▶ *Villa's third consecutive 2-1 victory over Ipswich* ▶ *Angel into double figures*

FA BARCLAYCARD PREMIERSHIP

A heavy fall at Pride Park

▶ The scoreline imparts the only information which really matters, but Villa supporters who made the short journey across the Midlands will tell you it could have been a vastly different story.

It wasn't just the biting wind which whipped across Pride Park that left the Villa faithful feeling an icy blast. The travelling band headed home feeling both cold and depressed after watching their team contrive to lose a match which should at least have yielded a point.

Not only did Villa hold the upper hand for lengthy periods, they were twice desperately close to scoring with fine second half efforts, only for Derby to sweep straight to the other end and deliver killer blows.

The upshot was a 3-1 result which makes no sense to anyone who braved the East Midland elements.

That, of course, was absolutely no consolation to manager John Gregory and his players. This was simply one of those occasions when nothing was destined to go right.

For all their possession, Villa simply could not find the vital cutting edge, with the exception of Juan Pablo Angel's excellent goal on the stroke of half-time.

That cancelled out Fabrizio Ravanelli's opener for the home side a minute earlier, but former Villa Park favourite Benito Carbone restored Derby's lead in the 67th minute and two minutes from time substitute Malcolm Christie added number three.

It was all very frustrating, even if Ravanelli had shown how it should be done in the 44th minute when he put Derby ahead with a well-taken goal.

Giorgi Kinkladze's corner was chested down by defender Chris Riggott, and as Villa hesitated, the Italian responded with a close-range shot on the turn which Peter Schmeichel could only help into the net.

Villa hit back with a fine equaliser just a minute later. Jlloyd Samuel's cross was flicked on by Dublin, and Angel displayed all his predatory instincts to shrug off Luciano Mawene and beat Poom with a low left-footer into the far corner.

Once the equaliser had gone in, a second goal looked imminent, and it almost arrived on 66 minutes when Angel nudged a short pass to Kachloul, whose low 20-yarder smacked against the right-hand post and rebounded across the face of goal.

But Villa were behind again within a minute as Derby launched a counter attack, and Schmeichel could do no more than tip Ravanelli's right wing cross to Carbone, who sent an angled shot into the far corner.

After Dublin and Angel had both headed wide, Villa were close to drawing level again in the 88th minute. Staunton's deep cross was headed down by Angel, and Merson looked a certain scorer until he was denied by Riggott's blocking tackle.

It was the last throw of the dice. The Rams went straight to the other end for Christie to slip the clinching goal past Schmeichel.

▶ A determined Steve Staunton challenges former Villa star Benito Carbone, watched by Carbone's fellow countryman Fabrizio Ravanelli.

MATCH 28

Date Saturday 22 December 2001
Venue Pride Park, 12 noon

DERBY COUNTY (1) 3
ASTON VILLA (1) 1

Attendance 28,001
Referee David Elleray
Assistants J. Holbrook and C. Bassindale

▶ DERBY COUNTY
white shirts, black shorts

1 Mart POOM (Gk)	
6 Chris RIGGOTT	
7 Benito CARBONE (70)	g67
10 Giorgi KINKLADZE (75)	
11 Fabrizio RAVANELLI (c)	g44
15 Danny HIGGINBOTHAM	
16 Luciano ZAVANGO	
17 Youl MAWENE	
23 Paul BOERTIEN	
37 Pierre DUCROCQ	
38 Francois GRENET	
Substitutes	
9 Deon BURTON (10)	
12 Malcolm CHRISTIE (7)	g88
24 Andy OAKES (Gk)	
19 Steve ELLIOTT	
31 Adam BOLDER	

▶ ASTON VILLA
platinum shirts, navy blue shorts

1 Peter SCHMEICHEL (Gk)	
3 Alan WRIGHT	
4 Olof MELLBERG	
6 George BOATENG (79)	
8 Juan Pablo ANGEL	g45
9 Dion DUBLIN	
10 Paul MERSON	
11 Steve STAUNTON	
15 Gareth BARRY (45)	
18 Steve STONE	
31 Jlloyd SAMUEL (45)	
Substitutes	
7 Ian TAYLOR	
12 Peter ENCKELMAN (Gk)	
17 Lee HENDRIE (31) ❑	
19 Bosko BALABAN (6)	
30 Hassan KACHLOUL (15)	

Before	P	W	D	L	F	A	pts
8 Villa	17	7	6	4	23	19	27
19 Derby	17	3	4	10	11	30	13
After	P	W	D	L	F	A	pts
8 Villa	18	7	6	5	24	22	27
18 Derby	18	4	4	10	14	31	16

▶ Villa beaten at Pride Park for the second consecutive season ▶ Kachloul returns after a four-game injury absence

33

FA BARCLAYCARD PREMIERSHIP

MATCH 29

A Boxing Day sucker punch

Date   Wednesday 26 December 2001
Venue Villa Park, 3.00pm

ASTON VILLA (1) 1
LIVERPOOL (1) 2

Attendance 42,602
Referee   Andy D'Urso
Assistants R. Booth and R. Gould

▶ Villa and Liverpool served up some appetising festive fayre for a capacity Boxing Day crowd, even if John Gregory and his players were ultimately left with a nasty taste.

The manager was ordered from the dug-out by referee Andy D'Urso after making comments to linesman Ray Gould over a dubious penalty award, but that was nothing compared with Gregory's disappointment at watching his side lose another match they could so easily have won.

Trailing to a bizarre goal after eight minutes, when Jari Litmanen gratefully slotted home a low shot after Peter Schmeichel's throw-out had struck D'Urso, Villa had battled back to be on level terms through Lee Hendrie.

But even though Litmanen hit the post from the spot kick which prompted such strong Villa protests, Liverpool ended a run of three games without a win when Vladimir Smicer stole in to claim their second goal in the 73rd minute.

Yet it could all have been so different, Ian Taylor, Paul Merson and Darius Vassell all having gone close before Scimcer pounced.

The visitors' early lead arrived in the most fortuitous of circumstances. Schmeichel had rushed from his line to collect a pass intended for Litmanen and with the danger having apparently subsided, Villa were regrouping as the keeper threw the ball out.

His clearance struck referee D'Urso on the back of his legs, however, and with the home defence totally off balance, Litmanen had the simple task of stroking his shot into the unguarded net from just outside the penalty area.

Villa hauled themselves level with a well-taken equaliser in the 20th minute. Moving on to George Boateng's pass, Juan Pablo Angel let fly with a tremendous angled drive which Jerzy Dudek could only parry, and when the ball fell invitingly to Hendrie, the midfielder rammed it home from 10 yards.

Then Boateng was on the receiving end of a harsh decision which presented the visitors with a penalty.

It appeared that Steven Gerrard merely tumbled over the Dutch midfielder's challenge as he cut in from the right, but an assistant referee immediately raised his flag and D'Urso pointed to the spot. Litmanen's kick had Schmeichel diving the wrong way, but struck the left hand post.

Villa were desperately unlucky not to go ahead in the 66th minute when substitute Ian Taylor met Vassell's low cross with a close-range shot which hit the near post and bounced across the danger zone. Even then, a goal looked certain as Merson moved in with a drive which deflected for a corner.

Then Vassell 's 20-yard left footer was tipped away at full stretch by Dudek, but just when Villa looked capable of translating their superiority into something more tangible they were rocked by Smicer's stunner.

Berger caught an otherwise impressive defence square as he knocked the ball over the top, leaving Smicer unmarked with only Schmeichel to beat.

▶ *It's celebration time for Villa as a shirt-less Lee Hendrie is congratulated by George Boateng after scoring Villa's equaliser.*

▶ ASTON VILLA
claret shirts with blue trim, white shorts

1	Peter SCHMEICHEL (Gk)	
3	Alan WRIGHT	
4	Olof MELLBERG	
6	George BOATENG ❑	
8	Juan Pablo ANGEL	
10	Paul MERSON (c)	
11	Steve STAUNTON	
17	Lee HENDRIE (46)	g20
22	Darius VASSELL	
30	Hassan KACHLOUL	
31	Jloyd SAMUEL (82)	
	Substitutes	
7	Ian TAYLOR (17)	
9	Dion DUBLIN	
12	Peter ENCKELMAN (Gk)	
15	Gareth BARRY	
18	Steve STONE (31)	

▶ LIVERPOOL
white shirts, black shorts

12	Jerzy DUDEK (Gk)	
2	Stephane HENCHOZ	
4	Sami HYYPIA (c)	
7	Vladimir SMICER (86)	g73
10	Michael OWEN	
15	Patrik BERGER	
16	Dietmar HAMANN	
17	Steven GERRARD (77)	
18	John Arne RIISE	
23	Jamie CARRAGHER	
37	Jari LITMANEN (68)	g8
	Substitutes	
9	Nicolas ANELKA (37)	
13	Danny MURPHY (17)	
21	Gary McALLISTER (7)	
22	Chris KIRKLAND (Gk)	
29	Stephen WRIGHT	

Before	P	W	D	L	F	A	pts
2 Liverpool	17	10	3	4	30	20	33
8 Villa	18	7	6	5	24	22	27
After	P	W	D	L	F	A	pts
2 Liverpool	18	11	3	4	32	21	36
8 Villa	19	7	6	6	25	24	27

▶ Hendrie's first goal since the September visit to Anfield ▶ Taylor returns after five-match absence

34

FA BARCLAYCARD PREMIERSHIP

Angel spot on for a point

▶ Juan Pablo Angel was the calmest man inside Villa Park as he salvaged a point with a penalty which carried all the hallmarks of a former Holte End hero.

It wasn't quite as cheeky as some of the spot kicks Dwight Yorke used to produce, but Angel's cool conversion in the fourth minute of stoppage time illustrated just how much the man from Colombia has matured since becoming Villa's £9.5million record signing.

John Gregory's side had spent virtually the whole of the second half seeking an equaliser to cancel out Les Ferdinand's 38th minute goal, and with the seconds ticking away, their search appeared to have been in vain.

But just when a third consecutive festive defeat was looming, Spurs' midfielder Darren Anderton inexplicably handled a Steve Stone cross which was going out, and Angel planted his kick into the centre of goal as Kasey Keller dived to his left.

Keller had earlier denied Villa with a string of outstanding saves, but there was no question that the home side deserved a point for their sheer resilience.

After an opening period in which both sides had kept the large crowd enthralled with some flowing football, Villa drove relentlessly at the Londoners, whose spirit of adventure was overtaken by a desire to hold what they had.

It was a pity the visitors did not maintain the ambition which had made the first 45 minutes so absorbing.

▶ *A ballet-like Paul Merson is well-balanced as he makes one of his trademark passes with the outside of his right foot.*

Both sides were committed to attack early on, and Darius Vassell delighted home supporters when some clever footwork left Chris Perry grounded before firing just wide of the near post.

But Gregory's side were fortunate not to go behind on 24 minutes when Ferdinand's downward header beat Schmeichel, only to come back off the inside of a post and into the 'keeper's arms.

It was Villa's turn to curse their luck eight minutes later, Merson ending a mazy run through the middle with a stinging right-footer which Keller found too hot to handle, the 'keeper recovering to palm away Kachloul's shot from the rebound.

A goal looked inevitable, but unfortunately it was the Londoners who grabbed it, Teddy Sheringham sending Ferdinand clear with a delightful flick. Schmeichel spread himself well and even got a foot to the striker's shot, but its momentum carried it just inside the right-hand upright.

The setback took the sting out of Villa and Spurs confidence grew, but the home side were close to an equaliser in the 52nd minute.

Steve Staunton cut a free-kick back to Alan Wright, whose shot cannoned off a defender before Lee Hendrie's low effort from the edge of the penalty area was tipped away by Keller.

When Angel and Vassell subsequently had headers saved by the 'keeper, it seemed Keller would have a clean sheet to mark his first appearance of the season, but he obviously hadn't counted on Anderton's hand ball or Angel's precision from 12 yards.

MATCH 30

Date Saturday 29 December 2001
Venue Villa Park, 3.00pm

ASTON VILLA (0) 1
TOTTENHAM H. (1) 1

Attendance 41,134
Referee Eddie Wolstenholme
Assistants R. Bone and N. Miller

▶ **ASTON VILLA**
claret shirts with blue trim, white shorts

1	Peter SCHMEICHEL (Gk)
3	Alan WRIGHT (72)
4	Olof MELLBERG
6	George BOATENG (88)
8	Juan Pablo ANGEL g90
10	Paul MERSON (c)
11	Steve STAUNTON
17	Lee HENDRIE
22	Darius VASSELL
30	Hassan KACHLOUL
31	Jlloyd SAMUEL
	Substitutes
7	Ian TAYLOR (6)
9	Dion DUBLIN
12	Peter ENCKELMAN (Gk)
15	Gareth BARRY
18	Steve STONE (3)

▶ **TOTTENHAM HOTSPUR**
white shirts, navy blue shorts

13	Kasey KELLER (Gk)
3	Mauricio TARICCO
4	Steffen FREUND
6	Chris PERRY
7	Darren ANDERTON
9	Les FERDINAND (83) ❑ g38
10	Teddy SHERINGHAM (c)
14	Gustavo POYET
23	Christian ZIEGE (85) ❑
26	Ledley KING
36	Dean RICHARDS
	Substitutes
1	Neil SULLIVAN (Gk)
8	Tim SHERWOOD
11	Sergei REBROV (9)
29	Simon DAVIES
30	Anthony GARDNER (23)

Before	P	W	D	L	F	A	pts
7 Spurs	19	8	3	8	30	26	27
8 Villa	19	7	6	6	25	24	27
After	P	W	D	L	F	A	pts
7 Spurs	20	8	4	8	31	27	28
8 Villa	20	7	7	6	26	25	28

▶ *Tottenham without a win at Villa Park since 1986* ▶ *Angel's second penalty conversion*

FA BARCLAYCARD PREMIERSHIP

Late, late and late again

▶ Villa were denied by a late goal for the third consecutive season as they kicked off 2002 with a hard-earned point against Sunderland at the Stadium of Light.

It could so easily have been three, but with just four minutes remaining, Brazilian defender Emerson Thome steered a header past Peter Schmeichel following a free-kick from Julio Arca.

On the balance of play, the equaliser was arguably no more than Peter Reid's men deserved, but it was galling for Villa to be denied yet again by a goal in the final 10 minutes.

Two seasons ago, Kevin Phillips popped up with an 82nd minute winner, while Gavin McCann's 83rd minute equaliser meant a 1-1 draw last March after the visitors had gone ahead through Julian Joachim.

This time, Thome's effort cancelled out a 60th minute effort from midfielder Ian Taylor, leaving John Gregory and his players frustrated once again on the homeward journey from Wearside.

Even so, a point wasn't a bad return from a match in which the manager was again forced into changes because of Juan Pablo Angel's groin strain.

Hardly surprisingly, Villa's defence were soon tested, Olof Mellberg clearing Jason McAteer's second minute cross before Darius Vassell fired into the side netting at the other end.

But Schmeichel came to the rescue in dramatic fashion after Quinn went down in the box and was adjudged to have been fouled by Jlloyd Samuel, even though there appeared to be no contact.

Phillips could hardly have struck the spot kick more firmly, but Schmeichel divied to his left to claw the ball to safety and ensured that justice was done.

▶ The turf is flying at the Stadium of Light as striker Darius Vassell lunges in to win this tackle in Villa's first match of 2002.

If the Black Cats generally held the upper hand, however, Villa almost went ahead just before half-time when Vassell's pace took him clear of Bernt Haas, only for the chance to be wasted when his delayed pass caught Dublin off balance.

Vassell was again lively on the resumption, turning smartly to meet Dublin's flick with a shot which was just wide, only for Sunderland to grasp the initiative as Alan Wright blocked a Jason McAteer shot and Schmeichel again denied Phillips by palming the striker's shot away for a corner.

There was another let-off when Quinn was unable to get his header on target after Arca had flicked on McAteer's cross, but Taylor showed how it should be done on the hour mark.

Stone played the ball out to Vassell on the right, and the striker's inch-perfect cross was met by the long-serving midfielder, who neatly headed down and past Sorensen.

As the Wearsiders went in search of an equaliser, Staunton and Mellberg were defiant at the heart of the Villa defence, only to see all their good work undone in the 86th minute.

MATCH 31

Date Tuesday 1 January 2002
Venue Stadium of Light, 3.00pm

SUNDERLAND (0) **1**
ASTON VILLA (0) **1**

Attendance 45,324
Referee Mike Riley
Assistants R. Booth and M. Atkinson

▶ **SUNDERLAND**
red and white striped shirts, black shorts

1	Thomas SORENSEN (Gk)
2	Bernt HAAS
3	Michael GRAY (c)
4	Claudio REYNA (22)
6	Emerson THOME g86
8	Gavin McCANN
9	Niall QUINN
10	Kevin PHILLIPS
16	Jason McATEER
18	Darren WILLIAMS
33	Julio ARCA
	Substitutes
11	Kevin KILBANE
19	Kevin KYLE
21	Paul THIRLWELL (4) ▢
24	George McCARTNEY
30	Jurgen MACHO (Gk)

▶ **ASTON VILLA**
claret shirts with blue trim, white shorts

1	Peter SCHMEICHEL (Gk)
3	Alan WRIGHT
4	Olof MELLBERG
7	Ian TAYLOR ▢ g60
9	Dion DUBLIN
11	Steve STAUNTON
17	Lee HENDRIE
18	Steve STONE ▢
22	Darius VASSELL ▢
30	Hassan KACHLOUL (67)
31	Jlloyd SAMUEL
	Substitutes
6	George BOATENG
10	Paul MERSON
12	Peter ENCKELMAN (Gk)
15	Gareth BARRY (30)
21	Thomas HITZLSPERGER

Before	P	W	D	L	F	A	pts
8 Villa	20	7	7	6	26	25	28
10 S'land	20	7	5	8	17	22	26
After	P	W	D	L	F	A	pts
9 Villa	21	7	8	6	27	26	29
10 S'land	21	7	6	8	18	23	27

▶ Villa still to win at the Stadium of Light   ▶ Juan Pablo Angel sidelined by a groin injury

FA CUP THIRD ROUND

A Ruud awakening

▶ Villa were just 13 minutes away from a famous FA Cup victory when their dreams were disrupted by an alarm call which left them wondering exactly what had gone wrong.

As the clock ticked away, John Gregory's side were on the brink of despatching Manchester United from the competition – only to be left stunned and shell-shocked by the surreal events which unfolded almost without warning.

Ian Taylor's second goal in consecutive games, plus a headed own goal from Phil Neville, had put Villa two-up and looking like clinching a fourth round place. But it was almost as if time had stood still as United, having looked a beaten side, responded with a three-goal blitz in the space of five devastating minutes.

Ole Gunnar Solskjaer prompted the revival with a low left foot drive, and Villa had barely recovered when £19million Dutch striker Ruud van Nistelrooy hooked home the equaliser after David Beckham had headed down Paul Scholes' left wing centre.

Van Nistelrooy, who had replaced first half substitute Luke Chadwick, then skipped through the home defence and took the ball around former United goalkeeper Peter Schmeichel to slot home what proved to be the winner.

It was, indeed, a bitter blow to the claret-and-blue faithful on a night when nothing had seemed quite normal.

There was real scare for Villa on 24 minutes when Beckham went racing through the middle, seemingly in an offside position. The flag stayed down, however, and there was enormous relief in the home camp as the England skipper's powerful rising drive was well held by Schmeichel.

Solskjaer's swerving drive was clutched by Schmeichel in the 40th minute, and two minutes later the striker superbly controlled a high ball before unleashing an angled shot just beyond the far post.

The lively Chadwick had two chances as Sir Alex Ferguson's outfit opened the second period in forceful fashion, sending one shot over from a good position and another wide. But just when Holte Enders were beginning to fear the worst, their favourites surged into a 52nd minute lead.

It was, in fact, their first on-target effort, but no-one was worrying too much about that as Taylor moved on to Hendrie's carefully threaded through ball, shrugged off Phil Neville and stabbed a low shot past the advancing Roy Carroll.

Two minutes later, the Villa faithful were in ecstasy, with Taylor again instrumental without even touching the ball. Paul Merson's lob was intended for the midfielder, but although Neville got there first, Taylor's presence forced the United defender to head past Carroll and over the line.

▶ Ian Taylor shapes up for the shot which gave Villa the lead despite the close attentions of Phil Neville.

In between times, Chadwick had hit the netting, and his latest miss prompted Ferguson to replace the substitute with Ruud van Nistelrooy.

With United looking to claw their way back, Solskjaer was wide with an 18-yard shot on the turn while Beckham long-range curler, although Angel was only inches away from making it 3-0 when he just failed to make contact with Samuel's cross right in front of goal.

It was to prove a costly miss, Solskjaer reducing the deficit with a left foot drive before van Nilstelrooy delivered his double whammy.

MATCH 32

Date Sunday 6 January 2002
Venue Villa Park, 7.00pm

ASTON VILLA (0) 2
MANCHESTER UTD. (0) 3

Attendance 38,444
Referee Graham Poll
Assistants P. Sharp and G. Turner

▶ **ASTON VILLA**
claret shirts with blue trim, white shorts

1 Peter SCHMEICHEL (Gk)	
3 Alan WRIGHT (86)	
4 Olof MELLBERG	
6 George BOATENG (86)	
7 Ian TAYLOR	g52
8 Juan Pablo ANGEL	
10 Paul MERSON (c) (86)	
11 Steve STAUNTON	
17 Lee HENDRIE	
22 Darius VASSELL ❑	
31 Jlloyd SAMUEL	
Substitutes	
2 Mark DELANEY	
12 Peter ENCKELMAN (Gk)	
15 Gareth BARRY (6)	
18 Steve STONE (3)	
20 Moustapha HADJI (10)	

▶ **MANCHESTER UNITED**
white shirts, black shorts

13 Roy CARROLL (Gk)	
2 Gary NEVILLE	
4 Juan Sebastian VERON	
6 Laurent BLANC ❑	
7 David BECKHAM	
8 Nicky BUTT (26)	
12 Phil NEVILLE	og54
16 Roy KEANE (c)	
18 Paul SCHOLES	
20 Ole Gunnar SOLSKJAER	g77
27 Mickael SILVESTRE	
Substitutes	
10 Ruud V. NISTELROOY (15) g80,82	
15 Luke CHADWICK (8) (56)	
17 Raimond VAN DER GOUW (Gk)	
28 Michael STEWART	
30 John O'SHEA	

▶ A first for Villa Park – a 7pm Sunday kick-off   ▶ Van Nistelrooy sets a United record by scoring in seven consecutive matches

FA BARCLAYCARD PREMIERSHIP

MATCH 33

Day of the avengers

Date Saturday 12 January 2002
Venue Villa Park, 3.00pm

**ASTON VILLA (2) 2
DERBY COUNTY (1) 1**

▶ Revenge wasn't exactly sweet, but it was certainly welcome as Villa edged two places up the Premiership with a hard-earned victory over Midland rivals Derby County.

If John Gregory's side had been more than a little unfortunate to lose the corresponding game at Pride Park three weeks earlier, they found the breaks going very much in their favour on this occasion.

It was the relegation-threatened Rams' turn to feel aggrieved as they were reduced to 10 men by the 24th minute dismissal of Francois Grenet, and then had a second half effort by Fabrizio Ravanelli ruled out for offside.

Not for the first time, playing against 10 men proved no easy option for Villa, and Derby actually looked more effective once they had recovered from the shock of losing their French midfielder.

From a Villa perspective, all the good things about this match happened before the interval when they produced some fluent football and deservedly led through a magnificent Darius Vassell finish and a Juan Pablo Angel header which gave the Colombian his ninth Premiership goal of the season.

Having won only once in their previous 13 league and cup matches, this was one where Villa desperately needed a result, and having survived Darryl Powell's equaliser and Ravanelli's disallowed effort, they achieved their objective.

Villa's bright opening certainly didn't reflect their poor record over the past couple of months as the energetic Paul Merson instigated some delightful moves, although Derby produced the first shot, Luciano Zavango firing past the far post from the left hand edge of the penalty area.

A clumsy challenge by the Argentine defender Zavango led to Villa's opening goal in the 11th minute.

After Zavango was cautioned for bringing down Merson just inside Villa's half, Peter Schmeichel launched a long free-kick which was flicked on by Angel, and Vassell's superb first touch enabled him to send a rising angled drive beyond Estonian goalkeeper Mart Poom and into the far corner.

That classic goal should have provided the springboard for an onslaught, but Villa went off the boil for a while and were pegged back by a sloppy 23rd minute equaliser.

Schmeichel's slip as he attempted to clear a Jlloyd Samuel back pass enabled Malcolm Christie to cut the ball back from the byline and although Samuel made a partial clearance, it hit the oncoming Darryl Powell and diverted into the net.

Over the course of the next few minutes, however, the outcome of the match was effectively decided.

Grenet's challenge on Lee Hendrie right in front of the dug-out was reckless to say the least, sending Villa's midfielder spinning into the air, and even though Gregory felt it did not warrant a red card, that was the punishment handed out by referee Mark Halsey.

Barely two minutes later, Villa were back in front, Ian Taylor moving on to Merson's well-measured pass to deliver a perfect right-wing cross which Angel met with a downward header to leave Poom helpless.

▶ *Juan Pablo Angel meets an Ian Taylor cross with the header which secured all three points for Villa.*

Attendance 28,881
Referee Mark Halsey
Assistants C. Boyeson and T. Kettle

▶ **ASTON VILLA**
claret shirts with blue trim, white shorts

1	Peter SCHMEICHEL (Gk)	
2	Mark DELANEY	
4	Olof MELLBERG ▫	
6	George BOATENG	
7	Ian TAYLOR (58)	
8	Juan Pablo ANGEL	g26
10	Paul MERSON (c) (90)	
11	Steve STAUNTON	
17	Lee HENDRIE (78)	
22	Darius VASSELL	g11
31	Jlloyd SAMUEL ▫	
	Substitutes	
12	Peter ENCKELMAN (Gk)	
15	Gareth BARRY (10)	
19	Bosko BALABAN	
20	Moustapha HADJI (17)	
30	Hassan KACHLOUL (7)	

▶ **DERBY COUNTY**
white shirts, black shorts

1	Mart POOM (Gk)	
4	Darryl POWELL	g23
6	Chris RIGGOTT	
11	Fabrizio RAVANELLI (c)	
12	Malcolm CHRISTIE	
15	Danny HIGGINBOTHAM	
16	Luciano ZAVANGO (68) ▫	
19	Steve ELLIOTT (22)	
23	Paul BOERTIEN ▫	
37	Pierre DUCROCQ	
38	Francois GRENET ▫	
	Substitutes	
9	Deon BURTON	
10	Giorgi KINKLADZE ▫ (19)	
17	Youl MAWENE	
24	Andy OAKES (Gk)	
31	Adam BOLDER (16)	

Before	P	W	D	L	F	A	pts
9 Villa	21	7	8	6	27	26	29
18 Derby	21	5	4	12	15	36	19

After	P	W	D	L	F	A	pts
7 Villa	22	8	8	6	29	27	32
19 Derby	22	5	4	13	16	38	19

▶ Villa maintain their 100 per cent Premiership home record over the Rams ▶ Delaney's first senior action since 5th December

FA BARCLAYCARD PREMIERSHIP

Such a happy Valley

▶ Darius Vassell and Juan Pablo Angel continued their emergence as one of the most effective striking partnerships in the top flight as Villa rediscovered their best form at The Valley.

The duo, match-winners against Derby in the previous game, reproduced the deadly formula in south London, and although Charlton skipper Graham Stuart reduced the deficit from a penalty rebound two minutes from time, there was never any question about the visitors' entitlement to all three points.

Villa looked destined for victory once Vassell had opened the scoring following their first attack on eight minutes. Mark Fish's misplaced pass enabled Jlloyd Samuel to play a fine pass inside to Vassell and although Jorge Costa lunged in with a desperate tackle, his contact succeeded only in sending the ball looping over goalkeeper Dean Kiely and into the far corner.

The visitors frequently threatened a second as skipper Paul Merson probed intelligently and Vassell produced footwork which frequently had the Londoners' defence mesmerised.

Jlloyd Samuel's frequent charges down the left added an extra dimension to Villa's attacks, even though the young full-back was a touch fortunate to escape punishment for a 21st minute challenge which left Luke Young needing lengthy treatment before he limped off eight minutes later.

It was George Boateng, though, who epitomised Villa's determination with a perpetual motion performance in midfield. That was never more evident than in the 42nd minute, when the Dutch international won a 40-60 challenge to set up the second goal.

Costa looked odds-on favourite to tidy up Moustapha Hadji's long clearance, but Boateng ran 40 yards to beat the Portuguese star with a brave header which was superbly controlled by Angel as he raced away down the right.

The Colombian striker cut inside and came up with the most clinical of finishes as he drilled a low angled right-foot shot beyond Kiely and in off the far post.

▶ *Darius Vassell's shot deflects off defender Jorge Costa to give Villa an eighth minute advantage at The Valley.*

By half-time, it could have been three, Kiely diving to tip the ball away from Angel's feet following a piercing Boateng pass, but Villa's defence were kept busy as Charlton stepped up the pace at the start of the second half but Euell was twice guilty of weak efforts right in front of goal and Schmeichel saved a Stuart header.

Although Villa were now under more pressure, they still mounted a succession of counter attacks. Hadji set up Vassell for a drive which flashed wide, while the Moroccan was not far off target with a spectacular 20-yard bicycle kick before Merson thought he had put the issue beyond doubt on 83 minutes.

The skipper nodded into an unguarded net after the diving Kiely had palmed away Vassell's stinging shot, only to be ruled offside.

Stuart then headed past Schmeichel after the Danish keeper had saved the midfielder's well-struck penalty with his legs, but they held on for three well-deserved points.

▶ *Villa's first win in London since their 4-2 in at Tottenham in April, 2000* ▶ *John Gregory's last game in charge*

MATCH 34

Date Monday 21 January 2002
Venue The Valley, 8.00pm

CHARLTON ATH. (0) **1**
ASTON VILLA (2) **2**

Attendance 25,681
Referee Rob Styles
Assistants G. Brittain and J. Holbrook

▶ **CHARLTON ATHLETIC**
red shirts, white shorts

1	Dean KIELY (Gk)	
3	Chris POWELL	
4	Graham STUART (c)	g88
9	Jason EUELL	
11	John ROBINSON	
17	Scott PARKER (89)	
19	Luke YOUNG (29)	
20	Claus JENSEN (68)	
21	Joanatan JOHANSSON	
27	Jorge COSTA ▫	
36	Mark FISH	
	Substitutes	
7	Chris BART-WILLIAMS	
13	Sasa ILIC (Gk)	
18	Paul KONCHESKY (19)	
24	Jonathan FORTUNE (17)	
29	Kevin LISBIE (20)	

▶ **ASTON VILLA**
platinum shirts, navy blue shorts

1	Peter SCHMEICHEL (Gk)	
2	Mark DELANEY	
4	Olof MELLBERG	
6	George BOATENG	
8	Juan Pablo ANGEL ▫	g42
10	Paul MERSON (c)	
11	Steve STAUNTON	
17	Lee HENDRIE (87)	
20	Moustapha HADJI	
22	Darius VASSELL	g8
31	Jlloyd SAMUEL	
	Substitutes	
12	Peter ENCKELMAN (Gk)	
14	David GINOLA	
15	Gareth BARRY (17)	
18	Steve STONE	
19	Bosko BALABAN	

Before	P	W	D	L	F	A	pts
8 Villa	22	8	8	6	29	27	32
10 Charlton	22	7	8	7	28	28	29
After	P	W	D	L	F	A	pts
7 Villa	23	9	8	6	31	28	35
10 Charlton	23	7	8	8	29	30	29

FA BARCLAYCARD PREMIERSHIP

A real sticking point

▶ The first match after a manager's departure is always going to be difficult, but Villa at least emerged with something to show from a testing occasion.

In an ideal world, they would have recorded their seventh consecutive home victory over an Everton side who have found Villa Park something of a graveyard in recent times. But with the upheaval of John Gregory's resignation six days earlier clearly still on many minds, this was a night when any sort of return was gratefully accepted.

Indeed, while Villa enjoyed greater territorial advantage in a largely uninspiring contest, the more clear-cut chances fell to the Toffees – even if the home side went closer to breaking the deadlock.

Skipper Paul Merson was desperately unlucky not to score in the 58th minute when his breathtaking run was followed by a rising right foot drive which left Everton goalkeeper Steve Simonsen helpless before crashing against the bar.

The opening exchanges were laced with caution, but the game suddenly came to life with a chance at either end in the space of 60 seconds.

Darius Vassell was not far off target with a far post header from Merson's 12th minute cross, but the visitors immediately posed a threat when Tony Hibbert knocked the ball inside from beyond the far post, forcing the diving Peter Enckelman to tip away one-handed.

Vassell again went close with a shot which took a deflection for a corner but Danny Cadamarteri's right wing centre for the visitors a few minutes later was menacing, finding the towering frame of Duncan Ferguson, whose downward header was clutched by Enckelman.

Merson then produced a drive which was blocked by Scott Gemmill before it could do any damage, but the skipper will have been disappointed when he shot tamely at Simonsen just before half-time after Vassell's knock down and Angel's precise pass had sent him on a run through the left hand channel.

That almost proved costly a minute later, Gemmill's ball over the top picking out Everton skipper Kevin Campbell, whose half-volley flew too high.

Merson was guilty of another poor finish two minutes after the break, sidefooting weakly and straight to Simonsen from outside the area following a neat lay-off from Dion Dublin, who had replaced the unwell Vassell at the interval.

But if most of what had gone before had been tame, the former England star brought Holte Enders to their feet with the game's most exciting piece of action on 58 minutes.

Collecting the ball on the touchline just inside his own half, Merson embarked on a scintillating run which had Everton players trailing in his slipstream before he cut inside to unleash a tremendous 25-yarder which smacked against the bar and went over.

Although Villa dominated for most of the second period, however, they experienced a few anxious moments in the closing stages before securing a point.

▶ *It's one against two at Villa Park, but Jlloyd Samuel comes away with the ball.*

MATCH 35

Date   Wednesday 30 January 2002
Venue   Villa Park, 7.45pm

ASTON VILLA (0) 0
EVERTON (0) 0

Attendance 32,460
Referee   Chris Foy
Assistants D. Babski and J. Devine

▶ **ASTON VILLA**
claret shirts with blue trim, white shorts

12	Peter ENCKELMAN (Gk)
2	Mark DELANEY
4	Olof MELLBERG
6	George BOATENG
8	Juan Pablo ANGEL ❑
10	Paul MERSON (c)
11	Steve STAUNTON
17	Lee HENDRIE (75)
20	Moustapha HADJI
22	Darius VASSELL (45)
31	Jlloyd SAMUEL
	Substitutes
9	Dion DUBLIN (22)
13	Boaz MYHILL (Gk)
15	Gareth BARRY
18	Steve STONE
30	Hassan KACHLOUL (17)

▶ **EVERTON**
blue shirts, white shorts

13	Steve SIMONSEN (Gk)
4	Alan STUBBS
6	David UNSWORTH
9	Kevin CAMPBELL (c)
10	Duncan FERGUSON ❑
15	Gary NAYSMITH ❑
17	Scott GEMMILL
19	Joe-Max MOORE
21	Danny CADAMARTERI (71)
27	Peter CLARKE ❑
28	Tony HIBBERT (25)
	Substitutes
1	Paul GERRARD (Gk)
14	Idan TAL
20	Alex CLELLAND (28)
29	Kevin McLEOD
30	Nick CHADWICK (21)

Before		P	W	D	L	F	A	pts
7	Villa	23	9	8	6	31	28	35
13	Everton	23	7	6	10	25	30	27

After		P	W	D	L	F	A	pts
7	Villa	24	9	9	6	31	28	36
12	Everton	24	7	7	10	25	30	27

▶ *Coaches John Deehan and Stuart Gray are caretaker managers* ▶ *Everton without a win in 14 league visits*

FA BARCLAYCARD PREMIERSHIP

Peter the great

▶ Peter Enckelman's value to the club was never more evident than on a breezy afternoon beside the Thames.

There was a succession of openings at both ends, and Enckelman's agility and anticipation were the major factors behind Villa's second consecutive goalless draw.

While the back four were once again solid, proving highly effective in subduing the triple threat of Louis Saha, Barry Hales and Steve Marlet, they were ultimately thankful to their underrated goalkeeper for three excellent saves which prevented the Londoners from snatching victory.

Enckelman denied Saha in the first half and Zat Knight and Hayles twice in the second to ensure Villa did not return home empty handed.

With a touch more composure in front of goal, in fact, Villa might well have established a commanding lead inside the opening 20 minutes.

It was just a pity Juan Pablo Angel was unable to accompany his deft touches with a killer instinct. When he delightfully controlled the ball on the edge of the penalty area after only four minutes, for instance, he let himself down with a wayward shot which flew high into the Hammersmith End terracing.

▶ *Mark Delaney and Steve Staunton can't bear to watch in this double challenge with Steve Marlet and Sylvain Legwinski.*

And when Hadji's low centre presented him with an even more inviting chance four minutes later, the former River Plate marksman sliced his eight-yard shot wide of the far post.

Some neat passes from Darius Vassell and skipper Paul Merson had paved the way for that opening, and such was Villa's early authority that they looked perfectly capable of controlling the whole match.

A deflected Hadji shot was collected with some difficulty by goalkeeper Edwin Van Der Sar, Vassell drilled a left foot effort just wide after the eager Boateng had dispossessed Sylvain Legwinksi and Van Der Sar had to get down smartly at the foot of a post to hold Steve Staunton's 25-yard free-kick.

Half an hour had elapsed before Fulham mustered their first attempt, French defender Alain Goma heading over a corner from Steed Malbranque, but three minutes later Enckelman had to be alert as he tipped Saha's close-range lob to safety.

Two minutes after the interval, Enckelman made an even better save, diving to his left to push Zat Knight's stinging low drive for a corner, but he was not alone in displaying his goalkeeping talents.

When Vassell received an astute return pass from Angel on 52 minutes, Van Der Sar kept out the young striker's low drive with his legs, while Fulham's keeper again denied the England under-21 international near the end.

Vassell will no doubt feel he should have done better with that one, shooting straight at Van Der Sar after Merson's clever flick had sent him racing clear.

Then the defiant Enckelman came up with two crucial late saves. He pushed aside a tremendous 70th minute angled drive from Hayles, and with the seconds ticking away he raced from his line to thwart the Fulham striker once again.

▶ *Villa's first visit to Craven Cottage for more than 27 years* ▶ *A second consecutive clean sheet*

MATCH 36

Date Saturday 2 February 2002
Venue Craven Cottage, 3.00pm

FULHAM (0) **0**
ASTON VILLA (0) **0**

Attendance 20,041
Referee Matt Messias
Assistants N. Miller and M. Atkinson

▶ **FULHAM**
white shirts, black shorts

1	Edwin VAN DER SAR (Gk)
2	Steve FINNAN
4	Andy MELVILLE (c)
7	Jon HARLEY
9	Steve MARLET
14	Steed MALBRANQUE
15	Barry HAYLES
16	Zat KNIGHT (64)
18	Sylvain LEGWINSKI
20	Louis SAHA ❏
24	Alain GOMA
	Substitutes
12	Maik TAYLOR (Gk)
19	Bjarne GOLDBAEK (16)
25	Abdeslam OUADDOU
29	Paul TROLLOPE
33	Callum WILLOCK

▶ **ASTON VILLA**
claret shirts with blue trim, white shorts

12	Peter ENCKELMAN (Gk)
2	Mark DELANEY
4	Olof MELLBERG
6	George BOATENG ❏
8	Juan Pablo ANGEL (78)
10	Paul MERSON (c)
11	Steve STAUNTON
17	Lee HENDRIE (86)
20	Moustapha HADJI ❏
22	Darius VASSELL
31	Jlloyd SAMUEL
	Substitutes
3	Alan WRIGHT
9	Dion DUBLIN
13	Boaz MYHILL (Gk)
18	Steve STONE (17)
30	Hassan KACHLOUL (8)

Before	P	W	D	L	F	A	pts
7 Villa	24	9	9	6	31	28	36
10 Fulham	23	7	10	6	23	23	31
After	P	W	D	L	F	A	pts
7 Villa	25	9	10	6	31	28	37
10 Fulham	24	7	11	6	23	23	32

FA BARCLAYCARD PREMIERSHIP

MATCH 37

Welcome back, Graham

▶ A point wasn't exactly what he wanted, but Graham Taylor's second coming was greeted by the sort of euphoria which hasn't been been witnessed at Villa Park for many a day.

The new manager was given a rapturous welcome as he walked down the touchline before the match, and Holte Enders remained upbeat throughout a pulsating contest which held the attention from first whistle to last.

That was no more than the occasion deserved, for Taylor's first match back in charge offered an abundance of promise.

Villa, in fairness, were ultimately a shade fortunate to hold on for a draw after skipper Paul Merson's 28th goal had been cancelled out by Frank Lampard's 65th minute equaliser.

While the home side had a couple of let-offs as Chelsea dictated the closing stages, however, it was no more than they deserved after an enterprising performance which was packed with some fine individual displays. After Sam Dalla Bona had fired too high for the visitors, Merson began to make an impact. The skipper curled a 20-yard shot wide after working a short free-kick routine with Jlloyd Samuel, and two minutes later he opened the scoring with an opportunist goal.

The initial menace was provided by Darius Vassell's darting run into the penalty area, and although the ball ran away from the England under-21 striker as he was challenged, Merson stuck out his left foot to send it into the roof of the net from six yards.

Villa almost scored again on 39 minutes, Hadji controlling Samuel's cross beyond the far post before blasting an angled drive across the face of goal.

But Chelsea's fine touch and movement made them equally dangerous and the visitors were twice close to equalising just before half time.

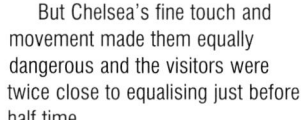

▶ *A special moment for Paul Merson as Villa's skipper celebrates scoring against his boyhood favourites Chelsea.*

Olof Mellberg blocked Eidur Gudjohnsen's shot, while a mix-up between Mark Delaney and Peter Enckelman almost put Villa in trouble before the ball was scrambled away for a corner.

The home side were under pressure following the flag kick, too, breathing a collective sigh of relief when Gudjohnsen fired wildly over from close range.

The early exchanges of the second half were even more frantic. Angel was only just wide with a free-kick after Vassell had been bundled over by John Terry just outside the penalty area, while Delaney came to Villa's rescue by blocking Gudjohnsen's well-struck shot.

It was just a pity that the equaliser followed a lengthy spell of Villa pressure.

Such was the home side's dominance at that juncture, in fact, that substitutes Gianfranco Zola and Mikael Forssell were kept waiting on the touchline for three or four minutes before they could make an entrance.

Unfortunately for Villa, Zola's introduction could not have been more effective, the Italian's beautifully-flighted through ball picking out Hasselbaink's run. The Dutch striker inelegantly headed sideways as Enckelman raced out to challenge, leaving Lampard the simplest of tasks to sidefoot into an unguarded net from 10 yards.

| Date | Saturday 9 February 2002 |
| Venue | Villa Park, 3.00pm |

ASTON VILLA (1) 1
CHELSEA (0) 1

Attendance	41,137
Referee	Paul Durkin
Assistants	G. Beale and D. Bryan

▶ **ASTON VILLA**
claret shirts with blue trim, white shorts

12	Peter ENCKELMAN (Gk)	
2	Mark DELANEY	
4	Olof MELLBERG (45)	
6	George BOATENG	
8	Juan Pablo ANGEL	
10	Paul MERSON (c)	g28
11	Steve STAUNTON	
17	Lee HENDRIE (57)	
20	Moustapha HADJI	
22	Darius VASSELL (87)	
31	Jlloyd SAMUEL ▫	
Substitutes		
9	Dion DUBLIN (22)	
13	Boaz MYHILL (Gk)	
15	Gareth BARRY (4)	
18	Steve STONE (17)	
19	Bosko BALABAN	

▶ **CHELSEA**
blue shirts, blue shorts

23	Carlo CUDICINI (Gk)	
6	Marcel DESAILLY (c)	
8	Frank LAMPARD	g65
9	Jimmy Floyd HASSELBAINK	
12	Mario STANIC	
14	Graeme LE SAUX	
17	Emmanuel PETIT	
18	Albert FERRER (63)	
22	Eidur GUDJOHNSEN (63)	
24	Sam DALLA BONA	
26	John TERRY (77)	
Substitutes		
1	Ed DE GOEY (Gk)	
10	Slavisa JOKANOVIC	
25	Gianfranco ZOLA (18)	
32	Mikael FORSSELL (22)	
36	Joe KEENAN (26)	

Before	P	W	D	L	F	A	pts
5 Chelsea	25	11	10	4	45	25	43
7 Villa	25	9	10	6	31	28	37
After	P	W	D	L	F	A	pts
5 Chelsea	26	11	11	4	46	26	44
7 Villa	26	9	11	6	32	29	38

▶ *Villa's seventh Premiership match without a defeat* ▶ *Chelsea remain unbeaten in this fixture since September 1994*

FA BARCLAYCARD PREMIERSHIP

Villa miss the boat

▶ Ruud van Nisterlrooy had almost single-handedly destroyed Villa's FA Cup dreams in January but this time he needed a little help to ensure that Graham Taylor's men returned home pointless from their Premiership visit to Old Trafford.

Where the Dutch striker had been so lethal in 34 minutes as a substitute at Villa Park, he was effectively shackled by Olof Mellberg and Steve Staunton for most of the match.

But van Nisterlrooy simply couldn't help but score five minutes after half-time when he was presented with what must rank as one of the easiest chances of his career.

There were groans all around the imposing arena as a United attack was broken up by George Boateng eight yards outside the penalty area, but having done the hard part of his job, Villa's tenacious defender inexplicably ran the ball back towards his own goal.

Mark Delaney's well-timed sliding tackle nudged the ball away from Ole Gunnar Solskjaer as the Norwegian striker prepared to shoot – but only as far as van Nisterlrooy, who calmly scored with a low shot on the turn from 12 yards.

It was a goal which accurately reflected the game – scrappy, untidy and littered with mistakes. United struggled to reproduce the flowing football which has taken them to the top of the table and Villa simply never got going as an attacking force.

The home side's failure to spark, it must be said, was due in no small measure to Villa's sheer resilience. Apart from Staunton and the towering Mellberg, they were also well served defensively by Delaney and Jlloyd Samuel, while Gareth Barry and Steve Stone were industrious in midfield.

Unfortunately, industry was the limit of the visitors' contribution to a hugely disappointing contest, and there was never much hope of them salvaging anything once van Nisterlrooy had accepted his 50th minute gift.

They managed only one serious threat of an equaliser, a low left foot drive in the 65th minute from Thomas Hitzlsperger which was well held by United goalkeeper Fabien Barthez.

Otherwise, though, the Frenchman was required to make only one save, having palmed away a well-struck 25-yarder from Juan Pablo Angel in the first half.

Villa just didn't get going up front, not least because the ploy of playing Angel as a lone striker with Hadji and Darius Vassell just behind him never really came off.

All three displayed some nice individual touches, but their combined efforts never produced the potent attacking unit Taylor would have liked.

But at least the introduction of Hitzlsperger offered plenty of promise on a day when rain, sleet and a swirling wind did nothing to aid the game's aesthetic value.

Apart from his shot, the 19-year-old German was confident and composed as he was given only his second taste of first team action.

▶ Olof Mellberg is just too late to prevent Ole Gunnar Solskjaer getting in a shot.

MATCH 38

Date Saturday 23 February 2002
Venue Old Trafford, 12 noon

**MANCHESTER UTD. (0) 1
ASTON VILLA (0) 0**

Attendance 67,592
Referee Jeff Winter
Assistants M. Atkinson and N. Miller

▶ **MANCHESTER UNITED**
red shirts, white shorts

1	Fabien BARTHEZ (Gk)	
2	Gary NEVILLE	
3	Denis IRWIN (86)	
4	Juan VERON	
6	Laurent BLANC	
7	David BECKHAM	
8	Nicky BUTT	
10	Ruud VAN NISTELROOY	g50
16	Roy KEANE (c)	
20	Ole Gunnar SOLSKJAER	
27	Mikael SILVESTRE	
Substitutes		
5	Ronny JOHNSEN (3)	
13	Roy CARROLL (Gk)	
21	Diego FORLAN	
18	Paul SCHOLES	
30	John O'SHEA	

▶ **ASTON VILLA**
platinum shirts, navy blue shorts

1	Peter SCHMEICHEL (Gk)
2	Mark DELANEY
4	Olof MELLBERG
6	George BOATENG
8	Juan Pablo ANGEL
11	Steve STAUNTON
15	Gareth BARRY
18	Steve STONE
20	Moustapha HADJI (64)
22	Darius VASSELL
31	Jlloyd SAMUEL (79)
Substitutes	
9	Dion DUBLIN (31)
12	Peter ENCKELMAN (Gk)
19	Bosko BALABAN
21	Thomas HITZLSPERGER (20)
30	Hassan KACHLOUL

Before	P	W	D	L	F	A	pts
1 Man Utd	27	17	3	7	66	28	54
7 Villa	26	9	11	6	32	29	38

After	P	W	D	L	F	A	pts
1 Man Utd	28	18	3	7	67	35	57
7 Villa	27	9	11	7	32	30	38

▶ Villa's first defeat in eight Premierhip matches ▶ Schmeichel's return to the club where he won the treble in 1999

FA BARCLAYCARD PREMIERSHIP

Vassell's late show

▶ Darius Vassell grabbed a stoppage time winner against the side who had denied Villa victory at the same late juncture in the corresponding fixture at Upton Park in December.

On that occasion, Jermain Defoe's last gasp equaliser for West Ham left the visitors frustrated, an emotion which turned to anguish four days later when they surrendered a two-goal lead against Arsenal before losing 3-2 right at the death.

The mid-winter depression, though, was well and truly forgotten, and a revitalised Villa outfit bounded enthusiastically to their first win under Graham Taylor.

As the clock wound down, most of the crowd were convinced they were about to witness the eighth consecutive Premiership draw between these teams.

But even as this highly-entertaining match went into overtime, Vassell's left foot volley flashed narrowly past the near post after his striking partner Juan Pablo Angel had flicked on a beautifully-floated through ball from substitute Paul Merson.

That, it seemed, was the final throw of the dice in Villa's attempt to transform one point into three, but there was still time for a winner. Jlloyd Samuel burst inside from the left flank and measured his low cross to perfection, Vassell getting in front of his marker to convert in deadly fashion from close range.

The late winner certainly put a different complexion on an afternoon which had looked ominous when Paolo Di Canio gave the Hammers the lead with a 13th minute penalty but rather more promising when Angel brought the scores level with his 23rd minute header.

West Ham's early enterprise was rewarded when Olof Mellberg's clumsy challenge on Defoe conceded a spot kick which Di Canio was determined to convert, having had his weak 12-yard effort saved by Peter Enckelman in the game at Upton Park.

The Italian hesitated momentarily on this occasion, too, but only to outwit Villa's acting captain Peter Schmeichel, who dived the wrong way as Di Canio calmly sidefooted his 50th Premiership goal.

Vassell came close to a 22nd minute equaliser when he nodded just past the far post, and a minute later Villa were on level terms.

Samuel, having made one of his many runs down the left, touched the ball into Barry's path, and the midfielder's superb cross was met at the far post by Angel, whose angled header was too clever for David James.

Thomas Hitzlsperger's full Villa debut was outstanding, the 19-year-old German defying his tender years with some solid tackling and intelligent distribution – not to mention two stinging left foot shots.

His first, just past the half hour mark, cannoned off James's legs with the 'keeper seemingly knowing little about it, although the former Villa man had to be at his best in the 73rd minute to tip away for a corner after Hiztlsperger had turned smartly to unleash another power drive from the edge of the area.

▶ Debut boy Thomas Hitzlsperger proves he's no slouch in this strong challenge on Joe Cole.

MATCH 39

Date   Saturday 2 March 2002
Venue Villa Park, 3.00pm

ASTON VILLA (1) 2
WEST HAM UNITED (1) 1

Attendance 37,341
Referee   Graham Barber
Assistants C. Bassindale and R. Pashley

▶ **ASTON VILLA**
claret shirts with blue trim, white shorts

1	Peter SCHMEICHEL (Gk)(c)	
2	Mark DELANEY	
4	Olof MELLBERG	
6	George BOATENG	
8	Juan Pablo ANGEL	g23
11	Steve STAUNTON	
15	Gareth BARRY	
20	Moustapha HADJI (78)	
21	Thomas HITZLSPERGER	
22	Darius VASSELL	g90
31	Jlloyd SAMUEL	
	Substitutes	
10	Paul MERSON (20)	
12	Peter ENCKELMAN (Gk)	
17	Lee HENDRIE	
19	Bosko BALABAN	
30	Hassan KACHLOUL	

▶ **WEST HAM UNITED**
blue shirts with claret trim, blue shorts

1	David JAMES (Gk)	
2	Thomas REPKA	
3	Nigel WINTERBURN	
7	Christian DAILLY	
8	Trevor SINCLAIR	
10	Paolo DI CANIO	g13
19	Ian PEARCE ❑	
25	Jermain DEFOE	
26	Joe COLE	
30	Sebastien SCHEMMEL	
33	Richard GARCIA (68)	
	Substitutes	
5	Vladimir LABANT (33)	
12	Paul KITSON	
17	Shaka HISLOP (Gk)	
20	Scott MINTO	
34	Grant McCANN	

Before	P	W	D	L	F	A	pts
7 Villa	27	9	11	7	32	30	38
11 W. Ham	27	9	7	11	30	42	34
After	P	W	D	L	F	A	pts
7 Villa	28	10	11	7	34	31	41
13 W. Ham	27	9	7	12	31	44	34

▶ Villa's first league win over the Hammers since April 1998   ▶ Thomas Hitzlsperger's full debut

A welcome whistle

▸ Were there any plus points to be taken from this match, Graham Taylor was asked after his side had crashed heavily at Ewood Park. The manager could think of only two – the sound of the final whistle and the fact that no-one had been sent off.

It was a chilling assessment of a poor Villa performance, and if the scoreline slightly flattered Blackburn, at least the new boss was brutally honest about his team's poor showing.

Blackburn, battling for Premiership survival, were full value for all three points as the visitors barely threatened and came off second best in nearly every 50-50 challenge.

It was an uphill battle from the seventh minute, when David Dunn opened the scoring with a blistering left footer, and although Taylor's men improved after half-time, their fate was sealed by two goals in the last six minutes from Damien Duff and Andy Cole.

Maybe the Worthington Cup holders were not three goals better, but there were no complaints from the claret-and-blue camp on a night when no-one emerged with any real credit.

Even strikers Juan Pablo Angel and Darius Vassell, the match-winners against West Ham three days earlier, were subdued, and although Vassell went close with one good effort, the Colombian was eventually replaced by Bosko Balaban.

▸ *Mark Delaney produces one of his trademark sliding tackles to win the ball from Damien Duff, but it was a brief respite.*

Blackburn were good value for their early lead. Matt Jansen had already seen a low drive deflected for a corner by Moustapha Hadji and Andy Cole had struck the bar with a close-range shot before the home side went ahead.

Turkish full-back Hakan Unsal delivered a 30-yard diagonal pass which found Dunn in space on the right, and the midfielder cut inside to unleash a fierce left footer from the edge of the penalty area to leave Peter Schmeichel motionless.

The visitors were struggling to get into their stride, although Hadji tested Brad Friedel with a long range effort before the Blackburn 'keeper produced an instinctive 21st minute save to keep his side's lead intact.

Vassell ghosted in at the near post to stab goalwards from Jlloyd Samuel's dipping centre from the left, and the American had to react smartly to claw the ball away as Villa's travelling contingent at the Darwen end were about to salute an equaliser.

But the visitors had a double let-off when Cole shot against a post, and and then collected the rebound to set up Duff for a low drive which Schmeichel saved, while the 'keeper needed a second attempt to hold Jansen's low left footer.

A double substitution gave Villa a more assertive look, but after Schmeichel had saved a Cole header, the 'keeper was given no chance on 84 minutes as Duff unleashed an angled drive which flew in off the inside of a post.

Five minutes later the misery was complete. As Cole moved on to a long through ball, Schmeichel came rushing out of his area and attempted a headed clearance, only to set up the former Manchester United man for a gently stroked shot which rolled in as Delaney tried to clear.

MATCH 40

Date Tuesday 5 March 2002
Venue Ewood Park, 8.00pm

BLACKBURN RVRS. (1) **3**
ASTON VILLA (0) **0**

Attendance 21,988
Referee Steve Bennett
Assistants P. Canadine and A. Garratt

▸ **BLACKBURN ROVERS**
blue and white halved shirts, white shorts

1 Brad FRIEDEL (Gk)	
3 TUGAY (65)	
4 Henning BERG	
7 Gary FLITCROFT (c)	
8 David DUNN	g7
9 Andy COLE	g88
10 Matt JANSEN (60)	
11 Damien DUFF	g85
14 Nils-Eric JOHANSSON	
22 Hakan UNSAL (56) ❏	
31 Lucas NEILL	
Substitutes	
15 Craig HIGNETT	
17 YORDI (10)	
18 Keith GILLESPIE (65)	
27 Alan MILLER (Gk)	
28 Martin TAYLOR (22)	

▸ **ASTON VILLA**
claret shirts with blue trim, claret shorts

1 Peter SCHMEICHEL (Gk) (c)
2 Mark DELANEY ❏
4 Olof MELLBERG
6 George BOATENG ❏
8 Juan Pablo ANGEL (72)
11 Steve STAUNTON
15 Gareth BARRY
20 Moustapha HADJI (45)
21 Thomas HITZLSPERGER (45)
22 Darius VASSELL
31 Jlloyd SAMUEL
Substitutes
10 Paul MERSON (20)
12 Peter ENCKELMAN (Gk)
17 Lee HENDRIE (21)
19 Bosko BALABAN (8)
30 Hassan KACHLOUL

Before	P	W	D	L	F	A	pts
7 Villa	28	10	11	7	34	31	41
18 Rovers	27	6	8	13	33	37	26
After	P	W	D	L	F	A	pts
7 Villa	29	10	11	8	34	34	41
18 Rovers	28	7	8	13	36	37	29

▸ *Villa's third consecutive defeat at Ewood, where they have won only once in eight Premiership visits*

Villa pay the penalty

MATCH 41

Date: Sunday 17 March 2002
Venue: Villa Park, 4.00pm

ASTON VILLA (0) 1
ARSENAL (1) 2

Attendance 41,520
Referee Steve Dunn
Assistants P. Sharp and S. Brand

▶ Apparently heading for a tame surrender to Arsenal's greater muscle power, Graham Taylor's men contrived to have a penalty saved and find themselves in an even deeper hole before deciding to make a scrap of it.

It was just a pity they left it until after the interval before deciding to treat the Gunners with less respect.

Throughout the opening period, Villa had been almost in awe of their high-riding opponents, who deservedly led through a 16th minute Edu goal.

But there was far more conviction about the home side after the break and they should have been level when they were awarded a 55th minute penalty.

Unfortunately, England goalkeeper David Seaman was equal to Gareth Barry's well-struck spot kick, and when Robert Pires conjured up a French fancy to make it 2-0 just past the hour mark, the match appeared to be over.

Dion Dublin, thankfully, had other ideas. Introduced as a half-time substitute, he had already begun to unsettle Arsenal's defence, and when he superbly headed in a 69th minute cross from Moustapha Hadji, there was suddenly every prospect of an equaliser.

Yet there had been little indication of a rousing finale as Arsenal did very much as they pleased throughout the first half, claiming the lead on 16 minutes.

Referee Steve Dunn's decision to penalise Hassan Kachloul for a challenge on Edu 25 yards out didn't go down too well with the Holte End, but disappointment turned to despair when the free-kick led to a scrappy goal.

▶ Moroccan midfielder Hassan Kachloul fires too high during this first half Villa raid, possibly distracted by Sol Campbell's lunging tackle.

Sylvain Wiltord's fierce drive was spilled by Peter Schmeichel and although the goalkeeper redeemed himself by throwing himself in the way of Vieira's follow-up shot, the ball ran to Edu for the Brazilian to stab in at close range.

But Dublin could not have been more effective after joining the action. The former Coventry striker had the beating of Igors Stepanovs, and also contributed to the move which led to Villa's penalty.

Thomas Hitzlsperger started the move after dispossessing Vieira and it was continued by Dublin and Hadji before Barry was sent sprawling by Dixon's challenge as he closed in on goal.

There wasn't a lot wrong with the young midfielder's spot kick, but Seaman flung himself across his line and saved one-handed before gathering the ball at the second attempt.

Villa were now increasing the tempo, only to fall victim to a sucker punch in the 61st minute. Fredrik Ljungberg's superb 40-yard picked out Pires with only George Boateng covering the danger, and the Frenchman deftly flicked the ball over the Dutch midfielder before cheekily lobbing over Schmeichel.

After Dublin had headed narrowly off target from Steve Staunton's curling free-kick, the substitute striker reduced the deficit on 69 minutes.

Barry sent Hadji racing down the left, and the Moroccan delivered a inch perfect cross which Dublin met with a glancing header which flashed into the far corner.

▶ **ASTON VILLA**
claret shirts with blue trim, white shorts

1	Peter SCHMEICHEL (Gk)	
2	Mark DELANEY	
4	Olof MELLBERG	
6	George BOATENG ❏	
11	Steve STAUNTON	
10	Paul MERSON (c) (79)	
15	Gareth BARRY	
21	Thomas HITZLSPERGER	
22	Darius VASSELL (45)	
30	Hassan KACHLOUL (45)	
31	Jlloyd SAMUEL	
	Substitutes	
9	Dion DUBLIN (22)	g69
12	Peter ENCKELMAN (Gk)	
17	Lee HENDRIE (10)	
18	Steve STONE	
20	Moustapha HADJI (30)	

▶ **ARSENAL**
bronze shirts, blue shorts

1	David SEAMAN (Gk)	
4	Patrick VIEIRA (c)	
7	Robert PIRES	g61
8	Fredrik LJUNGBERG (71) ❏	
10	Dennis BERGKAMP (77)	
11	Sylvain WILTORD	
12	LAUREN	
17	EDU	g16
22	Oleg LUZHNY ❏	
23	Sol CAMPBELL	
26	Igors STEPANOVS (45)	
	Substitutes	
2	Lee DIXON (26)	
18	Gilles GRIMANDI (8)	
24	Richard WRIGHT (Gk)	
25	KANU (10)	
27	Stathis TAVLARIDIS	

Before	P	W	D	L	F	A	pts
3 Arsenal	29	17	9	3	58	31	60
7 Villa	29	10	11	8	34	34	41
After	P	W	D	L	F	A	pts
2 Arsenal	30	18	9	3	60	32	63
7 Villa	30	10	11	9	35	36	41

▶ Juan Pablo Angel ruled out by a foot injury ▶ Villa suffer a double defeat at the hands of the Gunners

MATCH 42

Schmeichel the defiant

Date Saturday 23 March 2002
Venue Portman Road, 3.00pm

IPSWICH TOWN (0) 0
ASTON VILLA (0) 0

Attendance 25,247
Referee David Pugh
Assistants T. Massey and S. Gagen

▶ Having endured a few anxious moments in previous matches, Peter Schmeichel was back to his best to help Villa earn a draw at Portman Road.

The Danish goalkeeper made some excellent saves to deny an Ipswich Town outfit battling for Premiership survival, and while a goalless outcome against relegation-threatened opposition was not exactly what manager Graham Taylor wanted, a draw was the right result.

It wasn't a classic contest by any stretch of the imagination, and the game never really got going until after half-time, yet both sides had chances to grab victory.

George Burley's side had the better opportunities, yet Villa might well have scored in stoppage time as Thomas Hitzlsperger forced home 'keeper Matteo Sereni into a superb save and Jim Magilton almost conceded an own goal.

If the first half was tame fare, at least the tempo increased after the interval. The action had barely resumed when Schmeichel, moving one way to meet a George shot, suddenly found the ball diverted wickedly in the other direction by Bent's deflection, the Dane breathing a sigh of relief as the ball flashed just wide.

Villa's response came in the form of a header which Dublin sent narrowly wide from Mark Delaney's centre and a Boateng drive which flew too high after Vassell's exciting run had created the opening.

Ipswich substitute Magilton fired over after Delaney had been harshly booked for a handball which looked accidental, before Schmeichel's reflexes were tested by a stooping Stewart header from Jermaine Wright's cross. The 'keeper was falling as Stewart made contact, but improvised to keep out the close range effort with his feet.

There was an even bigger let-off on 69 minutes when Jamie Clapham's deep cross from the left was driven back across goal by George. Schmeichel again reacted smartly to parry Magilton's shot, but was helpless as the Ipswich veteran drove the rebound against his left hand post.

But Villa had by that stage begun to exert pressure of their own, with Steve Stone posing a threat down the right and Hitzlsperger increasingly combative in midfeld. The young German displayed immense confidence when accepting a Boateng pass before switching feet drive wide of the far upright, while Dublin nearly caught out Sereni when he met Olof Mellberg's free kick with a header which almost crept just under the bar.

Villa looked more likely to break the deadlock in the closing stages and in stoppage time they were twice desperately close to scoring.

Vassell's well-measured pass and Dublin's intelligent back-heel enabled Hitzlsperger to unleash a scorching drive which brought the save of the match as Sereni tipped it for a corner and right at the death there was almost an own goal.

Magilton's attempted headed clearance from Steve Staunton's inswinging corner flashed goalwards, forcing Sereni to tip the ball against the bar before it was cleared.

▶ *A relieved Peter Schmeichel gathers the ball after Ipswich striker Marcus Stewart has miskicked from a good position.*

▶ **IPSWICH TOWN**
blue shirts, white shorts

34	Matteo SERENI (Gk)
3	Jamie CLAPHAM
4	John McGREAL
5	Hermann HREIDARSSON
6	Mark VENUS
8	Matt HOLLAND (c)
11	Marcus STEWART (82)
14	Jermaine WRIGHT
15	Chris MAKIN (8)
33	Finidi GEORGE (82)
38	Marcus BENT
	Substitutes
1	Andy MARSHALL (Gk)
7	Jim MAGILTON (15)
9	Pablo COUÑAGO
10	Alun ARMSTRONG (11)
30	Martijn REUSER (33)

▶ **ASTON VILLA**
claret shirts with blue trim, white shorts

1	Peter SCHMEICHEL (Gk) (c)
2	Mark DELANEY ❏
4	Olof MELLBERG
6	George BOATENG
9	Dion DUBLIN ❏
11	Steve STAUNTON
15	Gareth BARRY
18	Steve STONE
21	Thomas HITZLSPERGER
22	Darius VASSELL
31	Jlloyd SAMUEL (79)
	Substitutes
7	Ian TAYLOR (31)
10	Paul MERSON
12	Peter ENCKELMAN (Gk)
19	Bosko BALABAN
20	Moustapha HADJI

Before	P	W	D	L	F	A	pts
8 Villa	30	10	11	9	35	36	41
17 Ipswich	30	8	7	15	38	49	31
After	P	W	D	L	F	A	pts
7 Villa	31	10	12	9	35	36	42
18 Ipswich	31	8	7	15	38	49	32

▶ *Villa's ninth Premiership clean sheet of the season* ▶ *Dion Dublin's first start since New Year's Day*

47

FA BARCLAYCARD PREMIERSHIP

Early goals not enough

▶ Villa headed back down the M6 wondering just how they had managed to lose a match which should have been won comfortably.

Even allowing for Bolton's understandable desire for three points to aid their fight against relegation, the visitors were left kicking themselves for failing to transform their first half superiority into an emphatic victory at the Reebok Stadium.

The setback of an early Mark Delaney own goal was overcome with apparent ease as Paul Warhurst also put the ball in his own net to bring the scores level and midfielder Ian Taylor marked his return to the starting line-up with a header which put the visitors 2-1 ahead by the 17th minute.

The only outcome at that juncture, it seemed, was a first away success since Taylor's return to the hot seat, but the manager was forced to watch in increasing frustration as his team conceded an equaliser from Fredi Bobic just before half-time and then found themselves sunk by Kevin Nolan's 76th minute free-kick.

By that stage, in fairness, Villa had lost much of their early impetus and they rarely looked likely to find a response as the game edged towards its conclusion.

Villa were stunned on nine minutes when Nolan, having had his long throw headed clear, unleashed a volley which struck Delaney on the chest and deflected wickedly inside Schmeichel's right hand post.

That disappointment, however, was merely temporary. Six minutes later, George Boateng moved on to a Taylor pass to deliver a menacing angled cross and Warhurst, desperately trying to prevent it reaching Villa's strikers, succeeded only in diverting the ball powerfully past bewildered goalkeeper Kevin Poole as he slid in for his attempted clearance.

Within two minutes, Taylor reached Thomas Hitzlsperger's inswinging corner just ahead of Crouch to beat Poole with a close range header, and Villa were not only ahead but looking perfectly capable of winning in style.

Sadly, it was not to be. Although Vassell was just unable to make contact when Hadji's angled shot flew across the goalmouth, Schmeichel saved well from French midfielder Youri Djorkaeff and Dean Holdsworth before the home side drew level three minutes before half-time.

The opening goal may have been unfortunate, but Villa's defence were caught napping as Djorkaeff floated a free-kick across the penalty area, and German striker Bobic slid in unmarked to prod past the unguarded goalkeeper.

Once again, it seemed no more than a minor inconvenience as Villa pushed forward after the interval, with Crouch constantly using his height to good effect – only for Bolton to claim victory with a controversial goal. Steve Staunton's challenge on Ricardo Gardner 25 yards out looked perfectly fair, but was punished not only by a free-kick but a yellow card before Nolan compounded the insult by curling his kick over Villa's defensive wall and into the top right hand corner.

▶ *Debut boy Peter Crouch climbs with Per Frandsen to put Bolton under presure at the Reebok Stadium, watched by Youri Djorkaeff.*

MATCH 43

Date: Saturday 30 March 2002
Venue: Reebok Stadium, 3.00pm

BOLTON WDRS. (2) 3
ASTON VILLA (2) 2

Attendance: 24,600
Referee: Rob Styles
Assistants: N. Miller and R. Lewis

▶ **BOLTON WANDERERS**
white shirts, navy blue shorts

30	Kevin POOLE (Gk)	
2	Bruno N'GOTTY	
6	Paul WARHURST	og15
8	Per FRANDSEN (27)	
10	Dean HOLDSWORTH ▢	
11	Ricardo GARDNER ▢	
13	Youri DJORKAEFF (67)	
15	Kevin NOLAN	g76
16	Fredi BOBIC	g42
25	Simon CHARLTON (c)	
34	Kostas KONSTANTINIDIS ▢	
Substitutes		
3	Mike WHITLOW (8)	
17	Michael RICKETTS (13)	
21	Rod WALLACE	
24	Anthony BARNESS	
35	Jeff CASSAR (Gk)	

▶ **ASTON VILLA**
claret shirts with blue trim, white shorts

1	Peter SCHMEICHEL (Gk) ▢	
2	Mark DELANEY (71)	og9
4	Olof MELLBERG	
6	George BOATENG	
7	Ian TAYLOR	g17
11	Steve STAUNTON ▢	
15	Gareth BARRY	
16	Peter CROUCH	
20	Moustapha HADJI	
21	Thomas HITZLSPERGER	
22	Darius VASSELL (71)	
Substitutes		
12	Peter ENCKELMAN (Gk)	
8	Juan Pablo ANGEL (22)	
19	Bosko BALABAN	
30	Hassan KACHLOUL	
31	Jlloyd SAMUEL (2)	

Before	P	W	D	L	F	A	pts
7 Villa	31	10	12	9	35	36	42
16 Bolton	31	7	12	12	34	48	33
After	P	W	D	L	F	A	pts
7 Villa	32	10	12	10	37	39	42
15 Bolton	32	8	12	12	37	50	36

▶ Peter Crouch makes his debut after signing from Portsmouth for £4.5m   ▶ Villa's first defeat at the Reebok Stadium

FA BARCLAYCARD PREMIERSHIP

Crouch stoops to conquer

▶ Holte Enders discovered a new hero as Peter Crouch marked his home debut with a fine header which earned a well-merited draw against Champions League contenders Newcastle United.

The former Portsmouth striker not only hit the target but did enough to earn a Man of the Match award from club sponsors ntl before making way for Darius Vassell when he began to tire in the closing stages.

It was just a pity Crouch's 26th minute header from Gareth Barry's cross was not scored in front of the massed ranks of home supporters in the Holte. But that hardly mattered as the new boy cancelled out Alan Shearer's third minute stunner.

More encouraging still was the fact that Villa more than matched their high-riding opponents and might well have claimed maximum points during wave after wave of menacing attacks during an absorbing first half.

They failed to do so only because of the defiance of Newcastle goalkeeper Shay Given, who produced a succession of excellent saves to earn his side a draw. This was a performance to warm claret-and-blue hearts, particularly as it featured fine displays from the likes of Barry, Crouch and Thomas Hitzlsperger, youngsters around whom manager Graham Taylor clearly intends building next season's team.

There was no shortage of class about this offering, and an abundance of spirit to overcome the blow of conceding such an early goal.

Shearer's strike, it must be said, was typical of the former England skipper's predatory instincts, even if there was a strong suspicion of offside.

A right wing cross from Keiron Dyer was headed away by Steve Staunton, but only as far as Laurent Robert, who was lurking just outside the penalty area.

The French midfielder controlled the ball on his chest before unleashing a volley which struck the inside of the left hand post. Shearer, standing barely six yards out, was left the simple task of tapping the rebound past a stranded Peter Schmeichel.

There was another scare for the home side when Dyer ghosted in to meet Nolberto Solano's long, high through ball with a close range volley which flashed narrowly wide, but Villa then settled to the task of finding an equaliser.

Crouch met Hadji's cross with a header which wasn't far off target, Hitzlsperger tried his luck with a 25-yard shot which carried no real power and then the new boys brought home fans to their feet with a superb leveller.

▶ Peter Crouch gets in front of Nikolas Dabizas to meet Gareth Barry's cross and mark his home debut with Villa's equaliser.

Gareth Barry delivered the sweetest of left wing centres, and Crouch got in front of Nikolas Dabizas to send a well-placed header past Given's despairing reach from 10 yards.

That was just the lift Villa needed, and they could easily have been ahead by half-time, with Ian Taylor, Angel, George Boateng and Mark Delaney all going close.

Not surprisingly, the tempo dipped after the interval, although one sustained attack ended with Hitzlsperger's volley thudding into the ground and skidding up for Staunton to get in a header which Given brilliantly pushed over at full stretch.

▶ Crouch scores on his home debut ▶ Shearer's 199th Premiership goal

---

MATCH 44

Date   Tuesday 2 April 2002
Venue   Villa Park, 7.45pm

ASTON VILLA (1) 1
NEWCASTLE UTD. (1) 1

Attendance   36,579
Referee   Steve Dunn
Assistants   D. Richards and P. Barnes

▶ **ASTON VILLA**
claret shirts with blue trim, white shorts

1 Peter SCHMEICHEL (Gk) (c)	
2 Mark DELANEY	
4 Olof MELLBERG	
6 George BOATENG (89)	
7 Ian TAYLOR	
8 Juan Pablo ANGEL	
11 Steve STAUNTON	
15 Gareth BARRY	
16 Peter CROUCH (76)	g26
20 Moustapha HADJI (76)	
21 Thomas HITZLSPERGER	
Substitutes	
12 Peter ENCKELMAN (Gk)	
18 Steve STONE (6)	
19 Bosko BALABAN (16)	
22 Darius VASSELL (20)	
31 Jlloyd SAMUEL	

▶ **NEWCASTLE UNITED**
black and white striped shirts, black shorts

1 Shay GIVEN (Gk)	
4 Nolberto SOLANO	
5 Andy O'BRIEN	
7 Jermaine JENAS	
8 Keiron DYER	
9 Alan SHEARER (c)	g3
16 Carl CORT (83)	
18 Aaron HUGHES	
24 Sylvain DISTIN	
32 Laurent ROBERT (83)	
34 Nikolas DABIZAS	
Substitutes	
3 Robbie ELLIOTT	
6 Clarence ACUNA (16)	
13 Steve HARPER (Gk)	
20 Lomana Tresor LUA LUA	
35 Olivier BERNARD (32)	

Before	P	W	D	L	F	A	pts
4 United	31	18	5	8	60	42	59
9 Villa	32	10	12	10	38	39	42
After	P	W	D	L	F	A	pts
4 United	32	18	6	8	61	43	60
9 Villa	33	10	13	10	38	40	43

49

FA BARCLAYCARD PREMIERSHIP

Sunk by the old boys

▶ Even before kick off at The Riverside, Villa must have feared the worst as they lined up against a side including three of their old boys.

After all, Gareth Southgate and Ugo Ehiogu had blunted their attack when Boro forced a goalless draw at Villa Park in November, while Benito Carbone had scored against them during his brief spell with Derby County a month later.

This time it was the Carbone-Ehiogu combination which did the damage, the diminutive Italian putting Boro ahead and the towering central defender grabbing the winner after Juan Pablo Angel's 16th goal of the season had brought Graham Taylor's men level.

If there was almost a feeling of inevitability about the goalscorers, though, Villa fans who made the long trip to Teesside will be only too aware that this was yet another match where their team's endeavours went sadly unrewarded.

Villa enjoyed a lion's share of possession but emerged with nothing to show for it. There wasn't a great deal wrong with his side's offering at The Riverside, and it should certainly have been sufficient to secure at least a draw. Instead, Ehiogu's 64th minute winner sent them home empty handed.

It was, needless to say, all very frustrating, particularly as new signing Peter Crouch again produced a display of immense promise, giving Southgate plenty to think about and providing an important "assist" for Angel's equaliser.

▶ *Almost two years after they were team-mates at Wembley, George Boateng and Benito Carbone are deadly rivals at The Riverside.*

By that stage, Villa should really have been in control. They were better side in the first half, and continued to dominate until the hour mark before falling away after the blow of Ehiogu's winner.

The visitors should really have capitalised on their early possession, when they stroked the ball around with confidence if not always total conviction.

Thomas Hitzlsperger came up with a touch of venom when his fierce 18th minute drive thudded into Southgate's midriff and Crouch had a header deflected for a corner as Taylor's men knocked the ball around in style, and half an hour had elapsed before Boro produced their first attempt on goal, substitute Dean Windass heading over from a Carbone flag kick.

Eight minutes later, unfortunately, the home side's second attempt resulted in them going ahead.

Olof Mellberg and Steve Staunton had previously stifled any hint of a Boro threat before goalkeeper Peter Schmeichel needed to concern himself but when French left-back Franck Queudrue lofted a high cross into the penalty area, Carbone emerged from an untidy challenge with Staunton to fire past the unguarded Dane from eight yards.

On the hour mark, Villa were level with a gem of a goal.

Using his height to good effect, Crouch climbed above Ehiogu to meet Gareth Barry's deep cross and head down to Angel, who instinctively drilled an unstoppable half volley past a helpless Schwarzer and into the roof of the net.

But just when the prospect of an away win seemed to be looming, the notion was dispelled within four minutes when Ehiogu headed in Carbone's corner.

MATCH 45

Date   Saturday 6 April 2002
Venue   The Riverside Stadium, 3.00pm

MIDDLESBROUGH (1) 2
ASTON VILLA (0) 1

Attendance   26,003
Referee   Graham Barber
Assistants   N. Bannister and G. Turner

▶ **MIDDLESBROUGH**
red shirts, red shorts

1	Mark SCHWARZER (Gk)	
6	Gareth SOUTHGATE (c)	
7	Robbie MUSTOE	
10	Benito CARBONE	g38
12	Jonathan GREENING	
17	Ugo EHIOGU	g64
26	Noel WHELAN (10)	
27	Robbie STOCKDALE	
31	Luke WILKSHIRE	
32	Allan JOHNSTON	
37	Franck QUEUDRUE	
	Substitutes	
5	Gianluca FESTA	
14	Michael DEBEVE	
20	Dean WINDASS (26)	
23	Carlos MARINELLI	
25	Mark CROSSLEY (Gk)	

▶ **ASTON VILLA**
platinum shirts, navy blue shorts

1	Peter SCHMEICHEL (Gk)	
2	Mark DELANEY	
4	Olof MELLBERG	
6	George BOATENG	
7	Ian TAYLOR	
8	Juan Pablo ANGEL	g60
11	Steve STAUNTON	
15	Gareth BARRY	
16	Peter CROUCH	
20	Moustapha HADJI (74)	
21	Thomas HITZLSPERGER	
	Substitutes	
12	Peter ENCKELMAN (Gk)	
18	Steve STONE	
19	Bosko BALABAN	
22	Darius VASSELL (20)	
31	Jlloyd SAMUEL	

Before	P	W	D	L	F	A	pts
9 Villa	33	10	13	10	38	40	43
10 Boro	33	11	9	13	32	39	42
After	P	W	D	L	F	A	pts
9 Boro	34	12	9	13	34	40	45
10 Villa	34	10	13	11	39	42	43

▶ *Angel's first away goal since January* ▶ *Ehiogu scores against Villa for the second time in three matches*

All in vain for valiant Villa

▶ An all-too-familiar scenario unfolded as Villa were left cursing the fact that a rousing second half display failed to yield any sort of return.

Just how Villa's dominance after the break went unrewarded will remain a mystery to anyone of claret and blue persuasion. The visitors' goal led a charmed life during the second period, particularly during a breathtaking finale which was agonisingly close to producing an equaliser on a number of occasions.

Unfortunately, none of those near misses will go down in the record books, which will show only that Mark Viduka's 28th minute goal presented Leeds with three points.

To make matters worse, the winning goal was a total catastrophe. Villa had survived a brief period during which Olof Mellberg received touchline treatment for a bloody nose, but just as the Swede was taking up his position in central defence, skipper Steve Staunton inexplicably passed to him from inside the penalty area.

With Mellberg unprepared, the ball slipped past him and straight to David Batty. Before Villa had time to re-organise, the Leeds midfielder swept forward and slipped short pass inside to Robbie Keane who, in turn, nudged the ball on for Viduka. The Australian cleverly flicked it past Mark Delaney before steering it past goalkeeper Peter Enckelman from 10 yards.

If the finish was classy, it was a sloppy goal from Villa's perspective, yet it offered a fair reflection of a first half in which Taylor's men simply never got going.

By the time Viduka pounced, in fact, Leeds had already had a Keane effort ruled out for offside, while Mellberg's magnificent intervention had denied the Irishman what looked a certain goal as he moved on to Lee Bowyer's piercing pass.

The home side could barely complain to be behind at the half-way stage, even though Peter Crouch and Juan Pablo Angel both went close with decent efforts before the Colombian suffered the indignity of being booked when he felt he should have had a penalty.

▶ *Left-back Gareth Barry and Leeds striker Alan Smith battle for possession during the second half.*

A superb 17th minute move involving Ian Taylor, Angel and Delaney ended with the South American appearing to be upended as he turned past Leeds skipper Dominic Matteo, only for referee Barry Knight to take the view that he had dived.

That was one of few Villa highlights in the first half, but it was a different story after the break as they attacked with far more menace, Crouch going desperately close to what would have been to a Goal the Month contender. Controlling Enckelman's long kick, the new boy deftly flicked the ball over Mills before beating Martyn with a an equally exquisite lob which just cleared the bar.

Samuel's angled half volley was brilliantly tipped over by Martyn, while Hitzlsperger's stinging shot was held by the 'keeper at the second attempt and Delaney's fierce drive flashed inches wide.

Then Martyn almost carried the ball over the line as Hitzlsperger's teasing lob dipped under the bar, the 'keeper somehow managing to scoop it away for a corner as he stumbled backwards.

MATCH 46

Date Saturday 13 April 2002
Venue Villa Park, 3.00pm

ASTON VILLA (0) 0
LEEDS UNITED (1) 1

Attendance 40,039
Referee Barry Knight
Assistants G. Beale and T. Massey

▶ **ASTON VILLA**
claret shirts with blue trim, white shorts

12	Peter ENCKELMAN (Gk)
2	Mark DELANEY ❑
4	Olof MELLBERG
6	George BOATENG (65)
7	Ian TAYLOR ❑
8	Juan Pablo ANGEL (65) ❑
11	Steve STAUNTON (c)
15	Gareth BARRY
16	Peter CROUCH
21	Thomas HITZLSPERGER
30	Hassan KACHLOUL (45)
	Substitutes
13	Boaz MYHILL (Gk)
18	Steve STONE (6)
19	Bosko BALABAN
22	Darius VASSELL (8)
31	Jlloyd SAMUEL (30)

▶ **LEEDS UNITED**
yellow shirts, yellow shorts

1	Nigel MARTYN (Gk)	
2	Gary KELLY	
3	Ian HARTE	
7	Robbie KEANE	
9	Mark VIDUKA	g28
11	Lee BOWYER ❑	
17	Alan SMITH	
18	Danny MILLS ❑	
19	Eirik BAKKE	
21	Dominic MATTEO (c)	
23	David BATTY ❑	
	Substitutes	
13	Paul ROBINSON (Gk)	
16	Jason WILCOX	
20	Seth JOHNSON	
27	Robbie FOWLER	
34	Frazer RICHARDSON	

Before	P	W	D	L	F	A	pts
6 Leeds	34	15	12	7	50	36	57
10 Villa	34	10	13	11	39	42	43
After	P	W	D	L	F	A	pts
6 Leeds	35	16	12	7	51	36	60
10 Villa	35	10	13	12	39	43	43

▶ *Peter Schmeichel signs for Manchester City after being told his one-year Villa contract will not be renewed*

Walker stands his ground

▸ Leicester City intend to call their new ground the Walkers Stadium. After this match, it's debatable whether the venue is being named after the Foxes' sponsors or their goalkeeper.

Villa's final visit to Filbert Street was one of utter frustration, and the main reason was undoubtedly Ian Walker.

The former Tottenham 'keeper may have suffered relegation less than a year after moving to the East Midlands, but he was as defiant as ever as Villa attempted to record their first win on this ground for nearly 15 years.

Although he was beaten by superb shots from England international Darius Vassell and Thomas Hitzlsperger, Walker produced a string of outstanding saves to earn the home side a creditable draw.

Post-match statistics showed that Villa had 13 efforts on target, but the fact that only two went in illustrates the quality of Walker's performance.

Villa were once again left cursing a succession of missed opportunities which went begging in the closing stages.

The game was in its final minute when George Boateng burst through the middle and set up Steve Staunton for a blistering low left-footer which cannoned off Walker's legs, and even in stoppage time the visitors managed to conjure up two more chances.

The manner in which Peter Crouch controlled substitute Hassan Kachloul's left wing cross was delightful in the extreme and the towering striker's flick and turn would have done justice to Dennis Bergkamp at his cheekiest.

Unfortunately, Crouch was unable to get sufficient power behind his close range shot, enabling Walker to tip away – but there was still time for Hitzlsperger to unleash a fierce left foot drive which the 'keeper clutched as he fell.

If those late saves were infuriating, though, Villa must have suspected it wasn't going to be their day as early as the 10th minute, when Crouch had an effort disallowed for offside.

Having absorbed that disappointment, Villa went ahead on 23 minutes, Crouch displaying great control before playing an inviting pass wide to Vassell, whose right foot drive arrowed beyond Walker and into the bottom right corner.

The lead lasted barely 60 seconds, Muzzy Izzet blasting a penalty past Peter Enckelman after Jlloyd Samuel's challenge on Ian Marshall, but only a further four minutes had elapsed before Villa regained their advantage.

It was a goal to savour for Hitzlsperger, who moved on to Steve Staunton's pass and darted between two opponents before firing hard and low into the bottom corner from just outside the penalty area with his "weaker" right foot.

But after Paul Dickov's shot had deflected off Staunton for a corner, the home side drew level again in the 67th minute.

Substitute Jon Stevenson looked offside as Robbie Savage lofted the ball into the penalty area, but the teenage striker prodded home after Enckelman had saved his first effort.

▸ *Thomas Hitzlsperger is flat out, but he's feeling sky high after scoring his first Villa goal.*

MATCH 47

Date Saturday 20 April 2002
Venue Filbert Street, 3.00pm

LEICESTER CITY (1) 2
ASTON VILLA (2) 2

Attendance 18,125
Referee Graham Poll
Assistants M. Short and K. Pike

▸ **LEICESTER CITY**
blue shirts, white shorts

1 Ian WALKER (Gk)	
2 Gary ROWETT	
3 Frank SINCLAIR	
6 Muzzy IZZET ❏	g24
8 Robbie SAVAGE	
14 Callum DAVIDSON (89)	
17 Stefan OAKES (51)	
18 Matt ELLIOTT (c)	
22 Paul DICKOV	
26 Lee MARSHALL (51)	
29 Matthew PIPER	
Substitutes	
28 Matthew HEATH (14)	
30 Michael PRICE (Gk)	
32 Jon STEVENSON (26)	g67
35 Jon ASHTON (17)	
38 Tom WILLIAMSON	

▸ **ASTON VILLA**
claret shirts with blue trim, claret shorts

12 Peter ENCKELMAN (Gk)	
2 Mark DELANEY	
4 Olof MELLBERG	
6 George BOATENG	
11 Steve STAUNTON (c)	
15 Gareth BARRY	
16 Peter CROUCH	
18 Steve STONE	
21 Thomas HITZLSPERGER	g27
22 Darius VASSELL (80)	g23
31 Jlloyd SAMUEL (80)	
Substitutes	
8 Juan Pablo ANGEL	
13 Boaz MYHILL (Gk)	
17 Lee HENDRIE	
19 Bosko BALABAN (22)	
30 Hassan KACHLOUL (31)	

Before	P	W	D	L	F	A	pts
10 Villa	35	10	13	12	39	43	43
20 Leicester	35	7	11	24	26	61	23
After	P	W	D	L	F	A	pts
10 Villa	36	10	14	12	41	45	44
20 Leicester	36	7	12	24	28	63	24

▸ Thomas Hitzlsperger's first senior Villa goal   ▸ Villa have never won a Premiership match at Filbert Street

FA BARCLAYCARD PREMIERSHIP

Darius double does the trick

▶ Sven Goran Eriksson probably didn't require a reminder of Darius Vassell's World Cup credentials, but the young striker provided one anyway on an afternoon of turning points at Villa Park.

Despite Vassell's dramatic arrival on the international scene, life on the domestic front had not been rosy of late, either for England's latest hot shot or his Villa team-mates.

Vassell's club form had faltered to the extent where he had been forced to settle for substitute appearances in three consecutive matches, while his goal at Leicester a week earlier had ended a barren spell of seven games.

But his first half double against Southampton brought Villa only their second success in 11 attempts under Graham Taylor's management – on a day, ironically, when they were not at their best.

Not that anyone was too concerned about the lack of aesthetic quality about Villa's latest offering. Having slipped from a secure seventh place to a tentative tenth over the previous four weeks, with just seven points gathered since Taylor's return to the hot seat, they were a team in desperate need of rediscovering the winning habit.

Thankfully, a vibrant first half performance was sufficient to clinch three important points, even if they subsequently surrendered the initiative to the Saints.

Although Gordon Strachan's men enjoyed a high percentage of second half possession, however, there was rarely much genuine threat to the home goal after James Beattie had reduced the deficit seven minutes after the interval.

Even so, the first half was one to savour as Taylor's troops marched forward relentlessly and with purpose to establish their two-goal advantage.

They were ahead after just eight minutes. Thomas Hitzlsperger's right wing corner was cleared, but when the German midfielder collected the ball and delivered a fine cross into a crowded goalmouth, Vassell stooped to send a header looping over goalkeeper Neil Moss.

Maybe the Saints' keeper should have done better with that one, but he had no chance when Vassell struck again three minutes before the break.

Towering striker Peter Crouch was the instigator of that one, displaying tremendous determination to win a midfield challenge before playing a short pass to Gareth Barry on the halfway line.

Spotting Vassell's run, Barry delivered a defence splitting through ball and without breaking his stride, the England striker volleyed firmly past Moss and into the bottom corner from just outside the penalty area.

In between Vassell's goals, Villa created a host of other opportunities as they pushed forward with invention.

▶ *Two-goal Darius Vassell and his England colleague Wayne Bridge are in determined mood as they contest a loose ball.*

Hitzlsperger curled a 20-yard free-kick only just the wrong side of the post, Barry headed wide from Mark Delaney's cross and Crouch somehow scooped over from close range when it looked easier to score.

The game was thrown wide open when Beattie converted Ormerod's low centre at point blank range, but Villa were not seriously inconvenienced again.

MATCH 48

Date Saturday 27 April 2002
Venue Villa Park, 3.00pm

ASTON VILLA (2) 2
SOUTHAMPTON (0) 1

Attendance 35,255
Referee David Elleray
Assistants P. Barston and J. Holbrook

▶ **ASTON VILLA**
claret shirts with blue trim, white shorts

12 Peter ENCKELMAN (Gk)	
2 Mark DELANEY	
3 Alan WRIGHT	
4 Olof MELLBERG ❏	
6 George BOATENG	
11 Steve STAUNTON (c) ❏	
15 Gareth BARRY (66)	
16 Peter CROUCH (66)	
18 Steve STONE (66)	
21 Thomas HITZLSPERGER	
22 Darius VASSELL	g8, 42
Substitutes	
8 Juan Pablo ANGEL (16)	
13 Boaz MYHILL (Gk)	
17 Lee HENDRIE	
20 Moustapha HADJI (18)	
31 Jlloyd SAMUEL (15)	

▶ **SOUTHAMPTON**
red and white striped shirts, black shorts

13 Neil MOSS (Gk)	
2 Jason DODD (c)	
3 Wayne BRIDGE	
5 Claus LUNDEKVAM	
6 Paul WILLIAMS	
9 James BEATTIE	g52
12 Anders SVENSSON	
18 Rory DELAP	
29 Fabrice FERNANDES (45)	
33 Paul TELFER	
36 Brett ORMEROD (80)	
Substitutes	
10 Kevin DAVIES (36)	
20 Tahar EL-KHALEJ	
21 Jo TESSEM (45) ❏	
26 Imants BLEIDELIS	
27 Scott BEVAN (Gk)	

Before	P	W	D	L	F	A	pts
10 Villa	36	10	14	12	41	45	44
13 Saints	36	11	9	16	42	51	42
After	P	W	D	L	F	A	pts
9 Villa	37	11	14	12	43	46	47
14 Saints	37	11	9	17	43	52	42

▶ Alan Wright's first game since January   ▶ Juan Pablo Angel receives Villa's Player of the Year award

FA BARCLAYCARD PREMIERSHIP

Signing off in style

▸ European football was again on Villa's horizon following a stylish performance which earned them a comprehensive victory at Stamford Bridge, cementing qualification for the InterToto Cup.

A result of this nature had been on the cards since Graham Taylor's return as manager in February, Villa at last finding the goals to match their invention.

Peter Crouch used his height to good effect to establish an interval advantage, with Darius Vassell celebrating his selection for England's World Cup squad by volleying the second on 63 minutes.

Eidur Gudjohnsen raised hopes of a Chelsea comeback by converting a 70th minute penalty, but substitute Dion Dublin, just back from a loan spell with Millwall, put the issue beyond doubt by heading the third goal after Alan Wright's fierce drive had struck the underside of the bar.

After a sluggish start, a well-delivered cross from Steve Stone was met by an angled Crouch header which was destined for the left hand corner before Carlo Cudicini stretched across his line to tip it away.

But in the 22nd minute the former Portsmouth striker's aerial presence was rewarded with a fine goal.

Vassell's tenacity won a corner off William Gallas, and when Stone delivered a teasing inswinger from the left, Crouch's downward header bounced beyond Cudicini's reach and into the top corner.

Villa's lead was kept intact by a combination of some dreadful finishing by young striker Carlton Cole, and three excellent saves from Peter Enckelman.

The Finn's sense of anticipation enabled him to thwart Mario Melchiot at close range after the Dutch defender had got away from Steve Staunton and he then held Cole's shot on the turn before diving full length to touch Zola's fierce angled drive to safety.

Although Enckelman did well to save with his feet from Cole in the 58th minute, that was merely the prelude to a sustained spell of dominance which deservedly brought a second Villa goal.

Vassell overhit a cross, but substitute Lee Hendrie refused to give up the cause, retrieving the ball in the far corner before slipping a short pass to Stone, whose centre was met by a stunning left-foot volley from Vassell to leave Cudicini helpless.

There could have been further goals, too, Cudinici producing acrobatic saves to keep out powerful headers from Hendrie and Crouch, both following Barry centres.

In between those two near misses, Gudjohnsen reduced the deficit by calmly sending Enckelman the wrong way from a 70th minute penalty after Delaney had been adjudged to bring down Sam Dalla Bona.

But somehow there was a feeling Villa were destined to finish on a high, and that's how it turned out. When the home side only partially cleared Barry's free-kick two minutes from time, Wright unleashed a ferocious 20-yard drive which bounced down off the underside of the bar. Dublin, having replaced Vassell just four minutes earlier, was only too happy to nod home the rebound.

▸ *Dion Dublin claimed Villa's final goal of the season, but the players acknowledge Alan Wright's contribution after his shot had crashed against the bar.*

MATCH 49

Date Saturday 11 May 2002
Venue Stamford Bridge, 3.00pm

CHELSEA (0) 1
ASTON VILLA (1) 3

Attendance 40,709
Referee Steve Bennett
Assistants A. Garratt and P. Barnes

▸ **CHELSEA**
blue shirts, blue shorts

23	Carlo CUDICINI (Gk)
8	Frank LAMPARD
11	Boudewijn ZENDEN (45)
13	William GALLAS
14	Graeme LE SAUX (c) (45)
15	Mario MELCHIOT
17	Emmanuel PETIT
25	Gianfranco ZOLA
26	John TERRY
30	Jesper GRONKJAER (45)
39	Carlton COLE
	Substitutes
1	Ed DE GOEY (Gk)
12	Mario STANIC
22	Eidur GUDJOHNSEN (30) g70
24	Sam DALLA BONA (11)
29	Robert HUTH (14)

▸ **ASTON VILLA**
claret shirts with blue trim, white shorts

12	Peter ENCKELMAN (Gk)
2	Mark DELANEY
3	Alan WRIGHT
4	Olof MELLBERG
6	George BOATENG
11	Steve STAUNTON (c)
15	Gareth BARRY
16	Peter CROUCH (84) g22
18	Steve STONE
21	Thomas HITZLSPERGER ❑ (53)
22	Darius VASSELL (84) g63
	Substitutes
8	Juan Pablo ANGEL (16)
9	Dion DUBLIN (22) g88
17	Lee HENDRIE (21)
20	Moustapha HADJI
39	Wayne HENDERSON (Gk)

Before	P	W	D	L	F	A	pts
5 Chelsea	37	17	13	7	65	35	64
9 Villa	37	11	14	12	43	46	47
After	P	W	D	L	F	A	pts
6 Chelsea	38	17	13	8	66	38	64
8 Villa	38	12	14	12	46	47	50

▸ *Villa's first win at Stamford Bridge since March 1988* ▸ *50th win over Chelsea*

FRIENDLIES

PRE-SEASON FRIENDLY
Date: Monday 16 July 2001
Venue: Supermarine Sports & Social

SWINDON SUPERMARINE (0) 0
ASTON VILLA (1) 4

Attendance: 1,210
Referee: K. Barnes
Assistants: P. Humphrey and S. Humphrey

▸ SWINDON SUPERMARINE
blue and white hooped shirts, blue shorts

1	Chris WEBB (45)
2	Vinnie PARKER (45)
3	Michael SILVANUS (45)
4	Lee HARTSHARN (45)
5	Matt JACK (45)
6	Peter FARROW (45)
7	Tony JOYCE (45)
8	Tony WILKINSON (45)
9	Neil MATTHEWS
10	Tate HULBERT
11	Sean WIMBLE

Second half team

1	Paul HAINES (1)
5	Paul BODEN (2)
6	Justin STEPHENS (3)
7	Matt SAYE (4)
7	Simon FUTCHER (5)
8	Mich CASEY (6)
9	Peter HORWAT (7)
11	Nathan Holt (8)
12	Richard HODGKISS (9)
12	Steve DAVIS (10)
15	Doug IMRIE (11)

▸ ASTON VILLA
claret and blue shirts, blue shorts

1	Boaz MYHILL	
2	Rob EDWARDS	
3	Danny JACKMAN (73)	
4	Michael STANDING (45)	
5	Danny HAYNES (14)	
6	Liam RIDGEWELL (73)	
7	Jay SMITH (80)	
8	Stephen COOKE	g24
9	Richard WALKER (45)	g81
10	Giovanni SPERANZA (45)	
11	Gavin MELAUGH (80)	g70

Substitutes

12	Andy MARFELL (9)	
14	Liam FOLDS (5)	
15	Leon HYLTON (6)	
16	Neil TARRANT (10)	
17	David BERKS (4)	g77

Returned to action

4	Michael STANDING (14)
6	Liam RIDGEWELL (3)
9	Richard WALKER (7)
10	Giovanni SPERANZA (11)

PRE-SEASON FRIENDLY
Date: Thursday 19 July 2001
Venue: The Buck's Head

TELFORD UNITED (3) 3
ASTON VILLA (0) 3

Attendance: 2,005
Referee: M. Fletcher
Assistants: S. Davies and K. Latham

▸ TELFORD UNITED
white shirts, black shorts

1	Ryan PRICE	
2	Mark ALBRIGHTON (61)	
3	Gareth HANMER	
4	Neil MOORE	
5	Jim BENTLEY	
6	Lee FOWLER	
7	Gary FITZPATRICK (45)	
8	Steve GAUGHAN (66)	
9	Steve ANTHROBUS	g17
10	Peter SMITH	
11	Steve PALMER (26)	g1, og65

Substitutes

12	Kevin PREECE (7)	
15	Jordan KING (8)	
16	Kevin DAVIES (11)	g42
17	Mick PORTER (2)	

▸ ASTON VILLA
claret shirts with blue trim, white shorts

1	Boaz MYHILL	
2	Gavin MELAUGH (62)	
3	Danny JACKMAN	
4	Rob EDWARDS	
5	Liam RIDGEWELL	
6	Thomas HITZLSPERGER (66)	
7	Jay SMITH (52)	
8	Stephen COOKE	
9	Richard WALKER (58)	
10	Stefan MOORE	g75
11	John McGRATH (50)	

Substitutes

12	Ryan AMOO	
14	Giovanni SPERANZA (6)	
15	Trialist (52)	
16	Michael STANDING (62)	g77
17	Trialist (58)	
18	Neil TARRANT (50)	

PRE-SEASON FRIENDLY
Date: Monday 23 July 2001
Venue: The Lamb

TAMWORTH (1) 2
ASTON VILLA (2) 3

Attendance: 1,606
Referee: M. Barnes
Assistants: S. Barrow and R. Orchard

▸ TAMWORTH
red shirts, red shorts

1	Darren ACTON	
2	Richard FOLLETT	
3	Robert MUTCHELL	
4	Mark TURNER	g83
5	Darren GROCUTT	
6	Robert GOULD	
7	David NORTON	
8	Gary MILLS	
9	Mark HALLAM (73)	
10	Lee WILSON (70)	g45
11	Ian McKENNA (12)	

Substitutes

12	Mykey PRICE (10)
14	Nick COLLEY (11)
15	Paul HATTON (9)

▸ ASTON VILLA
platinum shirts, navy blue shorts

1	Wayne HENDERSON (45)	
2	Rob EDWARDS	
3	Danny JACKMAN (76)	
4	Jonathan BEWERS	
5	Liam RIDGEWELL	
6	Thomas HITZLSPERGER	
7	Stefan MOORE	g45, 50
8	Stephen COOKE (76)	
9	Richard WALKER (45)	g20
10	Gavin MELAUGH (76)	
11	Neil TARRANT	

Substitutes

12	Jay SMITH (7)
13	Boaz MYHILL (45)
14	Michael STANDING (45)
15	Danny HAYNES (8)
16	David BERKS (10)
17	Liam FOLDS (3)
18	Andy MARFELL (11)

FRIENDLIES

PRE-SEASON FRIENDLY
Date: Saturday 28 July 2001
Venue: International Stadium

GATESHEAD (0) 0
ASTON VILLA (4) 4

Attendance: Not available
Referee: M. Clattenburg
Assistants: D. Roberts and I. Donaldson

▶ **GATESHEAD**
red shirts, red shorts

1	Adrian SWAN
2	Richie WATSON
3	Paul TALBOT
4	Rob BOWMAN
5	Rob JONES
6	Steve AGNEW (78)
7	Paul THOMPSON (70)
8	Steve BOWEY (20)
9	Lee ELLISON (58)
10	Rob PALMER
11	Richie ALDERSON (71)
	Substitutes
12	Lee FITZGERALD (6)
13	Chris LYNCH (11)
14	Phil ROSS (7)
15	Gareth McALINDON (8)
16	Wayne EDGCUMBE (9)

ASTON VILLA
claret shirts with blue trim, blue shorts

1	Boaz MYHILL
2	Jonathan BEWERS (45)
3	Jlloyd SAMUEL
4	Steve STAUNTON
5	Olof MELLBERG
6	Thomas HITZLSPERGER (45)
7	Moustapha HADJI (70) g32
8	Stephen COOKE (45)
9	Juan Pablo ANGEL g29, 44
10	Darius VASSELL (64) g28
11	Danny JACKMAN (45)
	Substitutes
12	Stefan MOORE (11)
14	Gavin MELAUGH (7)
15	Rob EDWARDS (2)
16	Jay SMITH (6)
17	Richard WALKER (10)
18	Michael STANDING (8)

UNDER-21 TOURNAMENT
Date: Saturday 11 August 2001
Venue: Belle Vue Stadium, Rhyl

ASTON VILLA (2) 5
JUVENTUS (0) 1

Attendance: Not available
Referee: M. Bridge
Assistants: Mr Petch and Mr Allsop

▶ **ASTON VILLA**
claret shirts with blue trim, blue shorts

13	Boaz MYHILL
2	Sean DILLON (10)
3	Danny JACKMAN (80)
4	Jonathan BEWERS
5	Danny HAYNES (57) g35
6	Liam RIDGEWELL
7	Jay SMITH
8	Michael STANDING
9	Stefan MOORE
10	Stephen COOKE (76) g37, 90
11	Thomas HITZLSPERGER
	Substitutes
1	Wayne HENDERSON
12	Gavin MELAUGH (5)
14	David BERKS (3)
15	Liam FOLDS (2)
16	Peter HYNES (10) g80, 85

▶ **JUVENTUS**
grey shirts, grey shorts

1	Mario ANDREA
2	Giorgio D'ANGELO (72)
3	Massimo TRIDON (53)
4	Sergio DE WINOT
5	Michele SCHINO
6	Marco CHIUMENTE
7	Gerado CLEMENTE (67)
8	Alex PEDERZOLI g78
9	Enrico CANAPE
10	Roni SILVA (45)
11	Jonothon ELLIOT
	Substitutes
12	Matteo RIZZO (2)
14	Gianluca ROMANO (45)
15	Francesco CESSARIO (3)
16	Ivano SORRENTINO (7)

PRE-SEASON FRIENDLY
Date: Sunday 12 August 2001
Venue: El Sardinero

RACING SANTANDER (0) 0
ASTON VILLA (2) 2

Attendance: 30,000
Referee: C. Caballero
Assistants: Not available

▶ **RACING SANTANDER**
white shirts, black shorts

1	Jose Ceballos VEGA
4	Claudio ARZENO
7	Julio ALVAREZ 62)
9	Javier MAZZONI (62)
10	Angel DORADO
12	Mahdi NAFTI
15	Alonso TXEMA (84)
16	SIERRA
18	MENA
21	Javier PINEDA
22	JUANMA
	Substitutes
14	MATEO (7)
20	BODIPO (9)
24	MORA (15)

▶ **ASTON VILLA**
claret shirts with blue trim, blue shorts

1	Peter SCHMEICHEL (45)
2	Mark DELANEY (45)
4	Olof MELLBERG (72)
5	ALPAY Ozalan (45)
8	Moustapha HADJI (73)
9	Juan Pablo ANGEL (80) g13, 16
11	Lee HENDRIE (45)
12	Hassan KACHLOUL
14	David GINOLA (84)
15	Steve STAUNTON
20	Sergei KANDEROV
	Substitutes
3	Gareth BARRY (4)
6	George BOATENG (11)
7	Steve STONE (2)
13	Peter ENCKELMAN (1)
16	Dion DUBLIN (9)
17	Darius VASSELL (14)
18	Alan WRIGHT (8)
19	Jlloyd SAMUEL (5)

ASTON VILLA REVIEW 2002 — FRIENDLIES

PRE-SEASON FRIENDLY
Date Wednesday 15 August 2001
Venue Crown Avenue

BOWERS UNITED (0) 0
ASTON VILLA (6) 10

Details of match officials not available

▶ **BOWERS UNITED**
red and white striped shirts, black shorts

1 Paul DENNIS
2 Barry SHORTER
3 Mickey WALSH
4 Lee GOODWIN
5 John WARNER
6 Darryl HERBERT
7 Jeff BRAZIER
8 Mark BARRY
9 Steve WARNER (85)
10 Lee BRANT (80)
11 Paul WILLIAMS
Substitutes
15 Paul DONOVAN (8)
16 Shane CAMPBELL (9)
17 Warren HAWTHORNE (10)

▶ **ASTON VILLA**
platinum shirts, white shorts

1 Wayne HENDERSON
2 Gavin MELAUGH
3 Thomas HITZLSPERGER (52) g35
4 Jonathan BEWERS
5 Michael STANDING
6 Liam RIDGEWELL
7 Jay SMITH (52) g24
8 Andrew MARFELL g30
9 Richard WALKER (52) g17, 26, 39
10 David BERKS g49
15 Danny JACKMAN (52)
Substitutes
12 Stephen COOKE (7) g70
13 Boaz MYHILL
14 Stefan MOORE (9) g63, 85
15 Danny JACKMAN (3)

FRIENDLY
Date Monday 10 September 2001
Venue Bodymoor Heath

ASTON VILLA (2) 4
NOTT'M FOREST (0) 1

Attendance Not available
Referee H. Hector
Assistants A. Marriner and A. Hendley

▶ **ASTON VILLA**
platinum shirts, navy blue shorts

1 Peter ENCKELMAN (55)
2 Steve STONE
3 Danny JACKMAN
4 Jlloyd SAMUEL
5 Steve STAUNTON
6 Gareth BARRY (68)
7 Moustapha HADJI (55)
8 Bosko BALABAN (45) g43
9 Stefan MOORE g5, 74
10 Stephen COOKE
11 David GINOLA (45)
Substitutes
12 Jay SMITH (7)
13 Boaz MYHILL (1)
14 Richard WALKER (45) g68
15 Thomas HITZLSPERGER (11)
16 Lee McGUIRE (6)
17 Cameron STUART (3)
19 Peter HYNES (14)

▶ **NOTTINGHAM FOREST**
red shirts, white shorts

1 Barry ROACH (45)
2 Niall HUDSON (45)
3 Alan ROGERS
4 Gareth EDDS
5 Kevin DANSON
6 Chris DOIG (45)
7 Andy GRAY
8 Jack LESTER (45)
9 Stern JOHN g88
10 David JOHNSON
11 Andy REID (60)
Substitutes
12 Gary JONES (2)
13 Pascal FORMAN (45)
14 Keith FOY (6)
15 David FREEMAN (11)
16 John THOMPSON (10)
17 LYNCH (45)

TESTIMONIAL MATCH
Date Thursday 2 May 2002
Venue Gay Meadow

SHREWSBURY TOWN (1) 5
ASTON VILLA (1) 2

Attendance 2,340
Referee R. Lewis
Assistants J. Holbrook and S. Gerard

▶ **SHREWSBURY TOWN**
blue shirts with yellow trim, blue shorts

1 Mark CARTWRIGHT (80)
2 Darren MOSS
3 Greg RIOCH
4 Mark ATKINS (59)
5 Mick HEATHCOTE (59)
6 Matt REDMILE
7 Ryan LOWE g51, 57, 90
8 Jamie TOLLEY (69)
9 Luke RODGERS g20, 83
10 Karl MURRAY
11 Chris MURPHY (80)
Substitutes
12 Leon DRYSDALE (5)
13 Tim HART (1)
14 Pete WILDING (4)
15 Mark CORBETT (11)
16 Neal McCANN (8)

▶ **ASTON VILLA**
claret shirts with blue trim, claret shorts

1 Wayne HENDERSON (45)
2 Mark DELANEY (76)
3 Alan WRIGHT (57)
4 Jamie McCOMBE (63)
5 Liam RIDGEWELL
6 Steve STONE (57)
7 Moustapha HADJI (63)
8 Lee HENDRIE g27
9 Stefan MOORE g87
10 Paul MERSON
11 Hassan KACHLOUL (57)
Substitutes
12 Jay SMITH (7)
13 Boaz MYHILL (1)
14 Danny JACKMAN (3)
15 Jonathan BEWERS
16 Gavin MELAUGH (6)
17 Stephen COOKE (2)
18 John McGRATH (11)
19 Rob EDWARDS (4)

57

The Weir and The Wonderful

Published later this year, *The Weir and The Wonderful* is a collection of pictures by Terry Weir, the former club photographer.

Many of the stunning black-and-white images have not previously been published, and each one is accompanied by an anecdote by the man who captured life at Villa Park, both on and off the pitch, for a quarter of a century.

This impressive volume will contain 224 landscape pages with a hardback cover and will be available from October, priced £19.95.

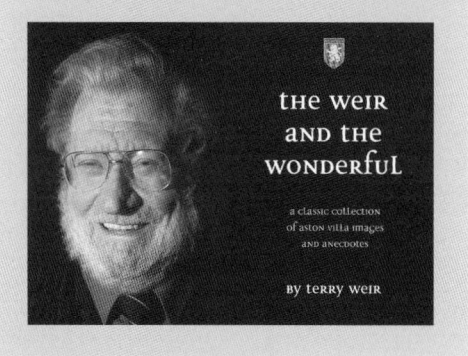

Children of the Revolution

Written by lifelong fan Richard Whitehead, this is the story of the 1970s from a Villa perspective, the decade in which the club shook off the cobwebs of years of decline and began to reassert itself as a force in football.

Starting with the boardroom revolution of 1968, it traces the years which followed. The days of relegation, midweek trips to Halifax, three Wembley finals – it's all captured in these pages.

The definitive work on one of the most vivid passages in Villa history, *Children of the Revolution* costs £14.95.

The Road to Rotterdam

Villa celebrated the 20th anniversary of their greatest achievement in May, and the story of the club's European Cup triumph is recalled in this book by *Villa News & Record* writer Rob Bishop.

Packed with pictures, including every Villa goal in the competition, the unforgettable story unfolds through the eyes of the 1981-82 squad, who come up with a host of personal memories. Price £12.99.

Villa Park 100 Years

Most fans like to think their club's home ground is special, but Villa fans are luckier than most. This richly-detailed and superbly illustrated centenary history pays tribute to Villa Park's unique setting – in the former grounds of a Jacobean stately home – and a heritage almost unrivalled in the annals of British sport.

Stadium expert and lifelong fan Simon Inglis has produced a comprehensive 'biography' of Villa Park, full of previously unpublished photographs and archive material. Price £24.95.

Stride Inside The Villa

In 1997, Steve Stride celebrated 25 years on the Villa payroll, initially as office boy and subsequently as secretary and director.

To mark the occasion, he committed to paper a wealth of stories about life at one of the nation's top clubs.

The result is the first book by a football club secretary, presented with the dry wit that has made this former Holte Ender one of football's most popular characters. Price £8.95.

Claret and Blue

The popular *Claret and Blue* magazine is being relaunched next season on a quarterly basis. The new publication will be issued free to all season ticket holders, but is also available on subscription at £12 for four issues. European rates are £16 for four issues, while subscribers in other parts of the world will be charged £20.

All publications are available from the club shop at the Villa Village, or contact the Publishing Department, Aston Villa FC, Villa Park, Birmingham, B4 6AX. (Telephone: 0121 327 2299, e-mail publishing@astonvilla-fc.co.uk.

Villa News and Record

The price of the club's official programme is being pegged at £2 for 2002-03, and it is also available on subscription. Home rates are £2.50 per issue, inclusive of post and packing.

ASTON VILLA REVIEW 2002 — TEAM GROUP

▶ Villa's First Team squad lineup for the start of the 2001–02 season. Back row: Alan Smith (assistant physio), Mark Delaney, Alpay Ozalan, Ian Taylor, Dion Dublin, Peter Enckelman, Peter Schmeichel (moved to Manchester City), Olof Mellberg, Jlloyd Samuel, Steve Staunton, David Ginola (moved to Everton), Jim Walker (physio). Front row: John Deehan (assistant manager), Moustapha Hadji, Steve Stone, George Boateng, Juan Pablo Angel, Paul Merson, John Gregory (now Derby County), Gareth Barry, Lee Hendrie, Darius Vassell, Alan Wright, Hassan Kachloul, Eric Steele (goalkeeping coach).

59

ASTON VILLA REVIEW 2002

MANAGEMENT

Little could Graham Taylor have imagined, when he took the role of non-Executive director last July, that seven months later he would be back at the sharp end of life at Aston Villa. To all intents and purposes, the former England boss was done with management, having stood down from a second term as Watford boss at the end of the 2000-01 campaign.

When he was invited to take up a behind-the-scenes role at Villa Park, he stressed there was no question of a return to the manager's chair, even at the club where he had been so successful more than a decade earlier. But in football, more than any other profession, you should never say never. John Gregory's resignation after almost four years at the helm prompted Villa to offer Taylor a second term in the hot seat – and the temptation was simply too strong.

After all, the Premiership had not even existed when he left Villa to become national coach in 1990 and, by his own admission, he would never have forgiven himself for giving up the opportunity of managing at this level.

▸ STUART GRAY

He quickly discovered, though, that life in the Midlands was going to be tougher the second time around.

In his first spell in charge, he had guided Villa back into the top flight just a year after they had been relegated, and subsequently led them to runners-up spot in the old First Division and qualification for the UEFA Cup.

Despite the mid-winter depression which had culminated with Gregory's resignation, a UEFA place was still possible when the new manager took over, but halting the decline was a task which proved too much even for a man of Graham Taylor's qualities.

▸ GRAHAM TAYLOR

▸ ERIC STEELE

Not that a disappointing sequence of results was received with any great vitriol by the vast majority of Villa supporters.

Maybe expectations were sky high when the new boss walked down the touchline to a rapturous ovation before his first match in charge, but the fans soon came to the realisation that the remainder of the campaign would be dedicated to assessing the strengths and weaknesses of the squad, rather than pushing towards the top of the table.

▸ JOHN DEEHAN

▸ KEVIN MacDONALD

Taylor learned a lot during those final 13 weeks, discovering which players he regarded as good enough to be involved in Villa's future, and introducing others he considered worthy of becoming a part of the grand plan.

In that respect, the closing weeks of the campaign were productive in spite of some disappointing results.

Gareth Barry, out in the cold for so long under the previous regime, was re-introduced to great effect; Thomas Hitzlsperger, previously restricted to just 15 minutes' senior football, responded magnificently to an extended run in the team; Peter Enckelman was at long last promoted to number one goalkeeper; Darius Vassell burst into the England side with stunning impact.

That quartet undoubtedly form the basis of the exciting new-look, younger line-up which the manager hopes will take Villa to honours over the next few seasons.

▸ GORDON COWANS

Taylor's appointment, of course, was not the only change of personnel behind the scenes.

The departure last summer of Steve Harrison and Paul Barron to Middlesbrough had created vacancies for a first team coach and goalkeeping coach, and these were filled by John Deehan and Eric Steele.

Deehan, a popular Villa striker in the 1970s, subsequently played for West Bromwich Albion and Norwich City before moving into coaching and was, in fact, in charge of England under-21s during Taylor's time as national team manager.

Steele, having begun his career with home town club Newcastle United, established himself as a dependable 'keeper for Peterborough, Brighton, Watford and Derby County, where he was working as goalkeeping coach before John Gregory persuaded him to move across the Midlands. Ironically, Gregory would travel in the opposite direction to become manager of the relegation-bound Rams after stepping down at Villa, being followed a few weeks later by chief scout Ross MacLaren, whose duties were assumed by Deehan.

There was another addition to the backroom team in November, former skipper Stuart Gray returning to the club in a coaching capacity after being sacked as manager of Southampton, a club he had also served as player and coach after leaving Villa in 1991.

The experience and knowledge of old boys Deehan and Gray was never more important than during the weeks following Gregory's resignation. Their presence meant the directors were able to deliberate over the best possible replacement rather than rushing into a decision, and the duo were in charge as joint caretaker managers for the matches at home to Everton and away to Fulham, both of which finished goalless.

Villa's reserves were again in the dependable hands of Kevin MacDonald, although it was at Academy level where the club enjoyed most success.

Although the under-19s' results were generally disappointing, coach Gordon Cowans – yet another former Villa player – derived enormous satisfaction from the progress made by a number of his young charges, either into the reserve ranks or the international stage at under-19 and under-20 level.

The under-17s, meanwhile, finished top of their Academy section and also headed their play-off group before missing out in the quarter-finals, but if that setback left coach Tony McAndrew disappointed, he and Cowans took great delight in coaxing Villa's youngsters to the club's first FA Youth Cup final for 22 years.

If it was a case of "as you were" for the reserves and Academy coaches, a similar situation existed among the rest of the staff.

The Academy set-up was overseen by director Bryan Jones and assistant director Steve Burns, while Youth Development Officer Alan Miller again scoured the continent in search of budding young talent – including one trip to snow-bound Turkey after he had been advised by Alpay to take his swimming trunks!

Paul Brackwell enjoyed his second season as Head of Education and Welfare, an important role in guiding the development of young players away from the football pitch, but if he and several other members of the backroom team were relative newcomers, Jim Walker has become almost a permanent fixture.

Appointed shortly after Taylor started his first spell as manager in 1987, the accomplished and hugely popular physio completed his 15th season of helping Villa's injured players back to fitness.

Walker has witnessed a lot of changes during his decade-and-a-half in the Bodymoor Heath treatment room, but will happily turn the clock back to when Graham Taylor was last at the helm – and Villa were challenging for the title!

▸ *TONY McANDREW*

▸ *BRYAN JONES*

▸ *STEVE BURNS*

▸ *JIM WALKER*

JUAN PABLO ANGEL

Born Medellin, Colombia
24 October, 1975.

Joined Villa January 2001 from River Plate, Argentina, £9.5m.

Villa debut as sub v Manchester United, Lge (a) 20/1/2001.

Any doubts about the wisdom of Villa's record transfer outlay were well and truly dispelled during Juan Pablo Angel's first full season in the Premiership.

Having struggled in his first few months at Villa Park, the Colombian striker signalled his intention to live up to his high-scoring reputation when he netted twice in the InterToto Cup final victory over Swiss club Basel.

He continued in scoring mode, too, including a brace against Bolton Wanderers which helped Villa to the top of the table in late October.

At one stage, Angel even looked capable of becoming the first Villa player to score 20 league goals in one season, and although he eventually fell well short of that target, his guile and graft made him a firm favourite with Holte Enders.

It was just a pity the second half of the season was overshadowed by speculation over his future because his wife Paula was unsettled in England.

Career Record

Season	Club	League Apps	Gls	Cups Apps	Gls
93-97	Nacional (Col)	54	8	-	-
97-98	River Plate (Arg)	12	2	-	-
98-99	River Plate (Arg)	32	12	-	-
99-00	River Plate (Arg)	38	29	-	-
00-01	Aston Villa	7 (2)	1	1	-
01-02	Aston Villa	26 (3)	12	4 (2)	4
Villa record		33 (5)	13	5 (2)	4
TOTAL		**169 (5)**	**64**	**5 (2)**	**4**

▶ Colombian Full international (22 caps, 5 goals).

BOSKO BALABAN

Born Rijeka, Croatia,
15 October, 1978.

Joined Villa August, 2001, from Dinamo Zagreb, £5.8m.

Villa debut as sub v Manchester United, Lge (h) 26/08/2001.

For the second consecutive season, Villa signed a striker who found considerable difficulty in adjusting to life in the Premiership.

Bosko Balaban arrived from Dinamo Zagreb with the reputation of a prolific marksman, just as Juan Pablo Angel had when signing from Argentine club River Plate seven months earlier.

Like the Colombian before him, though, Balaban struggled to settle in this country and his first team appearances proved to be few and far between.

He started only two matches – the second leg of the UEFA Cup-tie away to his fellow countrymen NK Varteks and the Worthington Cup-tie against Sheffield Wednesday – but otherwise had to settle for infrequent substitute appearances and has yet to complete a full 90 minutes for the first team. He was, however, on target four times for the reserves.

Career Record

Season	Club	League Apps	Gls	Cups Apps	Gls
95-96	Rijeka (Cro)	2	-	-	-
96-97	Rijeka (Cro)	17	1	-	-
97-98	Rijeka (Cro)	26	1	-	-
98-99	Rijeka (Cro)	23	4	-	-
99-00	Rijeka (Cro)	29	15	-	-
00-01	Dinamo Zagreb (Cro)	23 (2)	14	-	-
01-02	Dinamo Zagreb (Cro)	2	1	-	-
01-02	Aston Villa	- (8)	-	2 (1)	-
TOTAL		**122 (10)**	**36**	**2 (1)**	**-**

▶ Croatian Full international (12 caps, 6 goals).

NOTES ON PLAYER RECORDS

▶ Career records do not include cup-ties played for overseas clubs.

▶ Career records of goalkeepers Peter Schmeichel and Peter Enckelman list only the number of goals conceded for Aston Villa in the goals column.

Schmeichel scored one goal for Villa (at Everton, 20/10/01) was also on target six times for Hvidovre, twice for Brondby and once for Manchester United.

▶ All international records are up to 31st May 2002.

GARETH BARRY

Born Hastings,
23 February 1981.

Joined Villa on YTS terms in 1997, signed professional forms 23/2/98.

Villa debut as sub v Sheffield Wednesday, Lge (a) 2/5/1998.

If anyone epitomised the fluctuating fortunes of Villa's campaign, it was surely Gareth Barry. Thankfully, the versatile and talented youngster did it in the right order, finishing his season on a high note after his career had gone into reverse.

It was almost incredible that a player who has been capped six times by England should have to wait until December for his first Premiership start of the season, Even then, it was because of an injury crisis, and Barry found himself back on the subs' bench after four matches. But by the end of the season, the player who established himself as a central defender in the England set-up was well and truly back as a regular.

He was recalled to the line-up following Graham Taylor's appointment as manager, and operated equally effectively in midfield or at left-back.

Career Record

Season	Club	League Apps	Gls	Cups Apps	Gls
97-98	Aston Villa	1 (1)	-	-	-
98-99	Aston Villa	27 (5)	2	5	-
99-00	Aston Villa	30	1	13	-
00-01	Aston Villa	29 (1)	-	7 (1)	1
01-02	Aston Villa	16 (4)	-	6 (2)	-
TOTAL		**103 (11)**	**3**	**31 (3)**	**1**

▶ England international at Full (6 caps), Under-18 and Under-21 levels.

GEORGE BOATENG

Born Nkawkaw, Ghana,
5 September 1975.

Joined Villa July 1999 from Coventry City, £4.5m.

Villa debut v Newcastle United, Lge (a) 7/8/1999.

George Boateng was the only Villa player close to achieving an ever-present record, being involved in almost 50 matches throughout a gruelling season.

The Dutch midfielder would undoubtedly have benefited from a rest, but a shortage of back-up in his anchor role meant he had to soldier on.

He was regarded as an automatic choice by both John Gregory and Graham Taylor – and he also broke into Holland's senior team. Already an under-21 international, he made his full debut against Denmark and following up with another appearance in a 1-1 draw against England.

Career Record

Season	Club	League Apps	Gls	Cups Apps	Gls
94-95	Excelsior (Hol)	9	-	-	-
95-96	Feyenoord (Hol)	21 (3)	1	-	-
96-97	Feyenoord (Hol)	25 (1)	-	-	-
97-98	Feyenoord (Hol)	15 (3)	-	-	-
	Coventry City	14	1	5	-
98-99	Coventry City	29 (4)	4	6	2
99-00	Aston Villa	30 (3)	2	11	1
00-01	Aston Villa	29 (4)	1	8	-
01-02	Aston Villa	37	1	10 (1)	-
Villa record		96 (7)	4	29 (1)	-
TOTAL		**209 (18)**	**10**	**30 (1)**	**3**

▶ Dutch international at Full (2 caps) and Under-21 levels.

JONATHAN BEWERS

Born Kettering,
10 September 1982.

Joined Villa July 1997 as an Academy player.

Villa debut as sub v Tottenham Hotspur, Lge (a) 15/4/2000.

Apart from sitting on the bench for four matches (two InterToto Cup, two Premiership) the versatile defender didn't add to his single senior appearance, but was a regular for the reserves and continued his international education with the England under-19 team.

Career Record

Season	Club	League Apps	Gls	Cups Apps	Gls
99-00	Aston Villa	- (1)	-	-	-
00-01	Aston Villa	-	-	-	-
01-02	Aston Villa	-	-	-	-
TOTAL		**- (1)**	**-**	**-**	**-**

▶ England international at Under-17, Under-18 and Under-19 levels.

STEPHEN COOKE

Born Walsall, 15 February 1983.

Joined Villa Signed professional forms 15 February 2000.

Villa debut as sub v Celta Vigo, InterToto Cup, 2/8/2000.

A view from the substitutes' bench in the Worthington Cup-tie against Reading was the extent of midfielder Stephen Cooke's first team involvement, although he continued to make progress with the reserves, as well as breaking into the England under-19 squad.

Career Record

Season	Club	League Apps	Gls	Cups Apps	Gls
00-01	Aston Villa	-	-	- (1)	-
01-02	Aston Villa	-	-	-	-
loan	Bournemouth	6 (1)	-	-	-
Villa record		-	-	- (1)	-
TOTAL		**6 (1)**	**-**	**- (1)**	**-**

▶ England international at Under-16, Under-17 and Under-19 levels.

PETER CROUCH

Born Macclesfield, 30 January 1981.

Joined Villa March 2002 from Portsmouth for £4.5m

Villa debut v Bolton Wanderers, Lge (a) 30/3/2002.

A 6ft 6in striker, Peter Crouch arrived from Fratton Park just before the transfer deadline.

Born in Cheshire, Crouch was brought up in Ealing, London, and began his career as a YTS youngster with Spurs. With little prospect of first team football at White Hart Lane, he moved to QPR and then joined Pompey at the start of last season, scoring 19 goals for the south coast club.

That prolific output prompted Taylor to make his first venture into the transfer market since returning as manager, and it quickly became apparent he had made a sound investment. The new boy scored with an excellent header on his home debut against Newcastle, and also displayed remarkable ball control for a player of his height.

He also made his England under-21 debut just before joining Villa, and later scored in the 2-1 European Championship win over Switzerland.

Career Record

Season	Club	League Apps	Gls	Cups Apps	Gls
98-99	Tottenham	-	-	-	-
99-00	Tottenham	-	-	-	-
00-01	QPR	38 (4)	10	4 (1)	2
01-02	Portsmouth	37	18	2	1
01-02	Aston Villa	7	2	-	-
TOTAL		**82 (4)**	**30**	**6 (1)**	**3**

▶ England international at Youth and Under-21 levels.

MARK DELANEY

Born Haverfordwest, 13 May 1976.

Joined Villa March 1999 from Cardiff City, £500,000.

Villa debut as sub v Nottingham Forest, Lge (h) 24/4/1999.

After all of his injury problems the previous season, Mark Delaney would probably have been content merely to enjoy a clean bill of health in 2001-02. As it was, he did sustain a couple of injuries, but nothing to prevent him developing into one of the classiest full-backs in the Premiership.

Medial knee ligament damage kept him out for six matches over Christmas but otherwise he missed only a couple of games, and his extended tenancy of the right-back position saw him mature into a highly-accomplished footballer.

His tackling was of the highest order – and one challenge on Manchester United's Ryan Giggs drew comparisons with Bobby Moore's majestic tackle to dispossess Pele in the 1970 World Cup.

He also continued to be first choice for Wales, earning a number of call-ups for his country.

Career Record

Season	Club	League Apps	Gls	Cups Apps	Gls
98-99	Cardiff City	28	-	10 (2)	1
98-99	Aston Villa	- (2)	-	-	-
99-00	Aston Villa	25 (3)	1	5 (3)	-
00-01	Aston Villa	12 (7)	-	1 (1)	-
01-02	Aston Villa	30	-	9	-
Villa record		67 (12)	1	15 (4)	-
TOTAL		**95 (12)**	**1**	**25 (6)**	**1**

▶ Welsh international at Full (15 caps) and Under-21 levels.

DION DUBLIN

Born Leicester,
22 April, 1969.

Joined Villa November 1998 from Coventry City, £5.75m.

Villa debut v Tottenham, Lge (h) 7/11/1998.

If the previous campaign had been something of an anti-climax after his fairytale comeback from a broken neck in 2000, last season proved to be another low-key affair for Dion Dublin.

His starting appearances for Villa did not reach double figures as he was kept on the sidelines by the Darius Vassell-Juan Pablo Angel partnership, and he ended the season on loan to Millwall, whom he helped to reach the First Division play-offs.

If his Villa action was sporadic, however, he still came up with three trademark headed goals, against Liverpool, West Ham and Arsenal.

He was also on target with a more simple header after going on as a substitute in Villa's final match of the season at Chelsea.

Career Record

Season	Club	League Apps	Gls	Cups Apps	Gls
88-89	Cambridge United	12 (9)	6	1 (1)	1
89-90	Cambridge United	37 (9)	15	14 (2)	6
90-91	Cambridge United	44 (2)	16	13	7
91-92	Cambridge United	40 (3)	15	9	4
92-93	Manchester United	3 (4)	1	-	-
93-94	Manchester United	1 (4)	1	2 (3)	1
94-95	Manchester United	-	-	-	-
94-95	Coventry City	31	13	7	3
95-96	Coventry City	34	14	4 (1)	2
96-97	Coventry City	33 (1)	13	4 (1)	-
97-98	Coventry City	36	18	7	5
98-99	Coventry City	10	3	2	-
	Aston Villa	24	11	-	-
99-00	Aston Villa	23 (3)	12	5 (1)	3
00-01	Aston Villa	29 (4)	8	6 (1)	1
01-02	Aston Villa	9 (12)	4	6 (3)	2
loan	Millwall	5	2	-	-
Villa record		85 (19)	35	17 (5)	6
TOTAL		371 (51)	152	80 (13)	35

▶ At Cambridge also appeared in two Play-Offs, making 5 appearances, 2 goals. At Millwall, also appeared in Play-Offs, making two appearances, 1 goal.

▶ England Full international (4 caps).

PETER ENCKELMAN

Born Turku, Finland,
10 March 1977.

Joined Villa February 1999 from Jalkapallo TPS (Fin), for £200,000.

Villa debut as sub v Arsenal, Lge (a) 11/9/1999.

It's been a case of Patient Peter since his arrival at Villa Park, but the reliable keeper is hoping he can finally make the No 1 jersey his own in 2002-03.

Having been understudy to Mark Bosnich, David James and then Peter Schmeichel, Enckelman was promoted to first choice 'keeper following the announcement that Schmeichel's contract would not be renewed.

Even before the Dane's departure, however, Enckelman had more than proved his capabilities, producing sound performances whenever he was required to deputise. He was particularly impressive when standing in for consecutive matches against Everton, Fulham and Charlton in late January and early February, conceding just one goal in 180 minutes football.

Enckelman will be hopeful of plenty of opportunities to return similarly impressive figures next season.

Career Record

Season	Club	League Apps	Gls	Cups Apps	Gls
1995	TPS (Fin)	5 (1)	-	-	-
1996	TPS (Fin)	-	-	-	-
1997	TPS (Fin)	24 (1)	-	-	-
1998	TPS (Fin)	24	-	-	-
99-00	Aston Villa	9 (1)	9	4	1
00-01	Aston Villa	-	-	-	-
01-02	Aston Villa	9	10	4 (1)	5
Villa record		18 (1)	19	8 (1)	6
TOTAL		71 (3)	19	8 (1)	6

▶ Finland international at Full (3 caps) and Under-21 levels.

NEW PASTURES

Villa ventured into new pastures last season, playing in European competition in Croatia and Switzerland for the first time in their history.

They launched their InterToto campaign against Croatians Slaven Belupo before taking on Basel in the semi-finals.

Ironically, having never previously played in Croatia, they were back there for the first round UEFA Cup-tie against NK Varteks.

DAVID GINOLA

Born Gassin (France), 25 January 1967.

Joined Villa July 2000 from Tottenham Hotspur for £3m.

Villa debut v Leicester City, Lge (a) 19/8/2000.

An unhappy chapter in the flamboyant French winger's career was brought to an end when he left in February to join Everton.

It was clear from the opening weeks of the season that Ginola was not about to feature frequently on the left flank, even though his fleeting appearances suggested his flair could still provide an extra dimension to Villa's play.

The winger also scored a couple of goals in InterToto ties, only to find himself restricted to a watching brief once the Premiership got under way.

By mid-winter, he wasn't even in the squad and it was clear that things were not well between manager John Gregory and the player. Ironically, though, it was just after Gregory's departure to Derby that Ginola headed for Goodison Park.

Career Record

Season	Club	League Apps	Gls	Cups Apps	Gls
85-86	SC Toulon (Fra)	14	-	-	-
86-87	SC Toulon (Fra)	35	-	-	-
87-88	SC Toulon (Fra)	33	4	-	-
88-89	Racing Paris (Fra)	29	7	-	-
89-90	Racing Paris 1 (Fra)	32	1	-	-
90-91	Brest-Armorique (Fra)	33	6	-	-
91-92	Brest-Armorique (Fra)	17	8	-	-
	Paris St. Germain (Fra)	15	3	-	-
92-93	Paris St. Germain (Fra)	34	6	9	2
93-94	Paris St. Germain (Fra)	38	13	8	2
94-95	Paris St. Germain (Fra)	28	11	10	1
95-96	Newcastle United	34	5	6	-
96-97	Newcastle United	20 (4)	1	11 (1)	1
97-98	Tottenham Hotspur	34	6	6	3
98-99	Tottenham Hotspur	30	3	14	4
99-00	Tottenham Hotspur	36	3	6 (1)	2
00-01	Aston Villa	14 (13)	3	1	-
01-02	Aston Villa	- (5)	-	4 (4)	2
Villa record		14 (18)	3	5 (4)	2
TOTAL		**476 (22)**	**80**	**76 (6)**	**17**

▶ *NB Cup games in France are European competitions only.*

▶ *Full French international (17 caps, 3 goals).*

MOUSTAPHA HADJI

Born Ifrane, Morocco, 16 November 1971.

Joined Villa July 2001 from Coventry City, £4.5m.

Villa debut as sub v Slaven Belupo, InterToto Cup (h) 21/7/2001.

If they had not been aware of him before, Villa fans were certainly alerted to Moustapha Hadji when he pounced twice to give Coventry City a 2-0 interval lead in the final home match of 2000-01.

Those goals were not enough to prevent the Sky Blues from relegation as Villa stormed back to condemn them to First Division football with a 3-2 verdict, but Coventry's demotion made it inevitable they would sell one of their most prized assets.

Villa turned out to be the purchasers, striker Julian Joachim moving to Highfield Road in part exchange, and there's no question that it was good business for the club.

Although Hadji was a frequent observer from the subs' bench in the opening weeks, he quickly underlined his value when he broke into the side, operating effectively down the right flank and having the versatility to move up front whenever the need arose. He also scored one of Villa's best goals of the season, and it was just a pity his stunning last minute shot against Varteks was not enough to prevent a UEFA Cup exit on away goals.

Voted African Player of the Year in 1998, Hadji began his career with French club Nancy, and also played for Sporting Lisbon and Deportivo La Coruna before launching his Premiership career with Coventry.

Career Record

Season	Club	League Apps	Gls	Cups Apps	Gls
92-93	Nancy (Fra)	32	6	-	-
93-94	Nancy (Fra)	37	11	-	-
94-95	Nancy (Fra)	28	3	-	-
95-96	Nancy (Fra)	42	11	-	-
96-97	Sporting (Por)	27	3	-	-
97-98	Sporting (Por)	9	-	-	-
97-98	Deportivo (Esp)	10	-	-	-
98-99	Deportivo (Esp)	21	2	-	-
99-00	Coventry	33	6	3	-
00-01	Coventry	22 (1)	3	4 (1)	1
01-02	Aston Villa	17 (6)	2	5 (4)	1
TOTAL		**278 (7)**	**47**	**12 (5)**	**2**

▶ *Full Moroccan international (40 caps).*

LEE HENDRIE

Born Birmingham, 18 May 1977.
Joined Villa July 1993 as YTS trainee. July 1994 on professional forms.
Villa debut as sub v Queens Park Rangers, Lge (a) 23/12/1995.

After bouncing back to his best in 2000-01, Lee Hendrie never really managed to reproduce the sparkling form which had established him as one of the Premiership's brightest talents.

Indeed, the midfielder was so concerned about his general lack of spark that he requested to be rested from the match against Manchester United at Old Trafford – a decision he came to regret over the next few weeks.

With Thomas Hitzlsperger making such a big impact, the Birmingham-born midfielder found himself unable to break back into the line-up, although he was also hampered by a late-season injury.

Yet it had all started so promisingly. Hendrie was on target twice against Slaven Belupo in the InterToto Cup and some outstanding early performances not only earned him a new four-year contract, but prompted talk of a possible England recall as Sven Goran Eriksson contemplated his squad for the World Cup finals.

He also scored in a 3-1 win at Liverpool which ranked as the team's best performance of the campaign as well as netting the only goal in the return match against the Merseysiders at Villa Park on Boxing Day.

Those, unfortunately, were his only two Premiership goals and by the end of the season, his thoughts were focussed only on a Villa recall.

Career Record

Season	Club	League Apps	Gls	Cups Apps	Gls
94-95	Aston Villa	-	-	-	-
95-96	Aston Villa	2 (1)	-	-	-
96-97	Aston Villa	- (4)	-	1 (2)	-
97-98	Aston Villa	13 (4)	3	4 (3)	-
98-99	Aston Villa	31 (1)	3	5	-
99-00	Aston Villa	18 (11)	1	4 (5)	3
00-01	Aston Villa	26 (3)	6	2 (3)	-
01-02	Aston Villa	25 (4)	2	10	2
TOTAL		116 (29)	15	26 (13)	5

▶ England international at Full (1 cap) and Under-21 levels.

THOMAS HITZLSPERGER

Born Munich, Germany, 5 April 1982.
Joined Villa August 2000 from Bayern Munich. Free transfer.
Villa debut as sub v Liverpool, League (h) 13/1/2001.

No-one was more delighted about Graham Taylor's appointment than midfielder Thomas Hitzlsperger, whose career suddenly went into orbit following the club's managerial change.

Hitzlsperger, with just one substitute appearance to his name was beginning to wonder if he had a future at Villa Park until that crucial change of leadership.

On the night before his appointment was announced, Taylor watched the former Bayern Munich youngster in action for the reserves, liked what he saw, and immediately promoted him to the first team squad.

Less than two weeks later, Hitzlsperger was handed his first Premiership action of the season when he went on as substitute in front of over 67,000 at Old Trafford, and he has barely looked back.

Although he is still learning his trade, he grew in stature as the season drew to a close, and scored his first senior goal with a superb right foot shot in the 2-2 draw at Leicester.

He also broke into Germany's under-21 team and will undoubtedly be part of his country's plans in their qualification bid for the 2004 European Championships.

Career Record

Season	Club	League Apps	Gls	Cups Apps	Gls
00-01	Aston Villa	- (1)	-	-	-
01-02	Aston Villa	11 (1)	1	-	-
loan	Chesterfield	5 (1)	-	1	-
Villa record		11 (2)	1	-	-
TOTAL		16 (3)	1	1	-

▶ German international at under-18 and Under-21 levels.

ROTTERDAM REVISTED

The 2001-02 campaign marked the 20th anniversary of Villa's European Cup triumph, and a tribute dinner was staged to commemorate the event at the Hilton Metropole Hotel.

Attended by most of the members of the final squad, plus more than 600 supporters and various other Villa celebrities from down the years, the dinner celebrated Villa's 1-0 triumph over Bayern Munich in Rotterdam in May 1982.

The club also commissioned a mural, depicting triumphant skipper Dennis Mortimer and manager Tony Barton, which is now on display in the Holte End concourse.

HASSAN KACHLOUL

Born Agadir, Morocco, 19 February 1973.

Joined Villa July, 2001 from Southampton on a free transfer.

Villa debut v Slaven Belupo, InterToto Cup (h) 21/7/2001

Hassan Kachloul was snapped up on a Bosman transfer and it was something of a mixed season for the Moroccan midfielder. He was a regular until the end of November, but saw his fortunes decline after suffering concussion in the Worthington Cup-tie against Sheffield Wednesday.

He finished the match but later had no recollection of events. His condition gave cause for concern, but although he overcame that particular problem, a succession of other niggling injuries restricted his starting appearances.

Before that, Kachloul had scored a couple of important goals, clinching a home win over Charlton and netting a spectacular volley in a draw at Leeds.

Career Record

Season	Club	League Apps	Gls	Cups Apps	Gls
92-93	Nimes (Fra)	19	1	-	-
93-94	Nimes (Fra)	37	17	-	-
94-95	Nimes (Fra)	32	8	-	-
95-96	Dunkerque (Fra)	28	8	-	-
96-97	Metz (Fra)	7	-	-	-
97-98	St Etienne (Fra)	16	-	-	-
98-99	Southampton	18 (4)	5	2	-
99-00	Southampton	29 (3)	5	4 (1)	-
00-01	Southampton	26 (6)	4	3 (1)	1
01-02	Aston Villa	17 (5)	2	8 (1)	-
TOTAL		**227 (18)**	**48**	**17 (3)**	**1**

▶ Full Moroccan international (4 caps).

OLOF MELLBERG

Born Gullspang, Sweden, 3 September 1977.

Joined Villa July 2001 from Racing Santander (Spain), £5.6m.

Villa debut v Tottenham Hotspur, Lge (a) 18/8/2001.

Scandinavian footballers have invariably done well in the Premiership, and there was never any danger of Olof Mellberg proving an exception to the rule.

Signed from Spanish club Racing Santander for £5.6m, the Swedish central defender was composure personified from the moment he caught the eye with a superb debut against Spurs.

Mellberg's strong tackling and sense of anticipation made him one of the most reliable defenders in the top flight, and he would surely have been an ever-present but for the ankle injury he sustained in the second leg UEFA Cup clash away to NK Varteks.

That kept him out of the side for seven matches, but otherwise he was an automatic choice, forming sound partnerships alongside both Alpay Ozalan and Steve Staunton.

Career Record

Season	Club	League Apps	Gls	Cups Apps	Gls
1996	Dagefors (Swe)	22	-	-	-
1997	AIK Stockholm (Swe)	22	-	-	-
1998	AIK Stockholm (Swe)	21	-	-	-
98-99	R Santander (Esp)	25	-	-	-
99-00	R Santander (Esp)	37	-	-	-
01-02	R Santander (Esp)	36	-	-	-
01-02	Aston Villa	31	-	4	-
TOTAL		**194**	**-**	**4**	**-**

▶ Full Swedish international (21 caps).

JOHN McGRATH

Born Limerick, 27 March 1980.

Joined Villa Signed Professional forms in August 1999.

Villa debut as sub v Chelsea, League (a) 1/1/2001.

John McGrath's lengthy injury lay-off ensured there was little prospect of him adding to his senior appearances. A damaged ankle kept him out of action for four months.

Career Record

Season	Club	League Apps	Gls	Cups Apps	Gls
00-01	Aston Villa	- (3)	-	-	-
01-02	Aston Villa	-	-	-	-
TOTAL		**- (3)**	**-**	**-**	**-**

▶ Republic of Ireland Under-21 international.

PAUL MERSON

Born Northolt, Middlesex, 20 March 1968.

Joined Villa September 1998 from Middlesbrough, £6.75m.

Villa debut v Wimbledon, Lge (h) 12/9/1998.

After two seasons as Villa's undisputed Player of the Year, Paul Merson kept a somewhat lower profile in 2001-02, being hampered by injury problems.

A limited number of games meant Merson's goals were also at a premium, although he did have the satisfaction of scoring against one of his former clubs, Arsenal, at Highbury, and against his boyhood favourites Chelsea at Villa Park on the day Graham Taylor took charge for the first time.

Having now turned 34, the immensely-popular Merse is no longer able to cover the ground he used to, although there are few players in the Premiership with greater vision or the ability to make accurate passes over long distances.

Villa paid Middlesbrough £6.75m for his services four years ago and have received a good return on their investment.

Career Record

Season	Club	League Apps	Gls	Cups Apps	Gls
86-87	Arsenal	5 (2)	3	-	-
(loan)	Brentford	6 (1)	-	1 (1)	-
87-88	Arsenal	7 (8)	5	1 (1)	-
88-89	Arsenal	29 (8)	10	7 (1)	4
89-90	Arsenal	21 (8)	7	4 (3)	-
90-91	Arsenal	36 (1)	13	12	3
91-92	Arsenal	41 (1)	12	9	1
92-93	Arsenal	32 (1)	6	17	2
93-94	Arsenal	24 (9)	7	15 (1)	5
94-95	Arsenal	24	4	11 (1)	3
95-96	Arsenal	38	5	9	-
96-97	Arsenal	32	6	8	3
97-98	Middlesbrough	45	12	10	4
98-99	Middlesbrough	3	-	-	-
98-99	Aston Villa	21 (5)	5	1	-
99-00	Aston Villa	24 (8)	5	10 (2)	-
00-01	Aston Villa	38	6	7	-
01-02	Aston Villa	18 (3)	2	6	1
Villa record		101 (16)	18	24 (2)	1
TOTAL		**444 (55)**	**108**	**128 (10)**	**26**

▶ England international at Full (21 caps, 3 goals), Under-21 and 'B' levels.

ALPAY OZALAN

Born Izmir (Turkey), 29 May 1973.

Joined Villa July 2000 from Fenerbahce (Turkey), £5.6m.

Villa debut v Leicester City, Lge (a) 19/8/2000.

No-one was happier to see the end of a personally frustrating season than Alpay Ozalan, Villa's dependable and hugely popular central defender.

The Turkish international was a commanding figure at the heart of Villa's defence for the first few months of the campaign and was an ever-present until he was struck down by damaged ankle ligaments in the home match against Leicester City on the first weekend of December.

Initial medical reports indicated the former Fenerbahce player would be sidelined for no more than four weeks, but his absence eventually extended to more than four months, during which time he headed off to Germany for specialist treatment from Bayern Munich physio Dr Hans Wilhelm Muller-Wohlfahrt.

While Republic of Ireland international Steve Staunton proved a more-than-able deputy, Alpay was keenly missed by the Holte Enders with whom he has struck up a special affinity during his time as a Villa man.

Their affection for the popular Turk was never more evident than when he joined in the players' lap of appreciation after the final home match against Southampton. Even though he had not kicked a ball for nearly five months, Alpay received a rapturous ovation.

Career Record

Season	Club	League Apps	Gls	Cups Apps	Gls
92-93	Altay (Tur)	19 (4)	1	-	-
93-94	Besiktas (Tur)	8 (2)	-	-	-
94-95	Besiktas (Tur)	29	3	-	-
95-96	Besiktas (Tur)	31	2	-	-
96-97	Besiktas (Tur)	25	3	-	-
97-98	Besiktas (Tur)	26	1	-	-
98-99	Besiktas (Tur)	27	-	-	-
99-00	Fenerbahce (Tur)	29	3	-	-
00-01	Aston Villa	33	-	3	-
01-02	Aston Villa	14	-	10	-
Villa record		47	-	13	-
TOTAL		**241 (6)**	**13**	**13**	**-**

▶ Full Turkish international (62 caps, 4 goals).

JLLOYD SAMUEL

Born Trinidad & Tobago
29 March 1981.

Joined Villa July 1997 as YTS. January 1999 on professional forms.

Villa debut as sub v Chester City, Worthington Cup (h) 21/9/1999.

In his third full season as a professional, Jlloyd Samuel finally made the breakthrough to Villa's first team, with a little help from a trip to Kent.

Until he joined Gillingham on loan in October, there had seemed little prospect of the promising young full-back adding to the half dozen appearances he had made during the course of the previous two seasons. But Samuel benefited enormously from nine First Division games for the Gills, and when Villa were short of defensive cover for the match at West Ham on 5th December, he was hastily recalled.

He was soon making his seventh senior appearance, too, taking over in the second half when Mark Delaney suffered damaged medial knee ligaments.

Samuel held the right-back position for the next seven games during Delaney's absence and performed so well that he was then switched to his more natural left-back spot, where he continued to impress.

Although he was eventually rested, Samuel did more than enough to suggest he has a key role to play in Villa's future plans.

Career Record

Season	Club	League Apps	Gls	Cups Apps	Gls
99-00	Aston Villa	5 (4)	-	- (1)	-
00-01	Aston Villa	1 (2)	-	4	-
01-02	Aston Villa	17 (6)	-	1 (2)	-
loan	Gillingham	9	-	-	-
Villa record		23 (6)	-	1 (2)	-
TOTAL		**32 (6)**	**-**	**1 (2)**	**-**

▶ England international at Under-18, Under-20 and Under-21 levels.

KEEPING UP WITH HISTORY

Peter Schmeichel wrote himself into Villa's record books as the first goalkeeper in the club's history to score in a competitive match. He smashed the ball home in stoppage time at Goodison Park on 20th October after Darius Vassell had flicked on Steve Staunton's corner, although that memorable moment wasn't enough to prevent a 3-2 defeat at the hands of Everton.

PETER SCHMEICHEL

Born Gladsaxe, Denmark,
18 November 1963.

Joined Villa July, 2001, from Sporting Lisbon (Portugal) on a free transfer.

Villa debut v Slaven Belupo, InterToto Cup (h) 21/7/2001.

Villa pulled off the transfer coup of the year when Peter Schmeichel returned to the Premiership.

Having won an incredible treble with Manchester United in 1999, followed by two years in Portugal with Sporting Lisbon, Schmeichel was tempted back by the prospect of filling the void created by David James' departure.

Schmeichel's leadership qualities were such that he took over as captain whenever Paul Merson was out of the team. He also displayed an amazing spirit of adventure, frequently venturing upfield if Villa were trailing in the closing minutes – and even scored a stoppage time goal at Everton in October.

With Villa anxious to nurture Peter Enckelman's career, however, Schmeichel was informed his one-year contract would not be extended and he signed for newly-promoted Manchester City.

Career Record

Season	Club	League Apps	Gls	Cups Apps	Gls
83-84	Hvidovre (Den)	30	-	-	-
84-85	Hvidovre (Den)	28	-	-	-
85-86	Hvidovre (Den)	30	-	-	-
86-87	Brondby (Den)	23	-	-	-
87-88	Brondby (Den)	26	-	-	-
88-89	Brondby (Den)	26	-	-	-
89-90	Brondby (Den)	26	-	-	-
90-91	Brondby (Den)	18	-	-	-
91-92	Man Utd	40	-	13	-
92-93	Man Utd	42	-	6	-
93-94	Man Utd	40	-	-	-
94-95	Man Utd	32	-	11	-
95-96	Man Utd	36	-	9	-
96-97	Man Utd	36	-	13	-
97-98	Man Utd	32	-	12	-
98-99	Man Utd	34	-	22	-
99-00	Sporting (Por)	28	-	-	-
01-02	Sporting (Por)	22	-	-	-
01-02	Aston Villa	29	*37	7	8
TOTAL		578	37	113	8

* Schmeichel scored at Everton 20/10/01
▶ Full Danish international (129 caps, 1 goal).

STEVE STAUNTON

Born Drogheda, Ireland, 19 January 1969.

Rejoined Villa December 2000 from Liverpool. Free transfer.

Second Villa debut v Chelsea, League (a) 1/1/2001.

Steve Staunton could hardly have imagined, when he returned to Villa Park from Anfield, that his career would once again scale such lofty heights.

The dependable defender had cost Villa £1.1m when he signed from Liverpool in 1991, but this time he arrived on a free transfer. Liverpool's loss was Villa's gain, for Staunton has proved invaluable during his second spell in the Midlands.

Although he was regarded primarily as a back-up player at the start of the season, he found himself called into action after Olof Mellberg was injured and then landed a permanent central defensive role when Alpay was laid low.

Staunton's international career has also been revived, with him becoming the most capped Republic of Ireland player.

Career Record

Season	Club	League Apps	Gls	Cups Apps	Gls
86-87	Liverpool	-	-	-	-
87-88	Liverpool	-	-	-	-
loan	Bradford City	7 (1)	-	3	-
88-89	Liverpool	17 (4)	-	8	1
89-90	Liverpool	18 (2)	-	4 (2)	3
90-91	Liverpool	20 (4)	-	9	2
91-92	Aston Villa	37	4	6	-
92-93	Aston Villa	42	2	9	-
93-94	Aston Villa	24	3	9	-
94-95	Aston Villa	34 (1)	5	8	-
95-96	Aston Villa	11 (2)	-	3 (3)	1
96-97	Aston Villa	30	2	5	-
97-98	Aston Villa	27	1	11 (1)	1
98-99	Liverpool	31	-	8 (1)	-
99-00	Liverpool	7 (5)	-	4	1
00-01	Liverpool	- (1)	-	- (1)	-
	Aston Villa	13 (1)	-	3	-
loan	C Palace	6	1	-	-
01-02	Aston Villa	35 (3)	-	5	-
Villa record		248 (7)	17	59 (4)	2
TOTAL		**359 (24)**	**18**	**95 (8)**	**9**

▶ Full Republic of Ireland international (98 caps, 8 goals).

STEVE STONE

Born Gateshead, 20 August 1971.

Joined Villa March 1999 from Nottingham Forest for £5.5m.

Villa debut v Tottenham Hotspur, Lge (a) 13/3/1999.

Steve Stone found himself very much on the fringes of Villa's first team squad throughout last season, having to settle for just 13 Premiership starting appearances and half a dozen in cup competitions.

It really was a case of treading water for someone who had arguably been Villa's most improved player the previous season, prompting suggestions at one stage of a possible recall to the England set-up.

If Stone's career effectively stood still, however, his reliability and effectiveness were beyond question whenever his services were required by either John Gregory or Graham Taylor.

On more than one occasion, he breathed fresh life into the right of Villa's midfield when introduced as a substitute, although the man who netted a couple of goals during his nine-cap international career will be disappointed to have scored only once for Villa in 2001-02.

The former Nottingham Forest midfielder was on target with Villa's second as they established a 2-0 lead at Highbury before going down 3-2 to Arsenal.

Career Record

Season	Club	League Apps	Gls	Cups Apps	Gls
91-92	Nottingham Forest	- (1)	-	-	-
92-93	Nottingham Forest	11 (1)	1	- (1)	-
93-94	Nottingham Forest	45	5	9	-
94-95	Nottingham Forest	41	5	6	-
95-96	Nottingham Forest	34	7	16	2
96-97	Nottingham Forest	5	-	-	-
97-98	Nottingham Forest	27 (2)	2	-	-
98-99	Nottingham Forest	26	3	4	2
	Aston Villa	9 (1)	-	-	-
99-00	Aston Villa	10 (14)	1	5 (6)	2
00-01	Aston Villa	33 (1)	2	8	1
01-02	Aston Villa	14 (8)	1	6 (4)	0
Villa record		66 (24)	4	19 (10)	0
TOTAL		**255 (28)**	**27**	**54 (11)**	**7**

▶ Full England international (9 caps, 2 goals).

IAN TAYLOR

Born Birmingham, 4 June 1968.
Joined Villa December 1994 in straight swop deal with Guy Whittingham from Sheffield Wed.
Villa debut v Arsenal, Lge (a) 26/12/1994.

He has suffered his fair share of injuries down the years, but last season was undoubtedly the nadir of Ian Taylor's career.

It was apparent when the hard-tackling midfielder reported for pre-season training that his summer rest had not cured the knee problem which had troubled him since the end of the previous campaign. He duly underwent surgery which kept him out of action until mid-October, when he returned with a goal in the 2-0 home victory over Fulham.

That should have been the launch of an extended run in the side, but he was then laid low by a groin injury, once again returning to the starting line-up with a goal at Sunderland on New Year's Day and another in the third round FA Cup defeat by Manchester United.

Once again, however, he was sidelined for a lengthy spell by another knee injury, before calf and hamstring problems curtailed his campaign three matches early. Before that, however, he had made a third return to the side with a headed goal at Bolton, which once again underlined how effective a fit Ian Taylor can be.

Manager Graham Taylor certainly has a lot of faith in him, offering a one-year contract extension which the player signed in May.

Career Record

Season	Club	League Apps	Gls	Cups Apps	Gls
92-93	Port Vale	41	15	15	4
93-94	Port Vale	42	13	8	3
94-95	Sheffield Wednesday	9 (5)	1	2 (2)	1
	Aston Villa	21	1	2	-
95-96	Aston Villa	24 (1)	3	7 (2)	2
96-97	Aston Villa	29 (5)	2	3	1
97-98	Aston Villa	30 (2)	6	12	3
98-99	Aston Villa	31 (2)	4	4 (1)	-
99-00	Aston Villa	25 (4)	5	10 (2)	4
00-01	Aston Villa	25 (4)	4	6	1
01-02	Aston Villa	7 (9)	3	2	1
Villa record		185 (18)	28	46 (5)	12
TOTAL		**284 (32)**	**57**	**71 (7)**	**20**

DARIUS VASSELL

Born Birmingham, 30 June 1980.
Joined Villa July 1996 as YTS trainee. March 1998 on professional forms.
Villa debut as sub v Middlesbrough, Lge (h) 23/8/1998.

Darius Vassell started the campaign unsure about his place in the Villa line-up – and ended it as an England international bound for the World Cup finals.

The young striker earned a place in Sven Goran Eriksson's squad for Japan and South Korea after proving that he could reproduce his blistering domestic form on to the international stage.

Apart from reaching double figures for Villa, he marked his full international debut with a spectacular volley against Holland in February and followed up with a deflected goal in his third England game, a 4-0 victory over Paraguay.

Previously known as a bit-part player – albeit an effective one – Vassell really came of age as a footballer, showing he could handle a full 90 minutes and establishing himself as a first team regular despite the presence of more experienced strikers.

His substitute appearances still outnumber his senior starts, but that will undoubtedly change during the opening stages of 2002-03.

If his England debut goal was his crowning moment, the goal which gave him most satisfaction was the one against Manchester United in the opening Premiership home match.

Career Record

Season	Club	League Apps	Gls	Cups Apps	Gls
98-99	Aston Villa	- (6)	-	- (5)	2
99-00	Aston Villa	1 (10)	-	1 (4)	-
00-01	Aston Villa	5 (18)	4	2 (5)	1
01-02	Aston Villa	30 (6)	12	3 (5)	2
TOTAL		**36 (40)**	**16**	**6 (19)**	**5**

▶ England international at Full (5 caps, 3 goals), Under-21 and Under-18 levels.

DEADLY DARIUS

Darius Vassell became only the 15th Villa player to score on his England debut when he netted with a scissor kick in the 1-1 draw against Holland in Amsterdam in February.

Jlloyd Samuel, meanwhile, became the 25th Villa man to represent England under-21s – 25 years after John Deehan had been the first.

ALAN WRIGHT

Born Ashton-under-Lyme, 28 September 1971.

Joined Villa March 1995 from Blackburn Rovers, £900,000.

Villa debut v West Ham United, Lge (h) 18/3/1995.

It was very much a bitter-sweet season for long-serving defender Alan Wright. In November he joined the elite band of Villa players who have made more than 300 starts for the club, yet subsequently, he had to endure his longest spell out of the side since arriving more than seven years ago.

Left out after the FA Cup defeat by Manchester United in January, he had to wait until the penultimate game of the season for a recall, having being kept out by the impressive form of Jlloyd Samuel and Gareth Barry. For all that, his presence meant that Villa were probably better served at left-back than any club in the country, and the unruffled manner in which he accepted his demotion underlined what an outstanding professional he is.

As ever, he went about his business, both on the pitch and in training, with the quiet dedication which has been the trademark of his career. His reward was a return to the line-up for the last two matches.

Career Record

Season	Club	League Apps	Gls	Cups Apps	Gls
87-88	Blackpool	- (1)	-	-	-
88-90	Blackpool	14 (2)	-	3 (1)	-
89-90	Blackpool	20 (4)	-	9 (3)	-
90-91	Blackpool	45	-	12	-
91-92	Blackpool	12	-	5	-
	Blackburn Rovers	32 (1)	1	5	-
92-93	Blackburn Rovers	24	-	9	-
93-94	Blackburn Rovers	7 (5)	-	2	-
94-95	Blackburn Rovers	4 (1)	-	- (1)	-
	Aston Villa	8	-	-	-
95-96	Aston Villa	38	2	13	-
96-97	Aston Villa	38	1	7	-
97-98	Aston Villa	35 (2)	-	13	-
98-99	Aston Villa	38	-	7	-
99-00	Aston Villa	31 (1)	1	10	-
00-01	Aston Villa	35 (1)	1	8	-
01-02	Aston Villa	23	-	9	-
Villa record		246 (4)	-	67	-
TOTAL		**404 (18)**	-	**112 (5)**	-

▶ England Under-21 international.

Obituaries

STAN LYNN

Villa lost a true legend when Stan Lynn died in April at the age of 73. Noted for his thunderbolt shot, the tough-tackling Bolton-born full-back made 323 appearances for the club between 1950 and 1962, and played in the 1957 FA Cup-winning team.

Lynn began his career with Accrington Stanley in 1947, joining Villa three years later. Apart from the '57 Wembley triumph over Manchester United, Lynn also helped Villa to the old Second Division title in 1960 and played in the first leg of the League Cup final the following year before making the short trip across the city to join Blues.

His powerful shot brought him 38 goals for Villa, including a hat-trick against Sunderland in 1958. He ended his playing days with Stourbridge.

LES SEALEY

The build-up to Villa's opening Premiership home match against Manchester United last August was overshadowed by the death of former goalkeeper Les Sealey at the age of 43.

Sealey had given excellent service to both clubs, although it was at Coventry City that he began his career in the 1970s before joining Luton.

It was at Old Trafford, however, that he made his greatest impact, helping United to victory in the 1990 FA Cup final replay against Crystal Palace and a European Cup Winners' Cup final triumph over Barcelona 12 months later.

Sealey joined Villa on a free transfer from United in the summer of 1991 and made 22 appearances before returning to Manchester in January, 1993.

JOHN SHARPLES

Former Villa defender John Sharples died in September, aged 67. Born in Wolverhampton, Sharples played for two seasons as an amateur before turning professional in 1955.

He made 13 first team appearances in 1958-59 as a stand-in for Peter Aldis before joining Walsall and helping the Saddlers to promotion from the old Fourth Division to the old Second Division.

BRUCE NORMANSELL

Bruce Normansell, a former Villa director and vice-chairman, died in September, aged 84. He had served the club during the 1950s and 1960s, joining the board following the death in 1955 of his father Fred, who had been chairman for 19 years.

PREMIER STATS

FINAL TABLE

		P	W	D	L	F	A	W	D	L	F	A	W	D	L	F	A	Pts
1	Arsenal	38	12	4	3	42	25	14	5	0	37	11	26	9	3	79	36	87
2	Liverpool	38	12	5	2	33	14	12	3	4	34	16	24	8	6	67	30	80
3	Manchester United	38	11	2	6	40	17	13	3	3	47	28	24	5	9	87	45	77
4	Newcastle United	38	12	3	4	40	23	9	5	5	34	29	21	8	9	74	52	71
5	Leeds United	38	9	6	4	31	21	9	6	4	22	16	18	12	8	53	37	66
6	Chelsea	38	11	4	4	43	21	6	9	4	23	17	17	13	8	66	38	64
7	West Ham United	38	12	4	3	32	14	3	4	12	16	43	15	8	15	48	57	53
8	**Aston Villa**	38	8	7	4	22	17	4	7	8	24	30	12	14	12	46	47	50
9	Tottenham Hotspur	38	10	4	5	32	24	4	4	11	17	29	14	8	16	49	53	50
10	Blackburn Rovers	38	8	6	5	33	20	4	4	11	22	31	12	10	16	55	51	46
11	Southampton	38	7	5	7	23	22	5	4	10	23	32	12	9	17	46	54	45
12	Middlesbrough	38	7	5	7	23	26	5	4	10	12	21	12	9	17	35	47	45
13	Fulham	38	7	7	5	21	16	3	7	9	15	28	10	14	14	36	44	44
14	Charlton Athletic	38	5	6	8	23	30	5	8	6	15	19	10	14	14	38	49	44
15	Everton	38	8	4	7	26	23	3	6	10	19	34	10	14	14	45	57	43
16	Bolton Wanderers	38	5	7	7	20	31	4	6	9	24	31	9	13	16	44	62	40
17	Sunderland	38	7	7	5	18	16	3	3	13	11	35	10	10	18	29	51	40
18	Ipswich Town	38	6	4	9	20	24	3	5	11	21	40	9	9	20	41	64	36
19	Derby County	38	5	4	10	20	26	3	2	14	13	37	8	6	24	33	63	30
20	Leicester City	38	3	7	9	15	34	2	6	11	15	30	5	13	20	30	64	28

PREMIERSHIP ROLL OF HONOUR

Champions: Arsenal
Runners-up: Liverpool
Third place: Manchester United
Additional Champions League qualifiers: Newcastle United
UEFA Cup qualifiers: Leeds United, Chelsea, Blackburn Rovers and Ipswich Town*
InterToto Cup qualifiers: Aston Villa and Fulham
Relegated: Ipswich Town, Derby County and Leicester City
FA Cup winners: Arsenal
Worthington Cup winners: Blackburn Rovers
Promoted from Nationwide Division One: Manchester City, West Bromwich Albion and Birmingham City
*Ipswich qualify through the Fair Play system.

FACTS & FIGURES

Of the 380 games played in the Premiership, 165 resulted in home wins, 114 in away wins and 101 were drawn. A total of 1001 goals were scored at an average of 2.63 per game, with 557 scored by home teams and 444 by visiting teams.

Most goals scored: 87, Manchester United
Most home goals: 42, Arsenal
Most away goals: 47, Manchester United
Least goals scored: 29, Sunderland
Least home goals: 15, Leicester City
Least away goals: 11, Sunderland
Least goals conceded: 30, Liverpool
Least home goals conceded: 14, Liverpool
Least away goals conceded: 11, Arsenal
Most goals conceded: 64, Ipswich Town and Leicester City
Most home goals conceded: 34, Leicester City
Most away goals conceded: 43, West Ham United
Highest goals aggregate: 132, Manchester United
Lowest goals aggregate: 80, Fulham and Sunderland
Best home record: 41pts, Liverpool
Best away record: 47pts, Arsenal
Worst home record: 16pts, Leicester City
Worst away record: 11pts, Derby County
Highest home score:
Blackburn Rovers 7 West Ham United 1, 14.10.01
Highest away score: Ipswich Town 0 Liverpool 6, 9.2.02
Highest attendance:
67,683, Manchester United v Middlesbrough, 16.9.01
Lowest attendance:
15,412, Leicester City v Middlesbrough, 16.9.01

LEADING SCORERS
(including Cup & European games)

- 35 Ruud Van Nistelrooy (Manchester United)
- 32 Thierry Henry (Arsenal)
- 29 Jimmy Floyd Hasselbaink (Chelsea)
- 27 Michael Owen (Liverpool)
- 27 Alan Shearer (Newcastle United)
- 25 Ole Gunnar Solskjaer (Manchester United)
- 23 Eidur Gudjohnsen (Chelsea)
- 18 Andy Cole (Blackburn Rovers)
- 17 Fredrik Ljungberg (Arsenal)
- 17 Sylvain Wiltord (Arsenal)
- **16 Juan Pablo Angel (Aston Villa)**
- 16 David Beckham (Manchester United)
- 16 Robbie Fowler (Leeds United)

GOLDEN BOOT WINNER
(Premiership goals only)

- 24 Thierry Henry (Arsenal)

Other leading Premiership scorers:
- 23 Jimmy Floyd Hasselbaink (Chelsea)
- 23 Alan Shearer (Newcastle United)
- 23 Ruud Van Nistelrooy (Manchester United)
- 19 Michael Owen (Liverpool)
- 17 Ole Gunnar Solskjaer (Manchester United)
- 15 Robbie Fowler (Liverpool)
- 14 Marian Pahars (Southampton)
- 14 Eidur Gudjohnsen (Chelsea)
- 13 Andy Cole (Blackburn Rovers)
- **12 Juan Pablo Angel (Aston Villa)**
- 12 Michael Ricketts (Bolton Wanderers)
- **12 Darius Vassell (Aston Villa)**

PREMIERSHIP HAT-TRICKS
Robbie Fowler (Liverpool) v Leicester City 20.10.01
Paul Kitson (West Ham Utd) v Charlton Athletic 19.11.01
Ruud van Nistelrooy (Manchester Utd) v Saints 22.12.01
Robbie Fowler (Leeds Utd) v Bolton 26.12.01
Ole Gunnar Solskjaer (Manchester Utd) v Bolton 29.01.02
Jimmy Floyd Hasselbaink (Chelsea) v Spurs 13.03.02
Fredi Bobic (Bolton Wanderers) v Ipswich Town 6.4.02

HAPPY ANNIVERSARY

The Premier League celebrated its 10th anniversary in 2001-02, and attendances again showed a substantial increase. More than 13 million people passed through the turnstiles for league fixtures, at an average of 34,324 per match. Attendances have improved every year since the inception of the Premiership in 1992-93, as these figures illustrate:

Season	Av. att
92-93	21,125
93-94	23,040
94-95	24,271
95-96	27,550
96-97	28,434
97-98	29,190
98-99	30,580
99-00	30,707
00-01	32,821
01-02	34,324

THE GATE LEAGUE

		Total	Average
1	Manchester United	1,283,594	67,557
2	Newcastle United	976,079	51,372
3	Sunderland	888,136	46,744
4	Liverpool	780,182	43,343
5	Leeds United	755,287	39,751
6	Chelsea	742,383	39,072
7	Arsenal	723,036	38,054
8	**Aston Villa**	**665,223**	**35,011**
9	Tottenham Hotspur	665,015	35,000
10	Everton	604,841	33,602
11	West Ham United	564,410	31,356
12	Southampton	582,019	30,632
13	Derby County	571,735	30,091
14	Middlesbrough	540,719	28,458
15	Blackburn Rovers	493,551	25,976
16	Bolton Wanderers	476,867	25,098
17	Ipswich Town	464,263	24,434
18	Charlton Athletic	433,744	24,096
19	Leicester City	376,871	19,835
20	Fulham	367,519	19,343

TELEVISION STARS

Although Arsenal were crowned champions, Manchester United were the most popular club with BSkyB, making 15 live appearances on the satellite channel. Liverpool were second on 14, with the Gunners appearing on 13 occasions. In terms of total TV appearances, including coverage by Pay Per View and ITV, Liverpool were the most featured club with 37, compared with 36 each for Arsenal and United. The full table (total appearances in brackets):

	BSkyB	PPV	ITV
Liverpool (37)	14	6	17
Arsenal (36)	13	4	19
Manchester United (36)	15	6	15
Leeds United (29)	11	6	12
Newcastle United (26)	7	6	13
Chelsea (23)	7	6	10
Tottenham Hotspur (23)	7	5	11
Ipswich Town (20)	7	1	12
Blackburn Rovers (18)	4	6	8
Sunderland (17)	6	3	8
Bolton Wanderers (17)	5	1	11
Everton (17)	5	5	7
Aston Villa (16)	**6**	**4**	**6**
Charlton Athletic (16)	3	5	8
West Ham United (16)	3	4	9
Southampton (16)	3	4	9
Fulham (14)	6	2	6
Derby County (13)	3	3	7
Middlesbrough (12)	4	1	7
Leicester City (10)	3	2	5

FIRST TEAM APPEARANCES & GOALSCORERS

	LEAGUE Apps	Gls	FA CUP Apps	Gls	LEAGUE CUP Apps	Gls	UEFA CUP Apps	Gls	INTERTOTO CUP Apps	Gls	TOTAL Apps	Gls
Juan Pablo ANGEL	26 (3)	12	1	-	1	-	1 (1)	-	1 (1)	2	30 (5)	16
Bosko BALABAN	- (8)	-	-	-	1 (1)	-	1	-	-	-	2 (9)	-
Gareth BARRY	16 (4)	-	- (1)	-	-	-	- (1)	-	6	-	22 (4)	-
George BOATENG	37	1	1	-	1 (1)	-	2	-	6	-	47 (1)	1
Peter CROUCH	7	2	-	-	-	-	-	-	-	-	7	2
Mark DELANEY	30	-	-	-	1	-	2	-	6	-	39	-
Dion DUBLIN	9 (12)	4	-	-	1 (1)	1	- (1)	-	5 (1)	1	15 (15)	6
Peter ENCKELMAN	9	-	-	-	-	-	-	-	4 (1)	-	13 (1)	-
David GINOLA	- (5)	-	-	-	1 (1)	-	1 (1)	-	2 (2)	2	4 (9)	2
Moustapha HADJI	17 (6)	2	- (1)	-	2	-	2	1	1 (3)	-	22 (10)	3
Lee HENDRIE	25 (4)	2	1	-	2	-	1	-	6	2	35 (4)	4
Thomas HITZLSPERGER	11 (1)	1	-	-	-	-	-	-	-	-	11 (1)	1
Hassan KACHLOUL	17 (5)	2	-	-	2	-	2	-	4 (1)	-	25 (6)	2
Olof MELLBERG	32	-	1	-	1	-	2	-	-	-	36	-
Paul MERSON	18 (3)	2	1	-	-	-	-	-	5	1	24 (3)	3
ALPAY Ozalan	14	-	-	-	2	-	2	-	6	-	24	-
Jlloyd SAMUEL	17 (6)	-	1	-	-	-	-	-	- (2)	-	18 (8)	-
Peter SCHMEICHEL	29	1	1	-	2	-	2	-	2	-	36	1
Steve STAUNTON	30 (3)	-	1	-	2	-	-	-	2	-	35 (3)	-
Steve STONE	14 (8)	1	- (1)	-	1	-	1 (1)	-	4 (2)	-	20 (12)	1
Ian TAYLOR	7 (9)	3	1	1	1	-	-	-	-	-	9 (9)	4
Darius VASSELL	30 (6)	12	1	-	- (1)	-	1	-	1 (4)	2	33 (11)	14
Alan WRIGHT	23	-	1	-	1	-	2	-	5	-	32	-

UNUSED SUBSTITUTES

(figures in brackets refer to cup matches)

Peter Enckelman 29(6), Bosko Balaban 15(1), David Ginola 11(2), Gareth Barry 9(3), Boaz Myhill 8(4), Dion Dublin 4, Hassan Kachloul 4, Jlloyd Samuel 3(6), Juan Pablo Angel 3(4), Lee Hendrie 3, Paul Merson 3(1), Moustapha Hadji 3(1), Jonathan Bewers 2(2), Steve Staunton 1(6), Thomas Hitzlsperger 1(1), George Boateng 1, Ian Taylor 1, Alan Wright 1, Wayne Henderson 1, Stephen Cooke (1), Mark Delaney (1), Stefan Moore (1), Darius Vassell (1).

EVER-PRESENTS

▶ No player achieved an ever-present record during the 2001-02 campaign, although George Boateng was involved in every match. The only games he did not start were against Sheffield Wednesday in the Worthington Cup, when he went on as substitute for Moustapha Hadji, and the Premiership fixture at Sunderland, where he remained on the bench.

GOALSCORERS IN FRIENDLY GAMES

Stefan Moore 8, Richard Walker 6, Juan Pablo Angel 4, Stephen Cooke 4, Peter Hynes 2, Darius Vassell 1, Moustapha Hadji 1, Jay Smith 1, Andy Marfell 1, Thomas Hitzlsperger 1, Gavin Melaugh 1, Michael Standing 1, Danny Haynes 1, Bosko Balaban 1, Lee Hendrie 1, own goals 1.

HIGHEST AND LOWEST

Highest home attendance:
42,632 v Manchester United 26.08.01
Lowest home attendance:
23,431 v Reading (Worthington Cup, third round) 10.10.01
Highest away attendance:
67,592 v Manchester United 23.02.02
Lowest away attendance:
3,000 v Slaven Belupo (InterToto Cup, third round) 14.07.01
Biggest victory:
4-1 v Basel (InterToto Cup final, 2nd leg) 21.08.01
Heaviest defeat: 0-3 v Newcastle United (a) 02.11.01 and v Blackburn Rovers (a) 05.03.02

VILLA STATS

DEBUTANTS
▶ Six players made their Villa debuts this season:
Peter Schmeichel v Slaven Belupo (IT Cup) (h)
Hassan Kachloul v Slaven Belupo (IT Cup) (h)
Moustapha Hadji as sub v Slaven Belupo (IT Cup) (h)
Olof Mellberg v Tottenham Hotspur (a)
Bosko Balaban as sub v Manchester United (h)
Peter Crouch v Bolton Wanderers (a)

PENALTIES
▶ Villa were awarded three penalties during the season:
Scored: Juan Pablo Angel v Bolton Wanderers (h) (27.10.01) beat Steve Banks.
Scored: Juan Pablo Angel v Tottenham Hotspur (h) (29.12.01) beat Kasey Keller.
Missed: Gareth Barry v Arsenal (h) (17.03.02) saved by David Seaman.

▶ Penalties conceded were:
Louis Saha for Fulham at Villa Park (14.10.01), shot wide.
Paolo Di Canio for West Ham at Upton Park (05.12.01), Saved by Peter Enckelman.
Jari Litmanen for Liverpool at Villa Park (26.12.01), hit the post.
Kevin Phillips for Sunderland at the Stadium of Light (01.01.02), saved by Peter Schmeichel.
Graham Stuart for Charlton Athletic at The Valley (21.01.02), saved by Peter Schmeichel, but scored from the rebound.
Paolo Di Canio for West Ham at Villa Park (02.03.02), beat Peter Schmeichel.
Muzzy Izzet for Leicester City at Filbert Street (20.4.02), beat Peter Enckelman.
Eidur Gudjohnsen for Chelsea at Stamford Bridge (11.05.02), beat Peter Enckelman.

RED CARDS
▶ Two Villa players were sent off:
Dion Dublin against Southampton at St Mary's (24.9.01) for violent conduct. Later rescinded to a yellow card.
David Ginola against Leicester City (01.12.01) for violent conduct.
Manager John Gregory was ordered from the dug-out against Liverpool (26.12.01) for comments he made to a match official.

HOLTE END v WITTON END
▶ Of 59 goals scored at Villa Park in all competitions, 35 went in at the Holte End (19 for Villa, 16 against) and 24 at the Witton End (13 for Villa, 11 against).

▶ Four opposing players were sent off against Villa:
Steven Gerrard (Liverpool) at Anfield (8.9.01) for dangerous play.
Rory Delap (Southampton) at St Mary's (24.9.01) for a professional foul.
Alan Smith (Leeds United) at Elland Road (25.11.01) for violent conduct.
Francois Grenet (Derby County) at Villa Park (12.01.02) for dangerous play.

ARRIVALS
Hassan Kachloul 19.06.01 from Southampton on a free transfer.
Moustapha Hadji 05.07.01 from Coventry City for £4.5m.
Peter Schmeichel 12.07.01 from Sporting Lisbon on a free transfer.
Olof Mellberg 18.07.01 from Racing Santander (Spain) for £5.6m.
Bosko Balaban 11.08.01 from Dinamo Zagreb (Croatia) for £5.8m.
Peter Crouch 27.03.02 from Portsmouth for £4.5m.

DEPARTURES
Julian Joachim to Coventry City 05.07.01 in part exchange for Moustapha Hadji.
Gareth Southgate to Middlesbrough 11.07.01 for £6m.
David James to West Ham United 11.07.01 for £3.6m.
Richard Walker to Blackpool 20.12.01 for £50,000.
David Ginola to Everton 08.02.02 on a free transfer.

▶ Peter Schmeichel was released at the end of the season, and signed for Manchester City for the 2002-03 season. Michael Standing was released on 13.03.02 and subsequently joined Bradford City.

Loan spells:
▶ Thomas Hitzlsperger and Stefan Moore spent a month with Chesterfield; Jlloyd Samuel was at Gillingham for two months; Boaz Myhill went to Stoke City for one week; Danny Jackman had a three-month spell with Cambridge United, for whom he went on as substitute in the LDV Vans final at the Millennium Stadium; Stephen Cooke spent a month at Bournemouth. Dion Dublin went to Millwall from March until the end of the season, helping the Lions to the First Division play-off before returning for Villa's final match at Chelsea.

QUICK OFF THE MARK
▶ For the second consecutive season, Villa's fastest goal was scored by Dion Dublin, who was on target in the first minute against West Ham on 5th December. Dublin headed home Steve Stone's right wing cross to give Villa a flying start, although they had to settle for a 1-1 draw when Jermain Defoe equalised in stoppage time.

77

FA PREMIER RESERVE LEAGUE (NORTH)

Date	H/A	Opponent	Score
Aug 28	A	Everton *Walker*	1-1
Sept 5	H	**Bolton Wanderers** *Smith (2), S Moore*	3-1
Sept 25	A	Blackburn Rovers	0-5
Oct 3	H	Leeds United	0-2
Oct 17	H	**Liverpool** *Hitzlsperger, Balaban (pen)*	2-2
Oct 25	A	Manchester United	0-1
Nov 6	A	Manchester City	0-2
Nov 12	A	Newcastle United *Melaugh*	1-6
Nov 21	H	**Sheffield Wednesday** *L Moore, Barry*	2-1
Dec 6	H	Sunderland	0-1
Dec 11	A	Bradford City *Vassell*	1-4
Dec 19	H	Middlesbrough	0-3
Jan 8	A	**Leeds United** *S Moore, Hitzlsperger*	2-2
Jan 16	H	**Everton** *Ginola, Hitzlsperger, Stone, Hadji, Kachloul*	5-1
Jan 22	A	Bolton Wanderers *Balaban*	1-2
Feb 4	H	**Blackburn Rovers** *Cooke*	1-0
Feb 13	A	Middlesbrough	0-1
Feb 21	H	**Manchester United** *Cooke*	1-0
Mar 11	A	Sunderland	0-7
Mar 18	H	**Bradford City** *Balaban, McGrath*	2-0
Apr 3	H	**Manchester City** *Dillon*	1-1
Apr 8	A	Sheffield Wednesday	0-2
Apr 17	H	**Newcastle United** *Balaban*	1-0
Apr 22	A	Liverpool *Cooke, Hendrie*	2-4

Pick and mix not so sweet for reserves

▶ It's hardly surprising that Villa's second string didn't exactly set the FA Premier Reserve League on fire. Any manager will tell you a settled squad is a prerequisite of football success, and Kevin MacDonald most definitely didn't have that.

By the end of the campaign, MacDonald had utilised nearly 60 players over the course of a 24-match programme, ranging from first teamers in need of match practice to youngsters given the chance to step up from the club's Academy ranks.

In a team of fluctuating personnel, only Jon Bewers, Gavin Melaugh and Danny Jackman could be described as regulars. and such a mixture was never likely to produce a recipe for success.

They opened with a creditable draw against Everton at Goodison Park and followed up with a 3-1 victory over Bolton Wanderers in the opening home match, but that early promise soon evaporated into the grim reality of life at the wrong end of the table. By Christmas, they had collected just eight points from a dozen matches, but at least the New Year brought brighter fortunes.

By the end of the campaign they had more than trebled their points total, including a hard-earned win over a Newcastle United side who had thrashed them 6-1 in November.

The real success of the side was Thomas Hitzlsperger, who stepped up to the senior squad in February and quickly established himself as a first team regular. He and Melaugh found themselves on opposite sides then they made their respective under-21 debuts for Germany and Northern Ireland.

FINAL TABLE

		P	W	D	L	F	A	Pts
1	Manchester Utd.	24	12	7	5	47	28	43
2	Newcastle Utd.	24	13	3	8	46	28	42
3	Middlesbrough	24	12	6	6	36	26	42
4	Sunderland	24	12	4	8	43	28	40
5	Bolton W	24	12	3	9	45	40	39
6	Manchester City	24	10	7	7	40	28	37
7	Blackburn	24	11	4	9	41	30	37
8	Leeds Utd.	24	10	4	10	25	33	34
9	Liverpool	24	9	6	9	54	49	33
10	Everton	24	8	8	8	30	30	32
11	**ASTON VILLA**	**24**	**7**	**4**	**13**	**26**	**49**	**25**
12	Bradford City	24	5	6	13	27	56	21
13	Sheffield Wed.	24	2	4	18	26	59	10

FA PREMIER ACADEMY (UNDER-19)

Aug 25	A	Middlesbrough	1-2
		Pawley	
Sep 1	A	Bolton Wanderers	2-1
		Hynes, Husbands	
Sep 8	H	**Arsenal**	0-2
Sep 15	A	Wimbledon	2-1
		Cooke, Hynes	
Sep 22	H	**Charlton Athletic**	0-5
Sep 29	A	Southampton	0-3
Oct 6	A	Wolverhampton Wanderers	3-2
		Husbands, McGuire, S Moore (pen)	
Oct 13	H	**Norwich City**	1-4
		McGuire	
Oct 20	A	Birmingham City	3-3
		Rigdewell, Bewers, S Moore	
Nov 3	A	Ipswich Town	2-2
		Ridgewell, Husbands	
Nov 17	A	Leicester City	2-2
		Husbands (2)	
Nov 23	A	West Ham United	2-3
		Edwards, Dillon	
Dec 8	H	**Fulham**	1-2
		Husbands	
Dec 15	A	Watford	1-1
		Pawley	
Jan 12	H	**Ipswich Town**	1-3
		Stuart (pen)	
Feb 9	A	Fulham	1-1
		Hynes	
Feb 16	H	**Wolverhampton Wanderers**	1-1
		Pawley	
Feb 23	A	Norwich City	2-0
		Scullion, Pawley	
Mar 2	H	**Birmingham City**	5-1
		Husbands (3), Cooke, Scullion	
Mar 9	H	**Chelsea**	2-2
		Hynes (2)	
Mar 16	A	Bristol City	4-1
		Husbands, Scullion, S Moore, Edwards	
Mar 23	H	**West Ham United**	1-1
		S Moore	
Apr 16	H	**Millwall**	0-0
Apr 13	A	Tottenham Hotspur	2-3
		Hynes, Pawley	
Apr 20	H	**Leicester City**	1-2
		Pawley	

Caps galore for talented teenagers

▶ The table doesn't make particularly pleasant reading, particularly by comparison with the previous season's third place finish, but the blunt statistics tell only half a story.

While results were undeniably disappointing, Villa's under-19s, the objective at this age level is to groom players for the reserves, and in that respect there was plenty of reason for optimism.

The likes of Stephen Cooke, Jon Bewers, Stefan Moore, Leon Hylton, Rob Edwards, Michael Husbands, David Scullion, Peter Hynes, Sean Dillon, Liam Ridgewell, Boaz Myhill and Ben Willetts all represented Villa's reserves in varying degrees – with Cooke, Bewers and Moore even drafted into the first team squad during an injury crisis in December.

In addition, Cooke, Moore and Hylton were all in the England squad who clinched a place in the European under-19 championships, while Myhill played for England under-20s.

Another outstanding goalkeeping prospect, Wayne Henderson, represented the Republic of Ireland under-19s along with Hynes, while David Scullion broke into the Northern Ireland under-19 team and Cameron Stuart played for Scotland under-18s.

And Pierre Ennis, who missed a huge chunk of the season after going down with glandular fever, was voted the Republic of Ireland under-16 Player of the Year for the previous season.

FINAL TABLE

	P	W	D	L	F	A	Pts
1 Ipswich Town	26	17	7	2	69	38	58
2 West Ham Utd.	26	12	8	6	45	37	44
3 B'ham City	26	12	5	9	48	44	41
4 Fulham	26	9	6	11	44	47	33
5 Wolves	26	8	8	10	24	29	32
6 Leicester City	26	8	7	11	33	37	31
7 Norwich City	26	8	5	13	41	64	29
8 ASTON VILLA	**26**	**6**	**10**	**10**	**42**	**50**	**28**
9 Watford	26	7	7	12	28	44	28

Youth Cup triumph for Villa's young lions

▶ A week after the first team had played their final match, Villa's season ended on a glorious note when the club's youngsters lifted the AXA FA Youth Cup.

Despite a 1-0 defeat in the second leg of the final at Villa Park, Tony McAndrew's team claimed the trophy by virtue of their stunning 4-1 victory at Everton four days earlier. The display at Goodison Park was awesome, Villa cancelling out a 23rd minute Wayne Rooney goal when skipper Stefan Moore equalised on 37 minutes, and then cutting loose in the second half.

Moore added his second eight minutes after the interval, with Peter Hynes increasing the lead on 69 minutes and Stefan's younger brother Luke completing the scoring 10 minutes later.

Understandably, the return match was something of a formality, and despite an audience of 18,651, Villa were unable to reproduce the outstanding form they had displayed in previous ties.

Even so, they completed a 4-2 aggregate success to emulate the feat of their 1972 and 1980 counterparts in winning the country's most prestigious youth trophy.

Having reached the quarter-finals the previous season, Villa were exempt until the third round, although they might have been forgiven for thinking it was going to be a brief fling this time around.

Things looked bleak when they went a goal down at home to Wimbledon after only a minute, but Ryan Amoo equalised just before the hour mark, converting a penalty rebound to take the tie into extra-time before Peter Hynes grabbed the winner on 105 minutes.

An additional 30 minutes was again required for a fourth round thriller against Tranmere Rovers, Villa trailing three times before going through 4-3 with goals from Luke Moore, Amoo, Michael Husbands and Mark Atkinson.

Home advantage again proved important in the next round, David Scullion and Stefan Moore netting in the opening 20 minutes before goalkeeper Wayne Henderson produced some fine saves to keep the 2-0 scoreline intact.

Hitting the road for the first time was no great problem as Villa produced a stylish display to overcome Fulham 3-0 in the quarter-final at Craven Cottage. It wasn't until the 40th minute that the visitors went ahead, but two goals from Luke Moore before half-time, plus a third from Stefan on 52 minutes, ensured their passage to the last four.

The goalscoring roles were reversed in the semi-final home leg against Barnsley, Stefan netting twice – including a stoppage-time penalty – and Luke once as Villa established a 3-1 advantage.

Barnsley's performance that night suggested it would be tough in the return match at Oakwell, but in the event Villa won by the same margin to complete a 6-2 aggregate victory.

▶ Villa pile on the pressure but Everton 'keeper Andrew Pettinger punches clear to leave the home side frustrated in the second leg of the final.

Any early nerves were dispelled when Hynes opened the scoring after Steven Foley's shot had struck the bar and when Stefan Moore added number two in the 18th minute the tie was effectively over.

A glancing header from Steven Davis extended the lead before the home side grabbed a late consolation goal from the penalty spot. That set the scene for a two-leg final which attracted a total attendance of nearly 34,000 and saw Villa become one of only six clubs who have lifted the trophy on three or more occasions.

Manchester United lead the way with eight triumphs while Arsenal boast six victories. Villa, Everton, Tottenham and West Ham have all won it three times.

FA YOUTH CUP RESULTS

Date	H/A	Opponent	Score
Dec 4	H	**Wimbledon** (Rd 3) Amoo, Hynes (after extra-time)	2-1
Jan 23	H	**Tranmere Rovers** (Rd 4) L Moore, Amoo, Husbands, Atkinson (after extra-time)	4-3
Feb 6	H	**Brighton** (Rd 5) Scullion, S Moore	2-0
Mar 12	A	**Fulham** (Rd 6) L Moore (2), S Moore	3-0
Mar 27	H	**Barnsley** (S/F, 1st leg) S Moore (2), L Moore	3-1
Apr 9	A	**Barnsley** (S/F, 2nd leg) Hynes, S Moore, Davis	3-1
May 14	A	**Everton** (Final, 1st leg) S Moore (2), L Moore, Hynes	4-1
May 18	H	**Everton** (Final, 2nd leg) (Villa won 4-2 on aggregate)	0-1

ASTON VILLA REVIEW 2002

FA YOUTH CUP

▶ It's ours! Villa's youngsters celebrate with their coaching staff after winning the AXA FA Youth Cup. Although they lost 1-0 at home in the second leg of the final, their superb 4-1 triumph at Everton was enough to clinch the trophy.

81

FA ACADEMY (UNDER-17)

Aug 25	H	Middlesbrough	3-0
		L Moore (2), Brazil	
Sep 1	A	Bolton Wanderers	6-0
		L Moore (2), Atkinson (2), Davis, Brazil	
Sep 8	A	Arsenal	3-2
		L Moore (2), Atkinson	
Sep 15	A	Wimbledon	6-0
		L Moore (4), Baptist, Nolan	
Sep 22	H	**Charlton Athletic**	5-0
		L Moore (3), Baptist, Nolan	
Sep 29	A	Southampton	2-2
		L Moore (2)	
Oct 6	A	Wolverhampton Wanderers	5-0
		L Moore (3), Davis, O'Connor	
Oct 13	A	Tottenham Hotspur	0-2
Oct 20	A	Birmingham City	0-2
Oct 27	A	Watford	1-0
		Nolan	
Nov 3	A	Ipswich Town	2-1
		Foley, Atkinson	
Nov 17	H	**Leicester City**	1-1
		Nolan	
Nov 24	H	**West Ham United**	2-0
		Atkinson, Nolan	
Dec 8	H	**Fulham**	4-2
		L Moore, Foley, Brazil, Atkinson	
Jan 12	H	**Ipswich Town**	3-2
		Williams, Davis, L Moore	
Feb 9	A	Fulham	5-1
		Atkinson (3), Whittingham, Davis	
Feb 6	H	**Wolverhampton Wanderers**	2-1
		Davis, L Moore	
Feb 23	H	**Tottenham Hotspur**	1-1
		Marshall	
Feb 27	A	Leicester City	1-0
		Davis	
Mar 2	H	**Birmingham City**	0-0
Mar 5	A	West Ham United	0-1
Mar 9	H	**Watford**	1-0
		Ward	

Play-offs:

Mar 16	A	Middlesbrough	2-2
		Atkinson (2)	
Mar 23	H	**Manchester City**	2-1
		Atkinson, L Moore	
Apr 13	H	**Charlton Athletic**	4-1
		Atkinson, Foley, Davis, Baptist	
Apr 20	H	**Leeds United** (Quarter-final)	1-2
		L Moore	

Success marred by one off-day

▶ There was no question about Villa's most successful group of players throughout the season, even if their campaign ultimately ended with an unexpected jolt.

The under-17s were runaway winners of Group B, losing just three times in 22 matches and finishing 10 points clear of nearest rivals Birmingham City before heading their play-off section.

But just when glory appeared to beckon, the youngsters fell well below their own lofty standards in the quarter-finals, going down 2-1 at home to Leeds United despite holding an interval lead through Luke Moore.

That was Moore's 23rd Academy goal of the season, 18 of them coming in the opening seven matches when Villa were on fire and there was simply no stopping the prolific 15-year-old.

If Moore claimed most of the scoring honours, Mark Atkinson also played his part with a haul of 15, while the likes of Peter Whittingham and James O'Connor ensured that Villa also boasted one of the tightest defences in the country at this level.

The side produced a number of internationals, too, with Steven Foley and Steven Davis representing the Republic of Ireland at their respective age levels, while Luke Moore and Stuart Bridges were involved with England under-16s and under-17s respectively.

FINAL TABLE

	P	W	D	L	F	A	Pts
1 ASTON VILLA	22	15	4	3	53	18	49
2 Birmingham City	22	12	3	7	45	23	39
3 Leicester City	22	11	4	7	37	31	37
4 West Ham	22	10	5	7	28	25	35
5 Ipswich Town	22	10	3	9	43	38	33
6 Watford	22	8	4	10	24	33	28
7 Wolves	22	5	6	11	21	40	21
8 Fulham	22	5	5	12	29	61	20

Play-off table	P	W	D	L	F	A	Pts
1 ASTON VILLA	3	2	1	0	8	4	7
2 Middlesbrough	3	1	2	0	6	3	5
3 Manchester City	3	1	1	1	5	5	4
4 Charlton Ath	3	0	0	3	3	10	0

RESERVE & YOUTH TEAM APPEARANCES

	PREM. RESERVE LGE Apps	Gls	YTH ACC. U19 Apps	Gls	YTH ACC. U17 Apps	Gls	FA YTH CUP Apps	Gls
Gabriel Agbohlahor	-	-	-	-	- (1)	-	-	-
Ryan Amoo	-	-	12 (1)	-	-	-	4 (1)	2
Stefan Andersson	1	-	-	-	-	-	-	-
Mark Atkinson	-	-	-	-	24 (1)	14	- (5)	1
Bosko Balaban	11	4	-	-	-	-	-	-
Adam Baptist	- (2)	-	- (1)	-	16 (6)	2	-	-
Gareth Barry	7	1	-	-	-	-	-	-
David Berks	- (2)	-	-	-	-	-	-	-
Jonathan Bewers	24	-	12 (6)	1	-	-	-	-
Alan Brazil	-	-	-	-	3 (4)	3	-	-
Daniel Bridges	-	-	-	-	- (1)	-	-	-
Stuart Bridges	-	-	-	-	11 (5)	-	-	-
Gary Cahill	-	-	-	-	9 (6)	-	-	-
David Andrewartha	-	-	3 (2)	-	-	-	-	-
Rowan Caney	-	-	-	-	- (1)	-	-	-
Thomas Christensen	-	-	1	-	-	-	-	-
Stephen Cooke	15 (1)	3	8 (3)	2	-	-	-	-
Scott Cormell	-	-	1	-	17	-	2	-
Jamie Cunnington	-	-	4 (5)	-	-	-	-	-
Steven Davis	- (5)	-	-	-	20 (1)	7	8	1
Sean Dillion	4	1	19 (1)	1	-	-	-	-
Dion Dublin	1	-	-	-	-	-	-	-
Robert Edwards	9 (2)	-	18 (1)	2	-	-	-	-
Hjalgrim Elttor	1	-	2	-	-	-	-	-
Peter Enckelman	8	-	-	-	-	-	-	-
Steve Foley	- (4)	-	-	-	22	3	8	-
Steven Gahan	-	-	1	-	6	-	-	-
David Ginola	1	1	-	-	-	-	-	-
John Grady	-	-	-	-	5 (4)	-	-	-
Nick Green	-	-	-	-	2 (7)	-	-	-
Paul Green	-	-	-	-	2 (3)	-	-	-
Moustapha Hadji	2	1	-	-	-	-	-	-
Danny Haynes	2 (2)	-	-	-	-	-	-	-
Wayne Henderson	2	-	15	-	-	-	8	-
Lee Hendrie	4	1	-	-	-	-	-	-
Thomas Hitzlsperger	11	3	-	-	-	-	-	-
Michael Husbands	3 (1)	-	20 (4)	11	-	-	1 (4)	1

RESERVE & YOUTH TEAM APPEARANCES (continued)

	PREM. RESERVE LGE Apps	PREM. RESERVE LGE Gls	YTH ACC. U19 Apps	YTH ACC. U19 Gls	YTH ACC. U17 Apps	YTH ACC. U17 Gls	FA YTH CUP Apps	FA YTH CUP Gls
Leon Hylton	5	-	15 (2)	-	-	-	-	-
Peter Hynes	5 (4)	-	22 (3)	7	-	-	7 (1)	3
Danny Jackman	17	-	6 (3)	-	-	-	-	-
Aleksei Jermenko	-	-	2	-	-	-	-	-
Hassan Kachloul	5	1	-	-	-	-	-	-
Andy Marfell	3 (2)	-	-	-	-	-	-	-
Colin Marshall	- (1)	-	- (1)	-	21 (2)	1	3 (2)	-
John McGrath	7 (3)	1	-	-	-	-	-	-
Lee McGuire	2	-	12	2	-	-	-	-
Gavin Melaugh	18 (1)	1	-	-	-	-	-	-
Olof Mellberg	1	-	-	-	-	-	-	-
Paul Merson	2	-	-	-	-	-	-	-
Luke Moore	- (8)	1	-	-	21 (2)	23	8	5
Stefan Moore	10 (2)	2	5 (3)	4	-	-	8	7
Boaz Myhill	13 (2)	-	9	-	-	-	-	-
Alex Nicholas	-	-	1	-	-	-	-	-
David Nolan	- (1)	-	1	-	16 (6)	5	-	-
James O'Connor	3 (1)	-	-	-	24	1	6	-
Jamie Pawley	-	-	17 (3)	6	-	-	-	-
Antoni Pecora	-	-	1	-	20	-	-	-
Liam Ridgewell	10 (4)	-	15 (1)	2	-	-	8	-
Jlloyd Samuel	4	-	-	-	-	-	-	-
David Scullion	2 (2)	-	10 (1)	3	-	-	3 (4)	1
Paul Shane	-	-	-	-	1 (5)	-	-	-
Jay Smith	21 (1)	2	-	-	-	-	-	-
Michael Standing	5 (1)	-	-	-	-	-	-	-
Steve Stone	8	1	-	-	-	-	-	-
Cameron Stuart	-	-	23 (1)	1	-	-	- (4)	-
Ian Taylor	2 (2)	-	-	-	-	-	-	-
Darius Vassell	1	1	-	-	-	-	-	-
Richard Walker	2	1	-	-	-	-	-	-
Jamie Ward	-	-	-	-	- (1)	1	-	-
Andrew Wells	-	-	16 (2)	-	-	-	6	-
Peter Whittingham	4	-	-	-	25 (1)	1	8	-
Ben Willetts	1 (1)	-	15 (4)	-	-	-	-	-
Oliver Williams	-	-	-	-	20 (1)	1	-	-
Alan Wright	6	-	-	-	-	-	-	-

THE PREMIERSHIP • 1992-2002

		P	W	D	L	F	A	Pts	1993	1994	1995	1996	1997	1998	1999	2000	2001	2002
1	Manchester United	392	244	93	55	789	360	825	1st	1st	2nd	1st	1st	2nd	1st	1st	1st	3rd
2	Arsenal	392	195	110	87	598	346	695	10th	4th	12th	5th	3rd	1st	2nd	2nd	2nd	1st
3	Liverpool	392	189	100	103	643	408	667	6th	8th	4th	3rd	4th	3rd	7th	4th	3rd	2nd
4	Leeds United	392	167	111	114	543	437	612	17th	5th	5th	13th	11th	5th	4th	3rd	4th	5th
5	Chelsea	392	160	118	114	569	451	598	11th	14th	11th	11th	6th	4th	3rd	5th	6th	6th
6	**Aston Villa**	**392**	**154**	**115**	**123**	**491**	**434**	**577**	**2nd**	**10th**	**18th**	**4th**	**5th**	**7th**	**6th**	**6th**	**8th**	**8th**
7	Newcastle United	350	157	88	105	552	419	559	-	3rd	6th	2nd	2nd	13th	13th	11th	11th	4th
8	Tottenham H.	392	136	108	148	518	534	516	8th	15th	7th	8th	10th	14th	11th	10th	12th	9th
9	Blackburn Rovers	316	134	84	98	464	366	486	4th	2nd	1st	7th	13th	6th	19th	-	-	10th
10	Everton	392	119	111	162	479	538	468	13th	17th	15th	6th	15th	17th	14th	13th	16th	15th
11	West Ham United	350	122	92	136	420	475	458	-	13th	14th	10th	14th	8th	5th	9th	15th	7th
12	Southampton	392	119	99	174	466	581	456	18th	18th	10th	17th	16th	12th	17th	15th	10th	11th
13	Coventry City	354	99	112	143	387	534	409	15th	11th	16th	16th	17th	11th	15th	14th	19th	-
14	Sheffield Wed.	316	101	89	126	409	453	392	7th	7th	13th	15th	7th	16th	12th	19th	-	-
15	Wimbledon	316	99	94	123	384	444	391	12th	6th	9th	14th	8th	15th	16th	18th	-	-
16	Middlesbrough	270	79	82	109	313	382	316*	21st	-	-	12th	19th	-	9th	12th	14th	12th
17	Leicester City	270	78	75	117	306	390	309	-	-	21st	-	9th	10th	10th	8th	13th	20th
18	Derby County	228	67	62	99	251	331	263	-	-	-	-	12th	9th	8th	16th	17th	19th
19	Ipswich Town	202	57	53	92	219	312	224	16th	19th	22nd	-	-	-	-	-	5th	18th
20	Nottingham Forest	198	60	59	79	229	287	239	22nd	-	3rd	9th	20th	-	20th	-	-	-
21	Manchester City	202	53	64	85	221	287	223	9th	16th	17th	18th	-	-	-	-	18th	-
22	QPR	164	59	39	66	224	232	216	5th	9th	8th	19th	-	-	-	-	-	-
23	Sunderland	152	51	42	59	167	201	195	-	-	-	-	18th	-	-	7th	7th	17th
24	Norwich City	126	43	39	44	163	180	168	3rd	12th	20th	-	-	-	-	-	-	-
25	Charlton Athletic	114	32	36	46	129	162	132	-	-	-	-	-	-	18th	-	9th	14th
26	Crystal Palace	122	30	37	55	119	181	127	20th	-	19th	-	-	20th	-	-	-	-
27	Bolton Wanderers	114	26	31	57	124	194	109	-	-	20th	-	18th	-	-	-	-	16th
28	Sheffield United	84	22	28	34	96	113	94	14th	20th	-	-	-	-	-	-	-	-
29	Oldham Athletic	84	22	23	39	105	142	89	19th	21st	-	-	-	-	-	-	-	-
30	Bradford City	76	14	20	42	68	138	62	-	-	-	-	-	-	-	17th	20th	-
31	Fulham	38	10	14	14	36	44	44	-	-	-	-	-	-	-	-	-	13th
32	Barnsley	38	10	5	23	37	82	35	-	-	-	-	-	19th	-	-	-	-
33	Swindon Town	42	5	15	22	47	100	30	-	22nd	-	-	-	-	-	-	-	-
34	Watford	38	6	6	26	35	47	24	-	-	-	-	-	-	-	20th	-	-

Middlesbrough deducted 3 points in 96/97 season for failing to fulfil a fixture at Blackburn on 21.12.96. Final total of 7882 points takes this into account. Italicised positions denote relegated teams.

GRAHAM TAYLOR OBE

Even before his appointment as manager, Graham Taylor's services to football had received royal approval.

While still in his role as non-Executive director, he was awarded the OBE in the New Year's Honours List.

There was also an honorary MBE for Danish goalkeeper Peter Schmeichel, while former Villa striker Cyrille Regis received an honorary doctorate from the University of Wolverhampton.

DANE PACT

2002 was the year when AV joined forces with AB. Villa forged a partnership with Danish club Akademisk Boldklub of Copenhagen, geared towards co-operation between the two clubs on matters such as scouting, training and player development.

The idea had been on the anvil for almost 12 months, and manager Graham Taylor is hopeful Villa will forge similar links with other clubs across the Continent to enhance the club's knowledge of young foreign talent.

▶ *Manager Graham Taylor is the man in the middle as he displays the AB and Villa shirts at the launch of the partnership in Copenhagen.*

MAN OF THE MIDLANDS

Paul Merson received the 2001 Midlands Footballer of the Year award at a Football Writers Association dinner at Birmingham's Grand Moat House Hotel in November.

The former England midfielder was the fourth Villa recipient of the trophy, following Paul McGrath (1991), Mark Bosnich (1994) and Dwight Yorke (1996).

While Merse was voted top Midland man for the previous campaign, however, he relinquished his dominance of Villa's Player of the Year award, which he had won for two consecutive years.

That went to Juan Pablo Angel, with Mark Delaney getting the vote as Players' Player and Darius Vassell as Young Player of the Year.

Steve Staunton was Clubman of the Year, with Hassan Kachloul's spectacular volley at Leeds getting the nod as Goal of the Season.

MILLENNIUM FIRST

Danny Jackman has yet to kick a ball in competitive action for the first team, but he became the first Villa player to appear in a final at Cardiff's Millennium Stadium.

The teenage full-back went on as a 60th minute substitute for Cambridge United in the LDV Vans final, which they lost 4-1 to a Blackpool side for whom former Villa striker Richard Walker went on as an 84th minute sub. Jackman also played in one other LDV tie while on loan at Cambridge as well as making five league starts (plus two as sub) and scoring one goal.

Striker Stefan Moore, another player yet to sample senior action for Villa, also had his first taste of League football. He played one league game (plus one sub) and one cup-tie while on loan to Chesterfield.

JIM STRIKES GOLD

Villa fan Jim Lewis achieved a lifelong ambition when he was given a standing ovation by Holte Enders before the match against Arsenal on Sunday 17th March.

There was good reason for the fans' acclaim, too. Jim was holding aloft the Cheltenham Gold Cup, which his horse Best Mate had won three days earlier with jockey Jim Culloty resplendent in claret and blue.

DERBY DAYS

Two Midland derbies will return to Villa's fixture list next season following the promotion of our neighbours West Bromwich Albion and Birmingham City.

Albion achieved automatic elevation after clinching runners-up spot behind Manchester City in the First

Division, while Blues made it through the play-offs. They beat Millwall 2-1 on aggregate in the semi-finals and then faced Norwich City – who had knocked out Wolves in the other semi – at Cardiff's Millennium Stadium. The final finished 1-1 after extra-time before Blues won 4-2 on penalties.

JUST THE JOB, JACK

Long-serving Jack Watts was presented with a special lifetime award at the club's annual Awards Dinner to mark his devotion to Villa. Jack, who will be 84 on 26th August, has followed Villa for more than 70 years and entertains visitors with endless stories about the club's histories in his role as Tour Guide at Villa Park. He also helps to look after chairman Doug Ellis's guests on match days.

FIT FOR A PRINCE

Villa's new Trinity Road stand is fit for a Prince – and that's official.

Prince Charles was at Villa Park in November for the ceremony to mark the opening of the impressive structure.

The Prince later wrote to chairman Doug Ellis, complimenting the design of the stand, which replaced the Trinity Road stand which his grandfather, the Duke of York, had opened 77 years earlier.

It was a double mission for the Prince of Wales, who also presented the Prince's Trust awards at a dinner in the Holte Suite.

There was another high-profile visit in April when Sir Geoff Hurst, England's 1966 World Cup hat-trick hero, officially opened the new Academy indoor centre, based at the former Stumps venue in Witton Lane.

▶ *Prince Charles unveils the Trinity Road plaque, watched by chairman Doug Ellis, directors Steve Stride, Peter Ellis, Tony Hales, David Home, and Dion Dublin.*

DRIVING FORCE

Villa's shirts will be emblazoned by a new logo next season following the club's announcement of a two-year sponsorship deal with MG Rover. The Midlands biggest British car manufacturer gained "Premiership" status by linking up with Villa to extend the commercial partnership between the two companies to almost two decades.

Chairman Doug Ellis said: "The synergy between ourselves and MG Rover is very apparent, both in terms of success and importance to the region."

The name Rover will appear on Villa's home shirt, with the away shirt featuring the MG logo.

AND FINALLY...

For the second year running, Villa hosted the FA Carlsberg Vase and FA Umbro Trophy finals, the matches being staged on consecutive days.

Whitley Bay lifted the Vase, beating Tiptree United 1-0 on 11th May, while Yeovil were 2-0 winners over Stevenage Borough in the Trophy final less than 24 hours later. The club also hosted the FA Umbro Sunday Cup final, in which Britannia beat Little Paxton 1-0.

PLAYER OF THE MONTH

▶ Recipients of the 96.4BRMB/1152AM Capital Gold Player of the Month award:

September	**Juan Pablo Angel**	January	**Darius Vassell**	The 96.4BRMB/1152AM Capital
October	**Peter Schmeichel**	February	**Darius Vassell**	Gold Player of the Year trophy went
November	**Peter Schmeichel**	March	**Olof Mellberg**	to **Olof Mellberg**.
December	**Steve Staunton**	April	**Mark Delaney**	

87

VILLA'S RECORD IN EUROPEAN COMPETITIONS

1975-76 – UEFA CUP
Sept 17	R1/L1	A	Royal Antwerp (Belgium)	1-4	Graydon	
Oct 1	R1/L2	H	**Royal Antwerp**	0-1		*Agg. Score: Antwerp win 5-1*

1977-78 – UEFA CUP
Sept 14	R1/L1	H	**Fenerbahce (Turkey)**	4-0	Deehan 2, Gray, Little	
Oct 1	R1/L2	A	Fenerbahce	2-0	Deehan, Little	*Agg. Score: Villa win 6-0*
Oct 19	R2/L1	H	**Gornik Zabrze (Poland)**	2-0	McNaught 2	
Nov 2	R2/L2	A	Gornik Zabrze	1-1	Gray	*Agg. Score: Villa win 3-1*
Nov 23	R3/L1	H	**Athletic Bilbao (Spain)**	2-0	Iribar og, Deehan	
Dec 7	R3/L2	A	Athletic Bilbao	1-1	Mortimer	*Agg. Score: Villa win 3-1*
Mar 1	R4/L1	H	**Barcelona (Spain)**	2-2	McNaught, Deehan	
Mar 15	R4/L2	A	Barcelona	1-2	Little	*Agg. Score: Barcelona win 4-3*

1981-82 – EUROPEAN CHAMPIONS' CUP
Sept 16	R1/L1	H	**Valur (Iceland)**	5-0	Morley, Donovan 2, Withe 2	
Sept 30	R1/L2	A	Valur	2-0	Shaw 2	*Agg. Score: Villa win 7-0*
Oct 21	R2/L1	A	Dynamo Berlin (E. Germany)	2-1	Morley 2	*Agg. Score: 2-2, Villa*
Nov 4	R2/L2	H	**Dynamo Berlin**	0-1		*win on away goals*
Mar 3	QF/L1	A	Dynamo Kiev (USSR)	0-0		
Mar 17	QF/L2	H	**Dynamo Kiev**	2-0	Shaw, McNaught	*Agg. Score: Villa win 2-0*
Apr 7	SF/L1	H	**Anderlecht (Belgium)**	1-0	Morley	
Apr 21	SF/L2	A	Anderlecht	0-0		*Agg. Score: Villa win 1-0*
May 26	Final	N	Bayern Munich (W. Germany)	1-0	Withe	

Played at the 'De Kuip' Stadium in Rotterdam, Holland

1982-83 – EUROPEAN CHAMPIONS' CUP
Sept 15	R1/L1	H	**Besiktas (Turkey)**	3-1	Withe, Morley, Mortimer	
Sept 29	R1/L2	A	Besiktas	0-0		*Agg. Score: Villa win 3-1*
Oct 20	R2/L1	A	Dinamo Bucharest (Romania)	2-0	Shaw 2	
Nov 3	R2/L2	H	**Dinamo Bucharest**	4-2	Shaw 3, Walters	*Agg. Score: Villa win 6-2*
Mar 2	QF/L1	H	**Juventus (Italy)**	1-2	Cowans	
Mar 16	QF/L2	A	Juventus	1-3	Withe	*Agg. Score: Juventus win 5-2*

1982-83 – EUROPEAN SUPER CUP
Jan 19	L1	A	Barcelona (Spain)	0-1		
Jan 26	L2	H	**Barcelona**	3-0	Shaw, Cowans (pen), McNaught	*Agg. Score: Villa win 3-1*

1982-83 – WORLD CLUB CHAMPIONSHIP
Dec 12	–	N	Penarol (Uruguay)	0-2	

Played in Tokyo, Japan

1983-84 – UEFA CUP
Sept 14	R1/L1	A	Vitoria Guimaraes (Portugal)	0-1		
Sept 28	R1/L2	H	**Vitoria Guimaraes**	5-0	Withe 3, Gibson, Ormsby	*Agg. Score: Villa win 5-1*
Oct 19	R2/L1	A	Spartak Moscow (USSR)	2-2	Gibson, Walters	
Nov 2	R2/L2	H	**Spartak Moscow**	1-2	Withe	*Agg. Score: Spartak win 4-3*

1990-91 – UEFA CUP
Sept 19	R1/L1	H	**Banik Ostrava (Czechoslovakia)**	3-1	Mountfield, Platt, Olney	
Oct 2	R1/L2	A	Banik Ostrava	2-1	Mountfield, Stas og	*Agg. Score: Villa win 5-2*

| Oct 24 | R2/L1 | H | Inter Milan (Italy) | 2-0 | Neilsen, Platt | |
| Nov 7 | R2/L2 | A | Inter Milan | 0-3 | | Agg. Score: Inter win 3-2 |

1993-94 – UEFA CUP
| Sept 15 | R1/L1 | A | Slovan Bratislava (Slovakia) | 0-0 | | |
| Sept 29 | R1/L2 | H | **Slovan Bratislava** | 2-1 | Atkinson, Townsend | Agg. Score: Villa win 2-1 |

| Oct 19 | R2/L1 | A | Deportivo La Coruna (Spain) | 1-1 | Saunders | |
| Nov 3 | R2/L2 | H | **Deportivo La Coruna** | 0-1 | | Agg. Score: Deportivo win 2-1 |

1994-95 – UEFA CUP
| Sept 15 | R1/L1 | A | Inter Milan (Italy) | 0-1 | | Agg. Score: 1-1, Villa go through |
| Sept 29 | R1/L2 | H | **Inter Milan** | 1-0 | Houghton | after a penalty shoot-out |

| Oct 18 | R2/L1 | A | Trabzonspor (Turkey) | 0-1 | | Agg. Score: 2-2, Trabzonspor |
| Nov 1 | R2/L2 | H | **Trabzonspor** | 2-1 | Atkinson, Ehiogu | win on away goals |

1996-97 – UEFA CUP
| Sept 10 | R1/L1 | H | **Helsingborgs IF (Sweden)** | 1-1 | Johnson | Agg. Score: 1-1, Helsingborgs |
| Sept 24 | R1/L2 | A | Helsingborgs IF | 0-0 | | win on away goals |

1997-98 – UEFA CUP
| Sept 16 | R1/L1 | A | Girondins de Bordeaux (France) | 0-0 | | |
| Sept 30 | R1/L2 | H | **Girondins de Bordeaux** | 1-0 | Milosevic | Agg. Score: Villa win 1-0 |

| Oct 21 | R2/L1 | A | Athletic Bilbao (Spain) | 0-0 | | |
| Nov 4 | R2/L2 | H | **Athletic Bilbao** | 2-1 | Taylor, Yorke | Agg. Score: Villa win 2-1 |

| Nov 25 | R3/L1 | A | Steaua Bucharest (Romania) | 1-2 | Yorke | |
| Dec 9 | R3/L2 | H | **Steaua Bucharest** | 2-0 | Milosevic, Taylor | Agg. Score: Villa win 3-2 |

| Mar 3 | R4/L1 | A | Atlético Madrid (Spain) | 0-1 | | Agg. Score: 2-2, Atlético Madrid |
| Mar 17 | R4/L2 | H | **Atlético Madrid** | 2-1 | Taylor, Collymore | win on away goals |

1998-99 – UEFA CUP
| Sept 15 | R1/L1 | H | **Strømsgodset (Norway)** | 3-2 | Charles, Vassell 2 | |
| Sept 29 | R1/L2 | A | Strømsgodset | 3-0 | Collymore 3 | Agg. Score: Villa win 6-2 |

| Oct 20 | R2/L1 | A | RC Celta Vigo (Spain) | 1-0 | Joachim | |
| Nov 3 | R2/L2 | H | **RC Celta Vigo** | 1-3 | Collymore (pen) | Agg. Score: Celta Vigo win 3-2 |

2000-01 – INTERTOTO CUP
| July 16 | R3/L1 | A | Marila Príbram (Czech Republic) | 0-0 | | |
| July 22 | R3/L2 | H | **Marila Príbram** | 3-1 | Dublin, Taylor, Nilis | Agg. Score: Villa win 3-1 |

| July 26 | SF/L1 | A | RC Celta Vigo (Spain) | 0-1 | | |
| Aug 2 | SF/L2 | H | **RC Celta Vigo** | 1-2 | Barry (pen) | Agg. Score: Celta Vigo win 3-1 |

2001-02 – INTERTOTO CUP
| July 14 | R3/L1 | A | Slaven Belupo (Croatia) | 1-2 | Ginola | |
| July 21 | R3/L2 | H | **Slaven Belupo** | 2-0 | Hendrie 2 | Agg.Score: Villa win 3-2 |

| July 25 | SF/L1 | A | Stade Rennais (France) | 1-2 | Vassell | Agg. Score: 1-1, Villa |
| Aug 1 | SF/L2 | H | **Stade Rennais** | 1-0 | Dublin | win on away goals |

| Aug 7 | Final/L1 | A | Basel (Switzerland) | 1-1 | Merson | |
| Aug 14 | Final/L2 | H | **Basel** | 4-1 | Angel 2, Vassell, Ginola | Agg. Score: Villa win 5-2 |

2001-02 UEFA CUP
| Sep 20 | R1/L1 | H | **NK Varteks (Croatia)** | 2-3 | Angel 2 | Agg. Score: 3-3, Varteks |
| Sep 27 | R1/L2 | A | NK Varteks | 1-0 | Hadji | win on away goals |

VILLA'S ALL-TIME LEAGUE RECORD – CLUB BY CLUB

	P	W	D	L	F	A	W	D	L	F	A
		— Home —					— Away —				
Accrington	10	4	0	1	26	12	1	2	2	9	10
Arsenal	146	38	17	18	142	101	20	15	38	83	121
Barnsley	12	3	2	1	9	3	5	1	0	16	2
Birmingham City	96	23	13	12	82	60	16	12	20	68	74
Blackburn Rovers	136	36	17	15	141	90	18	12	38	90	147
Blackpool	62	16	9	6	65	39	10	7	14	44	51
Bolton Wanderers	132	36	15	15	142	86	17	13	36	69	129
Bournemouth	4	1	1	0	3	2	1	0	1	2	4
Bradford Park Avenue	10	4	0	1	12	4	1	2	2	8	16
Bradford City	32	11	2	3	35	12	5	5	6	21	24
Brentford	6	2	1	0	12	4	3	0	0	8	3
Brighton & Hove Albion	16	6	2	0	16	4	3	2	3	8	7
Bristol City	32	10	3	3	27	19	5	6	5	18	14
Bristol Rovers	8	3	1	0	8	3	2	1	1	4	4
Burnley	94	28	12	7	109	47	11	8	28	71	113
Bury	52	17	6	3	59	31	10	6	10	39	39
Cardiff City	44	14	3	5	39	20	8	2	12	23	30
Carlisle United	10	4	1	0	5	1	2	2	1	6	6
Charlton Athletic	44	12	6	4	47	23	7	7	8	28	37
Chelsea	110	27	15	13	106	77	18	10	27	67	80
Chesterfield	8	2	1	1	7	4	3	0	1	8	3
Coventry City	54	16	10	1	44	18	13	7	7	39	32
Crystal Palace	24	8	2	2	22	9	2	6	4	6	10
Darwen	4	2	0	0	16	0	1	1	0	6	2
Derby County	116	39	10	9	143	61	19	11	28	77	98
Doncaster Rovers	4	1	1	0	4	3	0	0	2	1	3
Everton	174	43	20	24	163	115	23	22	42	106	154
Fulham	36	9	5	4	32	22	2	6	10	20	34
Gillingham	2	1	0	0	2	1	0	1	0	0	0
Glossop	2	1	0	0	9	0	0	0	1	0	1
Grimsby Town	20	5	3	2	29	19	5	1	4	16	20
Halifax Town	4	1	1	0	2	1	1	0	1	2	2
Huddersfield Town	64	20	9	3	74	31	7	10	15	32	51
Hull City	16	4	3	1	21	8	2	2	4	7	12
Ipswich Town	44	13	6	3	44	19	6	5	11	22	31
Leeds United	76	18	10	10	61	45	8	14	16	37	60
Leicester City	80	18	9	13	80	62	6	12	22	53	96
Leyton Orient	10	4	1	0	8	3	1	2	2	3	6
Lincoln City	2	0	1	0	1	1	0	1	0	0	0
Liverpool	154	37	17	23	153	102	14	15	48	83	173
Luton Town	32	10	1	5	29	15	1	3	12	8	24

ASTON VILLA REVIEW 2002 — STATISTICS

	P	W (H)	D (H)	L (H)	F (H)	A (H)	W (A)	D (A)	L (A)	F (A)	A (A)
Manchester City	126	32	20	11	116	69	15	15	33	82	119
Manchester United	138	32	18	19	136	99	10	15	44	62	141
Mansfield Town	4	0	0	2	0	2	0	1	1	1	3
Middlesbrough	114	32	12	13	126	61	19	16	22	76	84
Millwall	18	4	4	1	14	8	3	2	4	9	12
Newcastle United	128	32	16	16	120	69	13	9	42	80	142
Northampton Town	2	0	0	1	1	2	0	0	1	1	2
Norwich City	46	14	6	3	42	25	4	7	12	28	41
Nottingham Forest	108	34	10	10	110	53	16	17	21	76	99
Notts County	66	23	7	3	83	29	12	8	13	49	52
Oldham Athletic	30	9	3	3	34	8	7	6	2	29	17
Oxford United	14	4	2	1	9	3	1	3	3	8	11
Plymouth Argyle	14	5	1	1	19	9	2	2	3	12	12
Portsmouth	60	19	7	4	73	39	8	7	15	42	65
Port Vale	4	2	0	0	3	0	0	1	1	4	6
Preston North End	98	37	3	9	108	44	13	11	25	64	90
Queen's Park Rangers	38	8	4	7	32	26	3	3	13	14	29
Reading	4	2	0	0	4	2	2	0	0	7	3
Rochdale	4	2	0	0	3	0	0	1	1	1	2
Rotherham United	8	3	0	1	8	3	2	1	1	6	3
Scunthorpe United	2	1	0	0	5	0	1	0	0	2	1
Sheffield United	120	40	12	8	145	55	17	16	27	85	111
Sheffield Wednesday	128	45	9	10	159	67	18	8	38	89	132
Shrewsbury Town	6	3	0	0	6	0	1	1	1	4	4
Southampton	54	14	9	4	43	19	7	7	13	28	45
Stockport County	2	1	0	0	7	1	1	0	0	3	1
Stoke City	88	31	7	6	108	36	13	13	18	54	66
Sunderland	146	46	14	13	145	89	14	23	36	91	139
Swansea City	14	7	0	0	19	0	4	0	3	12	10
Swindon Town	10	3	1	1	10	5	2	2	1	6	4
Torquay United	4	1	0	1	5	2	0	1	1	2	3
Tottenham Hotspur	118	26	16	17	94	80	19	11	29	92	114
Tranmere Rovers	4	2	0	0	3	0	1	1	0	2	1
Walsall	4	0	2	0	0	0	0	1	1	1	4
Watford	14	4	2	1	15	6	1	2	4	10	16
West Bromwich Albion	124	39	8	15	118	74	19	15	28	86	99
West Ham United	78	20	9	10	77	50	6	14	19	48	82
Wimbledon	26	6	2	5	22	12	3	5	5	20	21
Wolverhampton Wanderers	96	26	10	12	109	64	15	12	21	67	86
Wrexham	4	1	0	1	5	4	2	0	0	5	2
York City	4	2	0	0	5	0	1	1	0	2	1
TOTALS	**4052**	**1159**	**450**	**417**	**4170**	**2292**	**552**	**490**	**984**	**2568**	**3598**

VILLA'S ALL-TIME LEAGUE RECORD – SEASON BY SEASON

Season	Div	Teams	Pos	P	W	D	L	F	A	W	D	L	F	A	Pts	Cup Honours
1888-89	1	12	2nd	22	10	0	1	44	16	2	5	4	17	27	29	**(FAC Winners in 1886-87)**
1889-90	1	12	8th	22	6	2	3	30	15	1	3	7	13	36	19	
1890-91	1	12	9th	22	5	4	2	29	18	2	0	9	16	40	18	
1891-92	1	14	4th	26	10	0	3	63	23	5	0	8	26	33	30	FAC Runners-up
1892-93	1	16	4th	30	12	1	2	50	24	4	2	9	23	38	35	
1893-94	**1**	**16**	**1st**	**30**	**12**	**2**	**1**	**49**	**13**	**7**	**4**	**4**	**35**	**29**	**44**	
1894-95	1	16	3rd	30	12	2	1	51	12	5	3	7	31	31	39	**FAC Winners**
1895-96	**1**	**16**	**1st**	**30**	**14**	**1**	**0**	**47**	**17**	**6**	**4**	**5**	**31**	**28**	**45**	
1896-97	**1**	**16**	**1st**	**30**	**10**	**3**	**2**	**36**	**16**	**11**	**2**	**2**	**37**	**22**	**47**	**FAC Winners**
1897-98	1	16	6th	30	12	1	2	47	21	2	4	9	14	30	33	
1898-99	**1**	**18**	**1st**	**34**	**15**	**2**	**0**	**58**	**13**	**4**	**5**	**8**	**18**	**27**	**45**	
1899-00	**1**	**18**	**1st**	**34**	**12**	**4**	**1**	**45**	**18**	**10**	**2**	**5**	**32**	**17**	**50**	
1900-01	1	18	15th	34	8	5	4	32	18	2	5	10	13	33	30	FAC Semi-finalists
1901-02	1	18	8th	34	9	5	3	27	13	4	3	10	15	27	34	
1902-03	1	18	2nd	34	11	3	3	43	18	8	0	9	18	22	41	FAC Semi-finalists
1903-04	1	18	5th	34	13	1	3	41	16	4	6	7	29	32	41	
1904-05	1	18	4th	34	11	2	4	32	15	8	2	7	31	28	42	**FAC Winners**
1905-06	1	20	8th	38	13	2	4	51	19	4	4	11	21	37	40	
1906-07	1	20	5th	38	13	4	2	51	19	6	2	11	27	33	44	
1907-08	1	20	2nd	38	9	6	4	47	24	8	3	8	30	35	43	
1908-09	1	20	7th	38	8	7	4	31	22	6	3	10	27	34	38	
1909-10	**1**	**20**	**1st**	**38**	**17**	**2**	**0**	**62**	**19**	**6**	**5**	**8**	**22**	**23**	**53**	
1910-11	1	20	2nd	38	15	3	1	50	18	7	4	8	19	23	51	
1911-12	1	20	6th	38	12	2	5	48	22	5	5	9	28	41	41	
1912-13	1	20	2nd	38	13	4	2	57	21	6	8	5	29	31	50	**FAC Winners**
1913-14	1	20	2nd	38	11	3	5	36	21	8	3	8	29	29	44	FAC Semi-finalists
1914-15	1	20	13th	38	10	5	4	39	32	3	6	10	23	40	37	
First World War																
1919-20	1	22	9th	42	11	3	7	49	36	7	3	11	26	37	42	**FAC Winners**
1920-21	1	22	10th	42	11	4	6	39	21	7	3	11	24	49	43	
1921-22	1	22	5th	42	16	3	2	50	19	6	0	15	24	36	47	
1922-23	1	22	6th	42	15	3	3	42	11	3	7	11	22	40	46	
1923-24	1	22	6th	42	10	10	1	33	11	8	3	10	19	26	49	FAC Runners-up
1924-25	1	22	15th	42	10	7	4	34	25	3	6	12	24	46	39	
1925-26	1	22	6th	42	12	7	2	56	25	4	5	12	30	51	44	
1926-27	1	22	10th	42	11	4	6	51	34	7	3	11	30	49	43	
1927-28	1	22	8th	42	13	3	5	52	30	4	6	11	26	43	43	
1928-29	1	22	3rd	42	16	2	3	62	30	7	2	12	36	51	50	FAC Semi-finalists
1929-30	1	22	4th	42	13	1	7	54	33	8	4	9	38	50	47	
1930-31	1	22	2nd	42	17	3	1	86	34	8	6	7	42	44	59	
1931-32	1	22	5th	42	15	1	5	64	28	4	7	10	40	44	46	

ASTON VILLA REVIEW 2002 — STATISTICS

Season	Div	Teams	Pos	P	W	D	L	F	A	W	D	L	F	A	Pts	Cup Honours
1932-33	1	22	2nd	42	16	2	3	60	29	7	6	8	32	38	54	
1933-34	1	22	13th	42	10	5	6	45	34	4	7	10	33	41	40	FAC Semi-finalists
1934-35	1	22	13th	42	11	6	4	50	36	3	7	11	24	52	41	
1935-36	*1*	*22*	*21st*	*42*	*7*	*6*	*8*	*47*	*56*	*6*	*3*	*12*	*34*	*54*	*35*	
1936-37	2	22	9th	42	10	6	5	47	30	6	6	9	35	40	44	
1937-38	**2**	**22**	**1st**	**42**	**17**	**2**	**2**	**50**	**12**	**8**	**5**	**8**	**23**	**23**	**57**	FAC Semi-finalists
1938-39	1	22	12th	42	11	3	7	44	25	5	6	10	27	35	41	
Second World War																
1946-47	1	22	8th	42	9	6	6	39	24	9	3	9	28	29	45	
1947-48	1	22	6th	42	13	5	3	42	22	6	4	11	23	35	47	
1948-49	1	22	10th	42	10	6	5	40	36	6	4	11	20	40	42	
1949-50	1	22	12th	42	10	7	4	31	19	5	5	11	30	42	42	
1950-51	1	22	15th	42	9	6	6	39	29	3	7	11	27	39	37	
1951-52	1	22	6th	42	13	3	5	49	28	6	6	9	30	42	47	
1952-53	1	22	11th	42	9	7	5	36	23	5	6	10	27	38	41	
1953-54	1	22	13th	42	12	5	4	50	28	4	4	13	20	40	41	
1954-55	1	22	6th	42	11	3	7	38	31	9	4	8	34	42	47	
1955-56	1	22	20th	42	9	6	6	32	29	2	7	12	20	40	35	
1956-57	1	22	10th	42	10	8	3	45	25	4	7	10	20	30	43	**FAC Winners**
1957-58	1	22	14th	42	12	4	5	46	26	4	3	14	27	60	39	
1958-59	*1*	*22*	*21st*	*42*	*8*	*5*	*8*	*31*	*33*	*3*	*3*	*15*	*27*	*54*	*30*	FAC Semi-finalists
1959-60	**2**	**22**	**1st**	**42**	**17**	**3**	**1**	**62**	**19**	**8**	**6**	**7**	**27**	**24**	**59**	FAC Semi-finalists
1960-61	1	22	9th	42	13	3	5	48	28	4	6	11	30	49	43	**LC Winners**
1961-62	1	22	7th	42	13	5	3	45	20	5	3	13	20	36	44	
1962-63	1	22	15th	42	12	2	7	38	23	3	6	12	24	45	38	LC Runners-up
1963-64	1	22	19th	42	8	6	7	35	29	3	6	12	27	42	34	
1964-65	1	22	16th	42	14	1	6	36	24	2	4	15	21	58	37	LC Semi-finalists
1965-66	1	22	16th	42	10	3	8	39	34	5	3	13	30	46	36	
1966-67	1	22	21st	42	7	5	9	30	33	4	2	15	24	52	29	
1967-68	2	22	16th	42	10	3	8	35	30	5	4	12	19	34	37	
1968-69	2	22	18th	42	10	8	3	22	11	2	6	13	15	37	38	
1969-70	*2*	*22*	*21st*	*42*	*7*	*8*	*6*	*23*	*21*	*1*	*5*	*15*	*13*	*41*	*29*	
1970-71	3	24	4th	46	13	7	3	27	13	6	8	9	27	33	53	LC Runners-up
1971-72	**3**	**24**	**1st**	**46**	**20**	**1**	**2**	**45**	**10**	**12**	**5**	**6**	**40**	**22**	**70**	
1972-73	2	22	3rd	42	12	5	4	27	17	6	9	6	24	30	50	
1973-74	2	22	14th	42	8	9	4	33	21	5	6	10	15	24	41	
1974-75	2	22	2nd	42	16	4	1	47	6	9	4	8	32	26	58	**LC Winners**
1975-76	1	22	16th	42	11	8	2	32	17	0	9	12	19	42	39	
1976-77	1	22	4th	42	17	3	1	55	17	5	4	12	21	33	51	**LC Winners**
1977-78	1	22	8th	42	11	4	6	33	18	7	6	8	24	24	46	
1978-79	1	22	8th	42	8	9	4	37	26	7	7	7	22	23	46	
1979-80	1	22	7th	42	11	5	5	29	22	5	9	7	22	28	46	

VILLA'S ALL-TIME LEAGUE RECORD – SEASON BY SEASON (continued)

Season	Div	Teams	Pos	P	W	D	L	F	A	W	D	L	F	A	Pts	Cup Honours
1980-81	1	22	**1st**	42	16	3	2	40	13	10	5	6	32	27	60	
1981-82	1	22	11th	42	9	6	6	28	24	6	6	9	27	29	57	**EC Winners**
1982-83	1	22	6th	42	17	2	2	47	15	4	3	14	15	35	68	**ESC Winners**
1983-84	1	22	10th	42	14	3	4	34	22	3	6	12	25	39	60	LC Semi-finalists
1984-85	1	22	10th	42	10	7	4	34	20	5	4	12	26	40	56	
1985-86	1	22	16th	42	7	6	8	27	28	3	8	10	24	39	44	LC Semi-finalists
1986-87	*1*	*22*	*22nd*	*42*	*7*	*7*	*7*	*25*	*25*	*1*	*5*	*15*	*20*	*54*	*36*	
1987-88	2	23	2nd	44	9	7	6	31	21	13	5	4	37	20	78	
1988-89	1	20	17th	38	7	6	6	25	22	2	7	10	20	34	40	
1989-90	1	20	2nd	38	13	3	3	36	20	8	4	7	21	18	70	FMC Area Finalists
1990-91	1	20	17th	38	7	9	3	29	25	2	5	12	17	33	41	
1991-92	1	22	7th	42	13	3	5	31	16	4	6	11	17	28	60	
1992-93	P	22	2nd	42	13	5	3	36	16	8	6	7	21	24	74	
1993-94	P	22	10th	42	8	5	8	23	18	7	7	7	23	32	57	**LC Winners**
1994-95	P	22	18th	42	6	9	6	27	24	5	6	10	24	32	48	
1995-96	P	20	4th	38	11	5	3	32	15	7	4	8	20	20	63	**LC Winners**/FAC SF
1996-97	P	20	5th	38	11	5	3	27	13	6	5	8	20	21	61	
1997-98	P	20	7th	38	9	3	7	26	24	8	3	8	23	24	57	
1998-99	P	20	6th	38	10	3	6	33	28	5	7	7	18	18	55	
1999-00	P	20	6th	38	8	8	3	23	12	7	5	7	23	23	58	FAC Runners-up
2000-01	P	20	8th	38	8	8	3	27	20	5	7	7	19	23	54	
2001-02	P	20	8th	38	8	7	4	22	17	4	7	8	24	30	50	**ITC Winners 2001**

FAC = FA Cup; LC = League Cup; FMC = Full Members' Cup; EC = European Champions' Cup; ESC = European Super Cup; ITC = InterToto Cup. Championship seasons in **bold** type, relegation seasons in *italics*.

VILLA'S COMPLETE LEAGUE RECORD

	Played	Won	Drew	Lost	For	Against	Points
Home	2026	1591	450	417	4170	2292	2973
Away	2026	552	490	984	2568	3598	1707
Total	**4052**	**1711**	**940**	**1401**	**6738**	**5890**	**4680**

2pts for a win up to season 1980-81, 3pts for a win from season 1981-82

OTHER HONOURS

World Club Championship runners-up 1982-83

FA Charity Shield joint winners 1981-82

FA Charity Shield runners-up 1910-11, 1957-58, 1972-73

Premiership Prize Money League

1 Arsenal £8,835,400
2 Liverpool £8,393,630
3 Manchester United £7,951,860
4 Newcastle United £7,510,090
5 Leeds United £7,068,320
6 Chelsea £6,626,550
7 West Ham United £6,184,780
8 **Aston Villa** £5,743,010
9 Tottenham Hotspur £5,301,240
10 Blackburn Rovers £4,859,470
11 Southampton £4,417,700
12 Middlesbrough £3,975,930
13 Fulham £3,534,160
14 Charlton Athletic £3,092,390
15 Everton £2,650,620
16 Bolton Wanderers £2,208,850
17 Sunderland £1,767,080
18 Ipswich Town £1,325,310
19 Derby County £883,540
20 Leicester City £441,770

SUBSCRIBERS ROLL CALL — 2001/2002

1. Neil Gallagher
2. Simon A. J. Burley
3. The Fairfield Family
4. D. S. & Oliver Eagle
5. Tony Dacey
6. Yvonne Graves
7. John (Villa) Power
8. Ross Griffith
9. Brig Flounders
10. Geoff & Matt Baker
11. Robin D. Wilkes
12. The Berwick Family
13. J. R. Meek
14. Philip Gray
15. John Thompson
16. Gary P. Sewell
17. Paul J. Edwards
18. Darrell Hassam
19. Dean Woodhams
20. Dr Stephen Tovey
21. Mark Lench
22. Punky Schulz
23. Pete Boam
24. Mark Napier (Stafford)
25. Dr Mark Wilson
26. Clive & Michelle Platman
27. Richard Houghton (Nobby)
28. The Noden Family
29. Michael Rose
30. Ken Noon
31. Paul Noon
32. Peter Noon
33. Malcolm Taylor
34. Brian C. Seadon
35. Dave Andrews
36. Clare Briggs
37. John Briggs
38. David Ralphs
39. Tony Spraggon
40. The Sutton Family
41. David Woodley
42. Derek Day
43. Mark Ford
44. The Palmer Family (Ravenshead)
45. Jim Stelfox
46. H. John Desaulles
47. Martin Green (Bristol)
48. David Hodges (Southam)
49. Derek T. Hough
50. Wendy Jordan
51. Stephen J. Evans
52. Kevin A. Williams
53. Philip R. Haynes
54. Rachel Townsend
55. Frank Macdonald
56. Iris Barford
57. Andrew Collins
58. David Carter
59. Anthony Woolley
60. Andrew Mason
61. Adrian Thorne (Horsham)
62. Neil Strevens
63. Alex Ashford
64. Nigel & Ross Iwanski
65. Bill Willcox
66. The Dunbars
67. Paul & Jenny Bailey
68. Michelle Diggins
69. R. H. Fullbrook
70. M. A. Fullbrook
71. Simon Kerr-Edwards
72. Pete Abrahams
73. Mark Pearce
74. James Lawler
75. Warren H. McDivitt
76. Martin Greenslade
77. Adrian Batsford
78. Ciaran Hanley
79. Andrea Warren
80. Phillip (Tigger) Wall
81. Rob & Karen Wardle
82. Lars Nilsson
83. W. A. Harvey
84. Thomas Johansson
85. Susan Pudge
86. Andy Perry
87. Jodie Horton
88. George Deakin
89. Stuart Palmer
90. Jeff Corfield
91. Andy Campkin (Aylesbury)
92. David Knight
93. Simon Wilkes
94. Keith Andrew Taylor
95. Gareth Hubbard
96. David Richardson
97. Damien Witts
98. Tony, Matthew & Andrew Kenny
99. D. S. Willetts
100. John Foster
101. Stephanie Attenborough
102. Gareth C. Jones (Bones, Bristol)
103. Paul Duffin
104. Stuart T. Swann
105. Mr J. J. Howard
106. Adam Thomas Barrett
107. Rod & David Bevan
108. Ross Wright
109. Adrian Goddard
110. Jason Davis
111. Malcolm Cooper
112. Kevin Larkin
113. Julia Greenfield
114. Graham Carlin
115. Simon 'Wilf' Wheeler (Tamworth)
116. Geoff Clarke
117. Alex & Linda Groemminger
118. Robert Watson
119. S. J. Lavery
120. Philip J. Etheridge
121. Rod The Rocker
122. Karen Cook
123. Peter J. Ross (Belbroughton)
124. The Daly Family
125. Vera Ellen Ragsdale
126. Stephen Hill
127. Colin Brown
128. David John Edward Clayton
129. Robert Gough
130. John Lacey
131. Neil Harvey
132. Mark Whorton

SUBSCRIBERS ROLL CALL — 2001/2002

133 Alan F. Jasper	154 Nigel & Jacob Groves	175 Stephen Bishop
134 Sue & Mick Tilt	155 Gary & Natalie	176 Peter D. Jones
135 Gary Weaver	156 Michael Bates	177 Jason Norbury
136 Edmund Gajny	157 Keith Potter	178 Dan (The Villa Man) Renshaw
137 Paul Kenna	158 Thomas Edward Foster	179 Steve (Rennie) Renshaw
138 Paul Millard	159 R. O. Evans	180 Nigel & Simon Renshaw
139 Leo Osborn	160 Kevin Gledhill	181 Len Reading
140 Ken Buttery	161 Peter Gledhill	182 Paul Dorland
141 Joan Taylor	162 George Barker	183 Mitchell Willson
142 Gingerpud & Cadbury	163 Robert Smith Family	184 Arthur Bent
143 N. S. J. S. Casley	164 Geoff Underhill	185 Kevin Williams (Lower Holte)
144 Paul Casley	165 Ian James Ross	186 Mark Thackeray
145 Neal Sawyer	166 Antonio Durante (Rome)	187 Nigel Ainge
146 Bob Nicholls	167 Glynn C. Miller	188 H. J. McCranor
147 Clive Nicholls	168 Edward Knott	189 Roger Levicki
148 Richard Pargeter	169 The Hockenhull Family	190 Tim Levicki
149 James & Katie Flynn	170 Robert Moss	191 Andrew Levicki
150 Neil Jones (Holte End)	171 Eric Flavin M.B.E	192 John Ward
151 Eddie Mills (Weoley Castle)	172 Leigh McTiernan	193 Kenneth John Marriott
152 Robert Edward Garratt	173 Chris Newton	
153 Barry Geddis	174 Adrian Paul Rogers	